MW00826318

A Treatise
on the
Decorative Part
of
Civil Architecture

WILLIAM CHAMBERS

DOVER PUBLICATIONS, INC.
Mineola, New York

Bibliographical Note

This Dover edition, first published in 2003, is an unabridged reprint of the third edition of the work (first published in 1759), published by Joseph Smeeton, London, 1791. The original pagination, in which the main text starts on page seven, has been retained for authenticity, as have the broken letters and other typographical irregularities in the text.

Library of Congress Cataloging-in-Publication Data

Chambers, William, Sir, 1726-1796.
 A treatise on the decorative part of civil architecture / William Chambers.—Dover ed.
  p. cm.—(Dover pictorial archive series)
 Originally published: London : Printed by J. Smeeton, 1791.
 ISBN 0-486-42991-1 (pbk.)
  1. Decoration and ornament, Architectural—Early works to 1800. 2. Architecture—Details—Early works to 1800. I. Title. II. Series.

NA3310.C48 2003
729—dc21

2003053262

Manufactured in the United States of America
Dover Publications, Inc., 31 East 2nd Street, Mineola, N.Y. 11501

A

TREATISE

ON THE

DECORATIVE PART

OF

CIVIL ARCHITECTURE.

ILLUSTRATED BY

FIFTY ORIGINAL, and THREE ADDITIONAL PLATES,

Engraved by Old ROOKER, Old FOUDRINIER, CHARLES GRIGNION, and other eminent Hands.

By SIR WILLIAM CHAMBERS, K. P. S.

Surveyor General of HIS MAJESTY's Works; Treafurer, and Member of the ROYAL ACADEMY of ARTS in London; alfo of thofe of Paris, and Florence.

FRS. FAS. FSSS.

The THIRD EDITION, confiderably augmented.

LONDON;

PRINTED BY JOSEPH SMEETON, IN ST. MARTIN'S LANE, CHARING CROSS.

SOLD BY

T. CADELL, Bookfeller and Printer to the Royal Academy, Strand; I. and J. TAYLOR, Holborn; J. WALTER, Charing Crofs; R. ROBSON, New Bond Street; and R. SAYER, Fleet Street.

M.DCC.XCI.

T O

T H E   K I N G.

SIR,

THE prefent publication treats of an Art, often the amufement of YOUR MAJESTY's leifure moments; and which, in all ages, great princes have delighted to encourage: as one, amongft thofe moft ufeful to their fubjects; beft calculated to difplay the power and fplendor of their government; fitteft to convey to pofterity, the munificence, fkill, and elegance, of the times in which they flourifhed; the memorable events and glorious deeds, in which they were engaged.

THE indulgent reception afforded to the two former editions of this work, induced me, not only to enlarge, and attempt improvements, in this third Edition; but likewife to folicit the honour of its appearance, under the aufpices of YOUR MAJESTY's Patronage: and the condefcenfion with which that mark of Royal approbation was granted, proves YOUR MAJESTY's defire to promote, even the fmalleft advances, towards perfecting the Arts of Defign.

THE inftitution of a Royal Academy; an Exhibition, become fplendid under Royal Patronage; Englifh Productions of Art, contending for preeminence, with thofe of the firft Schools on the Continent; are events, unexpected, as unhoped for, till YOUR MAJESTY's Acceffion.

FOR

DEDICATION.

FOR the benefits derived from thefe events, Artifts of all degrees look up with reverence to the Throne: and fo powerful is the Example, fuch the Influence of Royal Patronage; that the fame fpirit of encouragement, has rapidly been diffufed, through all claffes of YOUR MAJESTY's Subjects; even men of inferior rank now afpire to Tafte in the fine arts; and by a liberality of Sentiment, formerly unknown, excite the artifts to emulate and excel each other: circumftances not only much to their own honour, but contributing greatly to augment the Splendor of the Nation; to improve its Tafte, and ftamp additional Value on its Manufactures; to extend its Commerce, and increafe the Profits arifing therefrom.

THAT YOUR MAJESTY may long Reign over happy nations, and continue with equal ardour a Patronage, which already has produced fuch beneficial effects; is the earneft wifh of

YOUR MAJESTY's

Moft dutiful Subject,

And ever faithful Servant,

WILLIAM CHAMBERS.

PREFACE.

AMONGST the various arts cultivated in fociety, fome are ufeful only; being adapted to fupply our natural wants, or affift our natural infirmities; others again, are inftruments of luxury merely; and calculated to flatter the pride, or gratify the defires of man: whilft others there are, contrived to anfwer many purpofes; tending at once to preferve, to fecure, to accommodate, delight, and give confequence to the human fpecies.

ARCHITECTURE, the fubject of our prefent enquiry, is of this latter kind; and when viewed in its full extent, may truly be faid to have a very confiderable part, in almoft every comfort, or luxury of life. The advantages derived from houfes only, are great, they being the firft fteps towards civilization, and having certainly great influence both on the body and mind. Secluded from each other, inhabitants of woods, of caves, or wretched huts; expofed to the inclement viciffitudes of feafons, and the diftreffing uncertainty of weather; men are generally indolent, dull and abject, with faculties benumbed, and views limited to the gratification of their moft preffing neceffities: but wherever focieties are formed, and commodious dwellings are found; in which, well fheltered, they may breath a temperate air, amid the fummer's heat or winter's cold; fleep, when nature calls, at eafe and in fecurity; ftudy unmolefted; converfe, and tafte the fweets of focial enjoyments; there they are fpirited, active, ingenious and enterprifing; vigorous in body, fpeculative in mind: agriculture and arts improve, they flourifh among them; the neceffaries, the conveniencies, and foon even the luxuries of life, become there abundant.

MERE ftrength however, even the fteadieft perfeverance, obtains with difficulty the defired produce; but inventions facilitate and fhorten labour, multiplying productions fo, as not only to fupply domeftic wants, but likewife to treafure up ftores for foreign markets.

ARCHITECTURE then fmooths the way for commerce; fhe forms commodious roads through marfhes or other grounds naturally impracticable, fills up vallies, unites, or levels mountains; throws bridges over deep or rapid waters, turns afide or deadens the fury of torrents; conftructs canals of navigation, builds fhips, and contrives ports for their fecure reception in the hour of danger: facilitating thus, the intercourfe of nations, the conveyance of merchandize from people to people.

A WELL regulated commerce is ever the fource of wealth; and luxury has ever been attendant on riches. As the powers of gratification increafe, fancy multiplies wants; till at length, indolence or pleafure, vanity and fuperftition, fears and refentments, give birth to a thoufand fuperfluous, a thoufand artificial cravings; the greater part of which could not be gratified, without the affiftance of architecture:

for

for splendid palaces, magnificent temples, costly dwelling houses, amphitheatres, theatres, baths and porticos, triumphal arches and bridges, mausoleums, and an endless number of similar inventions; are all, either necessary instruments of ease and pleasure; or striking testimonies of wealth, of grandeur and pre-eminence, either present or past.

NOR are there any other objects, whether necessary, or superfluous, so certainly productive of their design; so permanent in their effects, or beneficial in their consequences: fine furniture, rich dresses, brilliant equipages, numerous domestics; are only secondary attractions at first; they soon feel the effect of time; and their value fluctuates, or dies, with the fashion of the day. While the productions of architecture command general attention; are monuments lasting beyond the reach of modes; and record to latest posterity, the consequence, virtues, atchievements, and munificence of those they commemorate.

THE immediate and most obvious advantages of building are, employing many ingenious artificers, many industrious workmen and labourers of various kinds; converting materials of little value into the most stately productions of human skill; beautifying the face of countries; multiplying the conveniencies and comforts of life.

BUT these, however great, are not the most considerable: that numerous train of arts and manufactures, contrived to furnish and adorn the works of architecture, which occupies thousands, and constitutes many lucrative branches of commerce; that certain concourse of strangers, to every country celebrated for stately structures; who extend your fame, adopt your fashions, give reputation, and create a demand for your productions; are considerations of the highest consequence: in short, the advantages of building extend to the remotest ages, and at this day, the ruins of ANCIENT ROME, in a great measure support the splendor of the present; by the number of travellers who flock from all nations, to visit the ancient remains and modern magnificence of that famous city; and who, in the course of a few centuries, have there expended incredible sums of money, by long residence; and in the purchase of old pictures, antique statues, busts, basreliefs, urns, and other curious productions of art: of which, by some extraordinary good management, there is a treasure never to be exhausted: the waste of four hundred years is scarcely perceivable.

NOR is architecture less useful in defending, than prosperous in adorning and enriching countries: she guards their coasts with ships of war, secures their boundaries, fortifies their cities, and by a variety of artful constructions, controls the ambition, and frustrates the attempts of foreign powers; curbs the insolence, and averts the danger, the horror of internal commotions.

THUS architecture, by supplying men with commodious habitations; procures that health of body and vigor of mind, which facilitate the invention of arts: and when by the exertion of their skill or industry, productions multiply beyond domestic wants; she furnishes the means of transporting them to other markets: and whenever by commerce they acquire wealth, she points the way to employ their riches rationally, nobly, benevolently; in methods honorable and useful to them-
selves

felves and their defcendants; which add fplendor to the ftate, and yield benefit both to their cotemporaries and to pofterity: fhe farther teaches them to defend their poffeffions; to fecure their liberty and lives, from the attempts of lawlefs violence, or unreftrained ambition.

An art fo varioufly conducive to the happinefs of man, to the wealth, luftre and fafety of nations; naturally commands protection and encouragement: in effect, it appears, that in all civilized times, and well regulated governments, it has been much attended to, and promoted with unremitting affiduity; and the perfectioning of other arts, has ever been a certain confequence: for where building is encouraged; painting, fculpture, and all the inferior branches of decorative workmanfhip, muft flourifh of courfe; and thefe, have an influence on manufactures, even to the minuteft mechanic productions; for defign is of univerfal benefit, and ftamps additional value on the moft trifling performances, the importance of which, to a commercial people, is obvious; it requires no illuftration.

Let it not however be imagined, that building, merely confidered as heaping ftone upon ftone, can be of great confequence; or reflect honor, either on nations or individuals: materials in architecture, are like words in phrafeology; having feparately but little power; and they may be fo arranged, as to excite ridicule; difguft, or even contempt; yet when combined with fkill, expreffed with energy, they actuate the mind with unbounded fway. An able writer can move even in ruftic language, and the mafterly difpofitions of a fkilful artift, will dignify the meaneft materials; while the weak efforts of the ignorant, render the moft coftly enrichments defpicable. To fuch, the compliment of Apelles may juftly be applied; who, on feeing the picture of a Venus magnificently attired, faid to the operator; Friend; though thou haft not been able to make her fair, thou haft certainly made her fine.

Hitherto architecture has been confidered in a general light; under its different divifions of naval, military, and civil. I purpofe however in the prefent work, to confine myfelf to the laft of thefe branches, as being of more general ufe, and that, to which my own ftudy and practice have been more immediately directed.

It is not to be fuppofed, that fo difficult an art as architecture, after having lain many centuries abforbed in the general cloud of barbarifm, fhould at once, emerge in full perfection; or that the firft reftorers of the ancient manner of building, could at once, bring it to a degree of purity, incapable of farther improvement. With very little affiftance from books upon the fubject, and that, often obfcure, unintelligible, or erroneous; while they were labouring to feparate beauty from deformity; endeavouring to reftore to light, what length of time, cafualties, war and violence, had been active to deface; to anihilate; we muft neither cenfure with feverity their omiffions, nor wonder at their miftakes; yet with all due reverence for the memory of thofe illuftrious artifts, it may be remarked, that they left much undone; and taught many errors. Their meafures and defigns were, generally fpeaking, incorrect; their plates ill engraved; and the want of method, and of precifion in treating their fubject, renders the ftudy of it in their works, exceedingly difcouraging.

IT is indeed true, that later writers have, in a great meafure, fupplied their omiffions, and rectified their faults: few fubjects have been more amply treated of than architecture; nor any, by perfons better qualified; infomuch, that little re-mains either to be difcovered, or improved; every branch of the art having been maturely confidered, and brought very near the utmoft degree of certainty of which it is capable.

YET one thing of great ufe remained to be done; at leaft, in our language; which was, to collect in one volume, what lay difperfed in many hundreds, much the greater part of them written in foreign languages: and to felect, from mountains of promifcuous materials, a feries of found precepts, and perfect defigns.

WHOEVER has applied to the ftudy of architecture, will readily grant that there are few purfuits more perplexing: the vague foundation on which the more refined parts of the art are built, has given rife to fuch a multiplicity of jarring opinions, all fupported by, at leaft, plaufible arguments; that it is exceedingly difficult to difcriminate, or diftinguifh what is real, from that which is merely fpecious: the connexions which conftitute truth or fallacy, being often far diftant, beyond the fight of fuperficial obfervers. Whence, the merit of performances is too often mea-fured by the fame of the performer; by the tafte of the age in which they were produced; by vulgar report; party opinion; or fome other ftandard equally in-adequate: and not feldom by precepts delivered fome centuries ago, calculated for other climates, other men, and other cuftoms.

To obviate thefe inconveniencies, the author ventured, foon after his return from Italy, upwards of thirty years ago, to attempt fuch a compilation as is above mentioned; by a publication of the firft edition of the prefent work. He flattered himfelf, that if well conducted; it would greatly fhorten the labours of the ftudent, and lead him to truth, by eafy and more inviting paths; that it might render the ftudy of architecture, and its attendant arts, more frequent; ferve to promote true tafte, and to diffufe the love of *Vertu*, among perfons of high rank, and large for-tune; the fit encouragers of elegance.

HIS defign was, without biafs from national, or other prejudices; candidly to confider what had been produced upon the fubject: and to collect from the works or writings of others, or from his own obfervations, in all parts of Europe, famed for tafte; fuch particulars, as feemed moft interefting; or propereft to give a juft idea of fo very ufeful, and truly noble an art.

SENSIBLE that all ages had produced bad, or indifferent artifts; and that all men, however excellent, muft fometimes have erred; it was his intention, neither to be influenced by particular times, nor by the general reputation of particular per-fons: where reafon or demonftration could be ufed, he purpofed to employ them; and where they could not, to fubftitute in their places, generally admitted opi-nions. Abftrufe or fruitlefs arguments he wifhed carefully to avoid; nor was it his intention to perplex the unfkilful, with a number of indifcriminate examples: having judged it much more eligible to offer a few; calculated to ferve at once as ftandards for imitation, or guides to judge by, in fimilar productions. Precifion,

perfpicuity

perfpicuity and brevity, were to be attempted in the ftyle; and in the defigns, fimplicity, order, character, and beauty of form.

The difficulty and extent of fuch a tafk, undertaken early in life, rendered fuccefs very uncertain; and filled the writer's mind with many apprehenfions: but the indulgent encouragement, fo liberally extended to the two former publications of this work; and the frequent calls for a third: are pleafing teftimonies that his endeavours have not been wholly in vain. He ventures to confider the fale of two numerous editions, written upon a fubject rather inftructive than entertaining; and in a language generally unknown to foreign Artifts; as a proof of the utility of his undertaking: at leaft, in the country where he moft wifhed to have it ufeful. And ftimulated by a defire of rendering it ftill more deferving public notice; he has carefully revifed, and confiderably augmented this third edition: he does not prefume to fay improved it; but flatters himfelf the experience gained by thirty years very extenfive practice, fince the original publication; has enabled him to judge with fome degree of certainty, at leaft, of what might be left out, be added, or altered to advantage.

Amongst the additions to this third edition, there is an introductory difcourfe; defigned to point out, and briefly to explain, the requifite qualifications and duty of an architect, at this time: and in the courfe of the work, many additional hints, explanations, and elucidations, have been inferted; wherever they feemed, either neceffary for better underftanding the text; for the farther information of the reader; or for giving additional force, and greater authority, to what had been before advanced. It has farthermore been attempted, on different occafions, to point out to the ftudent the courfe he ought to fteer; the dangers he has to avoid; the object he muft conftantly keep in view.

To thefe additional articles in the text, are added four entire new plates; one of chimney pieces, the reft containing vafes, urns, and other ornamental pieces, defigned by the Author; and executed for their Majefties, his Grace the Duke of Marlborough, the Earl of Charlemont, and fome other perfons of high rank. Several of the old plates have alfo been altered; and it is hoped, fomewhat improved.

The favourable reception, this Treatife on the ornamental part of architecture has experienced, both in England, and abroad, is fuch, as certainly required a full difcharge, of the original engagement: by treating upon the Art, in its remaining branches. But fuch, and fo conftant, have been the Writer's avocations; that in the courfe of thirty years, it has never been in his power, properly to fet about, fo extenfive an undertaking: and a variety of concurring circumftances, render it lefs fo now, than ever. Loofe materials have, indeed, been abundantly collected; and many defigns have from time, to time, been made; with an eye to the general intention: but there are fo many more to make; fo much to correct and methodize; that he muft, however reluctantly, relinquifh the tafk: and confign the remainder, to the execution of fome future pen.

In the mean time, from the method throughout obferved, in treating the prefent fubject; it is prefumed; that this part may now be, as it has hitherto been, confidered as a diftinct work: in all refpects unconnected, with any thing that might, or

may

may follow: which form was originally fixed upon for the advantage of the fub-fcribers, as well as for the fecurity of the publifher; and has now been continued, partly from neceffity; and in part, for the benefit of purchafers: many of whom, have little or no occafion to ftudy any more of the art, than what the prefent publication contains: the remaining branches, though very important to builders; being of little fervice to connoiffeurs, or men of tafte; who afpire to be judges of the beauties, or deformities of a ftructure: without caring much about the reft; or having the fatigue, of entering into particulars; either concerning its value, its difpofition, or conftruction.

INTRODUCTION.

CIVIL ARCHITECTURE is that branch of the builder's art, which has for its objects all structures, either sacred or prophane, calculated to supply the wants and comforts; or to promote, extend, and diversify, the pleasures of life: either contrived to facilitate the business; give lustre to the duties; or display the state and distinctions of society. Its purpose is to erect edifices, in which strength and duration, shall unite with beauty, convenience, and salubrity; to ascertain their value; and to build them with every attention to safety, ease, and economy.

MANY, and singularly opposite, must be the qualities and attainments of him, who aspires to excel, in an art so variously directed. " Architecture," says father Laugier, " is of all useful arts, that which requires the most distinguished talents;
" there is perhaps as much genius, good sense, and taste requisite, to constitute a
" great architect; as to form a painter or poet of the first class. It would be a
" strange error to suppose it merely mechanical; and confined to digging founda-
" tions, or building walls, by rules of which the practice, supposes nothing more
" than eyes accustomed to judge of a perpendicular, and hands expert in the ma-
" nagement of a trowel. In contemplating the builder's art, all indeed that strikes
" a vulgar imagination, are, confused mounds of incommodious ruins; formless
" heaps of collected materials; dangerous scaffoldings; a frightful clatter of ham-
" mers, tools, and working machinery; an army of slovenly bespattered labourers
" and workmen: but these are only as it were, the rough bark of an art, the inge-
" nious mysteries of which, though only discoverable to few observers, excite the
" admiration of all who comprehend them. They perceive inventions of which the
" boldness, implies a genius, at once fertile and comprehensive; proportions of
" which the justness, announces a severe and systematic precision; ornaments of
" which the excellence, discovers exquisite and delicate feelings: and whoever is
" qualified to taste so many real beauties, will, I am certain, far from attempting to
" confound architecture with the inferior arts, be strongly inclined to rank it amongst
" those that are most exalted."

VITRUVIUS requires that the architect should have both ingenuity and applica-
tion, observing, that wit without labour, or labour without wit, never arrived at perfection. " He should," says he, " be a writer and draughtsman, understand geo-
" metry, optics, and arithmetic; be a good historian and philosopher, well skilled
" in music, and not ignorant in either physic, law, or astrology. The same author
" farther requires that he should be possessed of a great and enterprizing mind; be
" equitable, trusty, and totally free from avarice; without which, it would be im-
" possible to discharge the duties of his station with due propriety : ever disinterested,

B
" he

" he fhould be lefs folicitous of acquiring riches, than honour, and fame, by his pro-
" feffion."

AND Pythius, another ancient writer, cited by Vitruvius, infifted, that an architect fhould be more expert in every profeffion, connected with his art; than the
ableft profeffors of each art refpectively.

To this however Vitruvius does not affent; obferving, " that the human mind
" cannot arrive at perfection, in fo many difficult and various parts of knowledge.
" It is," fays he, " even rare in the courfe of a century to find a man fuperlatively
" excellent in any profeffion; why then is it expected, that an architect fhould
" equal Apelles in painting, Miro and Polycletes in fculpture, Hippocrates in me-
" dicine, Ariftoxenes in mufic, or Ariftarchus in purity of language: Pythius fhould
" have remembered, that every art confifts of two parts; theory, and practice: the
" latter of which, appertains peculiarly to its profeffors; but the former; is com-
" mon to them, and to the learned in general. If therefore an architect, be fuffi-
" ciently mafter in all the arts connected with his profeffion, to judge perfectly of
" the merit of their productions, it is the moft that fhould be infifted upon; and if
" fo qualified, he fhall not need to blufh at his own infufficiency."

IN fact, the bufinefs of an architect requires him rather to be a learned judge,
than a fkilful operator; and when he knows how to direct, and inftruct others, with
precifion; to examine, judge, and value, their performances with mafterly accuracy;
he may truly be faid to have acquired all that moft men can acquire; there are but
few inftances of fuch prodigies as Michael Angelo Bonarroti, who was at once the
firft architect, painter, geometrician, anatomift, and fculptor, of his time.

VITRUVIUS farthermore obferves, that an art enriched with fuch variety of
knowledge, is only to be learned by long and conftant application; and advifes his
cotemporaries never to affume the title of architects, till they are perfect mafters of
their own profeffion, and of the arts and fciences, with which it is connected: a caution, that even in the prefent times, may perhaps not be unneceffary.

IT will not readily occur, why a man fhould be either hiftorian, or philofopher;
mufician, or phyfician; lawyer, or aftrologer; before he ventures to commence architect. Our author, however, affigns his reafons; which, for the fake of brevity,
are here omitted. The curious reader will find them in the original book; to which
he is referred, for farther information.

SOME part of all this knowledge, though it might have been neceffary to an
artift of the Auguftan age, is not abfolutely fo now; fome part of it too, feems rather oftentatioufly introduced; more to enumerate the learned writers own qualifications, than fuch as were indifpenfably neceffary, to every man of his profeffion:
the remaining part fhall be mentioned in its place; while I venture to give an opinion, concerning the requifite qualifications of an architect: differing in fome particulars, from thofe above given; but more adapted, I flatter myfelf, to the wants,
cuftoms, and modes of life of our cotemporaries, as well as to the duties and avocations of a modern architect.

ARCHITECTURE,

ARCHITECTURE, being an active, as well as fpeculative art; in which exertions of the body, the organs of fenfe, and of utterance, are equally neceffary with efforts of the mind; it naturally follows, that fuch as intend to make it their profeffion, fhould enter the lifts with a good ftock of health, vigor and agility; they fhould neither be lame, nor unwieldy; neither aukward, flow, nor helplefs; neither pur-blind, nor deaf; nor have anything ridiculous about them, either natural or ac-quired. Their underftanding fhould be found; the fight and apprehenfion quick; the reafoning faculties clear, and unwarped by prejudices; the temper enterprizing, fteady, refolute; and though benevolent, rather fpirited than paffive, meek, or effeminate.

THE neceffity of thefe qualities, in one deftined to direct and manage great works, to govern and control numerous bands of clerks, infpectors, artifts, artificers, workmen and labourers; muft be fufficiently obvious. And as at the prefent time, few engage in any profeffion, till qualified for the world by a proper fchool educa-tion at leaft; it muft be fuppofed, that to a competent proficiency in the learned languages, the ftudent adds a thorough knowledge of his own; fo as to fpeak and write it, correctly at leaft, if not elegantly; that he is a good penman; verfed in accounts; a ready practitioner in arithmetic; and has received and profited by fuch other inftructions, as tend to fix the moral character; to inculcate integrity; to polifh the minds, and improve the manners of youth.

PROFICIENCY in the French and Italian languages is alfo requifite to him; not only that he may be enabled to travel with advantage, and converfe without difficulty, in countries where the chief part of his knowledge is to be collected; but alfo to underftand the many, and almoft only valuable books treating of his profeffion: the greater part of which, have never been tranflated. And as among feamen, there is a technical language, of which no admiral could be ignorant, without appearing ridiculous; fo in architecture, and the profeffions connected there-with, there are peculiar modes of expreffion, and terms of art, of which an architect muft by no means be ignorant; as that knowledge, impreffes upon the minds of the workmen, a refpectable idea of his abilities, confequently, a deference for his opi-nions; and farthermore enables him to explain to them intelligibly, what he intends, or wifhes to be performed.

To thefe qualifications, mental and corporeal, muft be united genius; or a ftrong inclination and bias of mind towards the purfuit in queftion: without which little fuccefs can be expected. This quality, whether it be * the gift of God, or a † fortuitous propenfity; whether innate, or acquired; has, not unaptly, been com-pared to thofe inftincts implanted by nature in different animals; by which, they are enabled to comprehend, and to perform certain things, with much eafe; while

---

* The Lord hath called Bezaleel, and hath filled him with the Spirit of God, in wifdom, in underftanding, and in knowledge, and in all manner of workmanfhip, and to devife curious works.

And he hath put it in his heart, that he may teach both he and Aholiab, them hath he filled with wifdom of heart to work all manner of work. Exodus, Chap. xxxv. v. 30, 31, 32, 33, 34.

† In the window of his mother's apartment, lay Spencer's Fairy Queen; in which he very early took delight to read, till, by feeling the charms of Verfe, he became, as he relates, irrecoverably a Poet. Such are the accidents, which, fometimes remembered, and per-haps fometimes forgotten, produce that particular defignation of mind, and propenfity for fome certain fcience or employment, which is commonly called genius. The true genius is a mind of large general powers, accidentally determined to fome peculiar direction. Sir Jofhua Reynolds, the great painter of the prefent age, had the firft fondnefs for his art excited by the perufal of Richardfon's Treatife. Dr. Johnfon's life of Cowley.

C

others,

others, not having the fame natural difpofition, neither comprehend, nor can per-form them: thus the man of genius; or he, whofe mind is peculiarly adapted to the contemplation of his fubject; comprehends with eafe, diftinguifhes with perfpicuity, treafures up with nice felection; whatever is ingenious, extraordinary, ufeful or elegant: his imagination ever active in a favourite purfuit, will abound in ideas, combinations and improvements, equally new, ftriking and agreeable; while he who miftakes his way, and applies to ftudies for which nature, or early impreffions, have not prepared him; labours fluggifhly; without relifh, as without effect; like Sify-phus, ever toiling up a hill, the fummit of which he is never to reach.

As many forts of knowledge, very oppofite in their natures, come under the architect's confideration; his genius muft be of a complex fort: endowed with the vivacity and powers of imagination, requifite to produce fublime or extraordinary compofitions; and at the fame time, with the induftry, patience, and penetration, neceffary to inveftigate mathematical truths; difcufs difficult, fometimes irkfome fub-jects; and enter into details of various forts, often as tirefome, as they are neceffary: a genius equally capable of expanding to the nobleft and moft elevated conceptions, or of fhrinking to the level of the meaneft and minuteft enquiries: as Doctor John-fon expreffes it; a mind, that at once comprehends the vaft, and attends to the minute.

DISPOSITIONS of this nature are feldom found, their conftituent qualities are in fome degree incompatible; and hence perhaps, chiefly arifes, the rarity of compleat mafters in the profeffion. The lively ftudent naturally ftrikes into the paths which afford moft fcope for his fancy; he exercifes himfelf in the arts of compofition, and in the different branches of defign; improves his knowledge of painting, fculpture, books, and ftructures; form his tafte, and turns his whole attention towards the fublimer parts of the art; neglecting all the while, the inferior knowledge; fo ufeful, fo abfolutely neceffary in practice; and of which a perfect mafter, can never be ig-norant. Ambitious to excel, he muft not neglect attainments, without which he cannot operate, while they may be purchafed at the expence of induftry, and fteady perfeverance.

A CELEBRATED Italian Artift, whofe tafte and luxuriance of fancy were un-ufually great, and the effect of whofe compofitions, on paper, has feldom been equalled; knew little of conftruction or calculation, yet lefs of the contrivance of habitable ftructures, or the modes of carrying real works into execution; though ftyling himfelf an architect. And when fome penfioners of the French academy at Rome, in the Author's hearing, charged him with ignorance of plans, he compofed a very complicated one, fince publifhed in his work; which fufficiently proves, that the charge was not altogether groundlefs. Indeed, it is not unfrequent in fome coun-tries of the continent, to find ingenious compofers and able draughtfmen, with no other reading than Vignola's rules, and without any fkill whatever in the executive parts; or knowledge of the fciences belonging thereto.

ON the other hand, the ftudent of a more faturnine caft, unable, or fearful perhaps, of foaring fo high; applies his powers to the operative and economical branches of the art, refting fatisfied in the parts of defign and compofition, to imitate or copy others; content, if by borrowing whatever falls in his way, he avoids any

ftriking

ſtriking abſurdities; and reaches that ſtate of mediocrity, which though it may eſcape cenſure, commands no praiſe.

IN countries where mechanics aſſume the profeſſion, and arrogate the title of architects; men of this ſort abound: they are by foreigners ſtiled portfolio artiſts; and their productions, collected without judgement, from different ſtores; muſt ever be diſcordant: without determined ſtile; marked character; or forcible effect: always without novelty; and having ſeldom either grandeur or beauty to recommend them. They are paſticcios in building; generally more imperfect than thoſe of the ſtage.

BUT though genius be the baſis of excellence, it can alone, produce but little: the richeſt ſoil when neglected, affords no other crop than weeds; and from the happieſt diſpoſition without culture; without knowledge of rules to guide, or judgement to reſtrain; little more can be expected, than capricious conceits; or luxuriant extravagancies.

OF mathematical knowledge, geometry, trigonometry, and conick ſections, ſhould be underſtood; as teaching the conſtruction, properties, contents, and diviſions of the forms uſed in building. Likewiſe mechanicks and hydraulicks, which treat of the formation, and aſcertain the effects of all kinds of machinery, ſimple, or complex, uſed in building: likewiſe of the raiſing, conveyance, and application of water; as well for the common uſes of life, as to produce many extraordinary effects; very ornamental in gardening, and efficacious in manufactures.

THESE ſciences farthermore, treat of the gravitation of bodies; and in what manner, and by what laws, they move, and act upon each other, under different circumſtances; with many other particulars, of frequent and material uſe in an art, where vaſt weights are to be moved; and in which, ſtructures of whatever form, muſt be calculated to carry great and indeterminate burthens; to ſtand the ſhock of heavy laden carriages; and to reſiſt the utmoſt fury of the elements.

BY opticks, particularly that part which is called perſpective, the artiſt is enabled to judge with preciſion, of the effects of his compoſitions, when carried into execution; and alſo to repreſent them more pleaſingly in deſign; as well for his own ſatisfaction, as to give his employers a more perfect idea of his intentions, than could be collected from geometrical drawings. And an acquaintance with the other branches, will be uſeful on many occaſions; in the diſtribution of light, to produce particular ſtriking effects; and in the diſpoſal of mirrors, to create deceptions; multiply objects; and raiſe ideas of far greater, than the real magnitude, or extent, of that which is exhibited to view.

AS to a painter, or ſculptor, ſo to an architect; a thorough maſtery in deſign, is indiſpenſably neceſſary; it is the ſine qua non; and the *mai a baſtanza* of *Carlo Maratt*, is full as applicable in one art, as in the others; for if the architect's mind be not copiouſly ſtored with correct ideas of forms; and habituated by long practice, to vary and combine them, as the fancy operates: or if his hand has not the power of repreſenting with preciſion and force, what the imagination ſuggeſts; his com-

D poſitions

pofitions will ever be feeble, formal, and ungraceful: and he will ftand unqualified to difcharge the principal part of his duty; which is, to invent and difpofe all that enters into his defign; and to guide the painter, fculptor, and every other artift or artificer, by advice, and precife directions; as far, at leaft, as relates to the outline and effect of their performances: that all may be the effort of one mind, maf-ter of its object; and all the parts be calculated, to produce a general uniformly fupported whole: which never can be the cafe, where artifts and artificers are left to themfelves; as each, naturally enough, confiders the perfection of his own part; fometimes without comprehending, and always without attention, to the whole com-pofition. Even Bernini, though an able architect; could feldom refrain from facrificing architecture, to the graces of fculpture and painting; the ill confequences of which, is fufficiently confpicuous in feveral of his works; but particularly, in his piazza of St. Peter's; where the ftatues placed upon the colonades, inftead of ftand-ing upright, as they fhould do, in all fuch fituations; are fo whimfically contorted, that at a little diftance, they feem to be performing a dance, and very confiderably injure the effect, of that magnificent approach, to the firft building in the Chriftian world.

To the knowledge, practice, and facility of hand, juft mentioned; compofers in architecture muft unite a perfect acquaintance with all kinds of proportions; having relation either to the grandeur, beauty, ftrength, or convenience of ftruc-tures: their variations, as occafions require; and the different effects which fituation, diftance, light, or other circumftances have upon them: which is a fcience of very confiderable difficulty; and only to be attained, by much experience, and clofe obfervation.

He farthermore muft be well verfed in the cuftoms, ceremonies, and modes of life of all degrees of men, his cotemporaries; their occupations and amufements; the number and employments of their domefticks, equipages and appurtenances; in what manner the bufinefs allotted to each is performed, and what is requifite or proper, to facilitate the fervice; with many other particulars, which though feemingly tri-fling, muft not be unknown to him, who is to provide for the wants, and gratify the expectations of all.

Neither muft he be ignorant of ancient hiftory, fable and mythology; nor of antiquities; as far as relates to the ftructures, fculpture, ornaments, and utenfils of the Egyptians, Greeks, Romans, and Etrurians; as the eftablifhed ftile of decora-tion, collects its forms, combinations, fymbols, and allufions, from thefe abundant fources; which time, and the concurring approbation of many ages, have rendered venerable.

The painter's canvas, and the fculptor's block, are their ultimate objects; but the architect's attention muft at once be directed, to the grandeur or beauty, ftrength, duration, fit contrivance, and economical execution of his compofitions: qualities, that ever clafh; and which it often is exceedingly difficult to reconcile. His different plans, elevations, and fections, muft all be confidered at the fame time; and like the parts of a piece of mufick, be contrived to harmonize, and fet each other off to moft advantage.

To

To the excellence of the defigner's art, muft yet be added, the humbler, though not lefs ufeful fkill, of the mechanick and accountant; for however able the draughtfman, he fhould not deem himfelf an architect, nor venture upon practifing in that capacity; till mafter of the executive parts of this profeffion.

THESE imply, an acquaintance with all the known, approved methods of building, every kind of ftructure fecurely, and for duration. How difficulties arifing from fituation, nature of foils, or other adventitious circumftances, are to be furmounted; and precifely, what precautions the occafion may require; in order to avoid fuperfluous expence, by avoiding to employ fuperfluous remedies.

THEY farther imply, a power of conducting large works, with order and economy; of meafuring correctly according to eftablifhed ufages; of regulating the accounts with accuracy; of employing with difcernment; directing and govern⸗ ing with fkill and temper; many men of different profeffions; capacities, and difpofitions: all without violence, or clamour; yet with full effect.

To maftery in thefe particulars, muft be added, proficiency in all the arts, liberal or mechanick, having relation to the building or adorning ftructures: a capacity of determining exactly, the goodnefs of the different materials ufed; with the degree of perfection, and confequent value at all times, of every kind of work: from the ftately, fplendid productions of the pencil, and chiffel; to the moft trifling objects employed in a fabrick: together with all the circumftances conftituting their value; as upon thefe, its occafional fluctuation muft depend.

CONSIDERABLE as this detail may feem, it is yet infufficient. A builder, like a chemift, muft analyze his fubftances; be fo much mafter of the conftituent parts of his compofition; their neceffary forms and dimenfions; that, as thofe of the profeffion term it, he may be able to take the whole building to pieces; and eftimate from his defigns, the total amount of the ftructure, before a fingle ftone is prepared.

To ignorance, or inattention in this particular; of which, for ferious reafons, no architect fhould ever be ignorant, or carelefs; muft be afcribed, the diftrefsful, often the ruinous uncertainty, of common eftimates: for fome, who condefcend to eftimate their own productions, know perhaps, but imperfectly, how their defigns are to be carried into execution; and confequently omit in the valuation, much that muft be done. And fome, who being too great for fuch minute inveftigations, employ others to eftimate; without defcribing thoroughly the manner in which they intend to proceed; leave them fo much in the dark, that even if capable, they can do little more than guefs at the value; and are feldom or ever right in their con⸗ jectures.

OTHERS there are, who being either unqualified, or too idle to calculate themfelves, and perhaps, too parfimonious to employ any other perfon; (for it is a work of time, and confiderable expence), value by the fquare; an operation, both eafy and expeditious; but of all, the moft fallacious; excepting in common build⸗ ings; of fimilar forms and dimenfions, built and finifhed in the fame manner: where, the amount of what has been done, may be a guide to value by. But in

E   extraordinary

extraordinary works, thefe rapid eftimators never hit the mark; and are generally fo far wide of it, as to draw fhame and reproaches on themfelves; regret, difficulties, fometimes ruin; both on the employer, and the tradefmen employed.

As one, in whofe honour and judgement the employer confides; and to whom the employed look up for protection and juftice; as mediator, and judge between them; on fubjects generally important: the architect's fkill, vigilance, and activity, fhould equal the confequence of his ftation; and ftudious to fuftain his character, attentive to juftify the confidence repofed in him, he muft neither inadvertently, nor otherwife, bring on unexpected ruinous expences; neither countenance, nor fuffer impofition on the one hand; oppreffive parfimony, or ill directed liberality on the other.

Let it not however, be inferred, from any thing here faid, that errors in eftimation proceed on every occafion, from the ignorance, or inadvertency of the architect: thofe who build, are often whimfical themfelves; or advife with fuch as are: they are pleafed to-day, difgufted to-morrow, with the fame object: hence alterations commence; deviation, fucceeds to deviation; their firft ideas are extended, improved and varied, till by infenfible gradations, both the form and value, of the original defign are entirely changed.

All that in fuch cafes the architect can do, and in difcharge of his duty fhould do; is, at the time, to notify by written information, the confequences of the alterations taking place. I fay written, for words are foon forgot; or if remembered, explained away; and fometimes denied. But written teftimony admits of no equivocation, it cannot be difputed, and will fix the blame, where it fhould be fixed; not on the architect's want of care or judgement; but on the builder's wavering difpofition.

Ornamental gardening, which in Italy, France, and other countries of the European continent, conftitutes a part of the architect's profeffion; is here in other hands: and, with a few exceptions, in very improper ones. Should that pleafing art be ever practifed by men, who have made compofition in general, a ftudy; who by having feen much, have ftored the fancy with copious imagery; and by proficiency in the arts of defign, formed a correct and elegant tafte; we might expect to find much more variety, and far higher perfection in works of that fort, than can now be expected, or is yet to be boafted of.

It feems almoft fuperfluous to obferve, that an architect cannot afpire to fuperiority in his profeffion, without having travelled; for it muft be obvious, that an art founded upon reafoning and much obfervation, is not to be learnt without it; books cannot avail; defcriptions, even drawings or prints, are but weak fubftitutes of realities: and an artift who conftantly inhabits the fame place, converfes with the fame people, and has the fame objects always obtruding on his view; muft neceffarily have very confined notions; few ideas, and many prejudices. Travelling roufes the imagination; the fight of great, new, or uncommon objects, elevates the mind to fublime conception; enriches the fancy with numerous ideas; fets the reafoning faculties in motion: he who has beheld with attentive confideration, the venerable remains of ancient magnificence; or ftudioufly examined the fplendor of modern times, in the productions of the fublime Bonarotti, Bramante, Vignola, Palladio,

Palladio, Raphael, Polidore, Peruzzi, Sanfovino, San Michaeli, Amanato, Bernini, Pietro da Cortonna, and many other original mafters; whofe works are the ornament and pride of the European continent; muft have acquired notions, far more extenfive, and fuperior to him, whofe information has been gleaned, from the copiers, or feeble imitators, of thefe great men; and their ftupendous works: he muft be in compofition more animated, varied and luxuriant; in defign, more learned, correct, and graceful: ever governed by a tafte formed at the fountain's head, upon the pureft models; and impreffed with the effect of thofe great objects, which fome time or other in life, have been the admiration of moft who either claim diftinction, or afpire to elegance; he muft always labour with greater certainty of fuccefs.

By travelling, a thorough knowledge of different countries, their language and manners, are alone to be attained in perfection: and by converfing with men of different nations, we learn their opinions; hear their reafons in fupport of them; and are naturally led to reafon in our turn: to fet afide our national prejudices, reject our ill-founded maxims, and allow for granted, that only which is clearly proved; or is founded on reafon, long experience, and careful obfervation.

Thus habituated to confider with the rigour of critical accuracy, we learn to fee objects in their true light; without attention, either to cafual approbation or diflike: to diftinguifh truth through the veil of obfcurity, and detect pretence however fpecioufly fuftained. Travelling to an artift, is as the univerfity to a man of letters, the laft ftage of a regular education; which opens the mind to a more liberal and extenfive train of thinking, diffufes an air of importance over the whole man, and ftamps value upon his opinions: it affords him opportunities of forming connections with the great, the learned, or the rich; and the friendfhips he makes while abroad, are frequently the firft caufes of his reputation, and fuccefs at home.

Of the ORIGIN, and PROGRESS of BUILDING.

BUILDINGS were certainly among the firft wants of mankind; and architecture muft, undoubtedly be claffed, among the earlieft antediluvian arts. Scripture informs us, that Cain built a city: and foon after the deluge, we hear of many cities; and of an attempt to build a tower that fhould reach the fky: a miracle ftopped the progrefs, and prevented the completion of that bold defign.

The firft men, living in a warm climate, wanted no habitations: every grove afforded fhade from the rays of the fun, and fhelter from the dews of the night; rain fell but feldom, nor was it ever fufficiently cold, to render clofer dwellings than groves, either defirable or neceffary, even in the hours of repofe: they fed upon the fpontaneous productions of the foil, and lived without care, as without labour.

But when the human fpecies increafed, and the produce of the earth, however luxuriant, was infufficient to fupply the requifite food; when frequent difappointments drew on contention, with all its train of calamities, then feparation became neceffary; and colonies difperfed to different regions: where frequent rain, ftorms and piercing cold, forced the inhabitants to feek for better fhelter than trees.

At firſt they moſt likely retired to caverns, formed by nature in rocks; to hollow trunks of trees; or to holes, dug by themſelves in the earth; but ſoon diſguſted with the damp and darkneſs of theſe habitations, they began to ſearch after more wholeſome and comfortable dwellings.

The animal creation pointed out both materials, and manners of conſtruction; ſwallows, rooks, bees, ſtorks; were the firſt builders: man obſerved their inſtinctive operations, he admired; he imitated; and being endued with reaſoning faculties, and of a ſtructure ſuited to mechanical purpoſes, he ſoon outdid his maſters in the builder's art.

Rude and unſeemly, no doubt, were the firſt attempts; without experience or tools, the builder collected a few boughs of trees, ſpread them in a conick ſhape, and covering them with ruſhes, or leaves and clay; formed his hut: ſufficient to ſhelter its hardy inhabitants at night, or in ſeaſons of bad weather. But in the courſe of time, men naturally grew more expert; they invented tools to ſhorten and improve labour; fell upon neater, more durable modes of conſtruction; and forms, better adapted than the cone, to the purpoſes for which their huts were intended. They felt the want of convenient habitations, wherein to taſte the comforts of privacy, to reſt ſecurely, and be effectually ſcreened from troubleſome exceſſes of weathers. They wanted room to exerciſe the arts, to which neceſſity had given birth; to depoſit the grain, that agriculture enabled them to raiſe in abundance; to ſecure the flocks, which frequent diſappointments in the chace, had forced them to collect and domeſticate. Thus ſtimulated, their fancy and hands, went arduouſly to work, and the progreſs of improvement was rapid.

That the primitive hut was of a conick figure, it is reaſonable to conjecture; from its being the ſimpleſt of ſolid forms: and moſt eaſily conſtructed. And wherever wood was found, they probably built in the manner above deſcribed; but, ſoon as the inhabitants diſcovered the inconvenience of the inclined ſides, and the want of upright ſpace in the cone; they changed it for the cube: and, as it is ſuppoſed, proceeded in the following manner.

Having, ſays Vitruvius, marked out the ſpace to be occupied by the hut; they fixed in the ground, ſeveral upright trunks of trees, to form the ſides; filling the intervals between them with branches, cloſely interwoven, and ſpread over with clay. The ſides thus compleated, four beams were laid on the upright trunks; which being well faſtned together at the angles of their junction, kept the ſides firm; and likewiſe ſerved to ſupport the covering or roof of the building; compoſed of ſmaller trees, placed horizontally, like joiſts: upon which were laid ſeveral beds of reeds, leaves, and earth or clay.

By degrees, other improvements took place; and means were found to make the fabrick laſting, neat, and handſome: as well as convenient. The bark and other protuberances were taken from the trees that formed the ſides, theſe trees were raiſed above the dirt and humidity on ſtones; were covered at the top with other ſtones; and firmly bound round at both ends with ozier or cords, to ſecure them from ſplitting. The ſpaces between the joiſts of the roof, were cloſed up with

clay

clay or wax, and the ends of them either fmoothed, or covered with boards. The different beds of materials that compofed the covering, were cut ftraight at the eaves, and diftinguifhed from each other by different projections. The form of the roof too, was altered; for being, on account of its flatnefs, unfit to throw off the rains which fometimes fell in great abundance; it was raifed in the middle, on trees difpofed like rafters; after the form of a gable roof.

THIS conftruction, fimple as it appears, probably gave birth to moft of the parts that now adorn our buildings; particularly to the orders; which may be confidered as the bafis, of the whole decorative part of architecture: for when ftructures of wood were fet afide, and men began to erect folid, ftately edifices of ftone; having nothing nearer to imitate, they naturally copied the parts, which neceffity introduced in the primitive hut; infomuch that the upright trees, with the ftones and cordage at each end of them, were the origin of columns, bafes, and capitals; the beams and joifts, gave rife to architraves and frizes; with their triglyphs, and metopes: and the gable roof, was the origin of pediments; as the beds of materials forming the covering, and the rafters fupporting them, were of cornices; with their corona, their mutules, modillions, and dentils.

THAT trees were the originals of columns feems evident, from fome very ancient Egyptian ruins ftill exifting; in which are feen columns compofed of many fmall trees tied together with bandages, to form one ftrong pillar; which, before ftone was in ufe, became a neceffary operation in a country, where no large timber was to be had; and in which, the ftupendous fize of their ftructures, conftituted the principal merit. Herodotus defcribes a ftately ftone building, which ftood in the court of the temple of Minerva at Sais, the columns of which were made to imitate palm trees.

THE form of the bundle pillar abovementioned, though deriving its exiftence from neceffity, is far from difagreeable; it was evidently a beauty in the eyes of the ancient Egyptians, fince it was imitated by them in ftone: and it feems more natural to fuppofe, that fluted columns, owe their origin to the intermediate hollows, between the trees compofing thefe pillars, than to the folds of a woman's garment; to which they have but very little refemblance.

VITRUVIUS, the only remaining ancient writer upon the decorative part of architecture, afcribes almoft every invention in that art to the Greeks: as if till the time of Dorus, it had remained in its infant ftate; and nothing had till then appeared worth notice. And moft, if not all the modern authors, have ecchoed the fame doctrine. Yet, if ancient hiftory be credited, * the Egyptians, Affyrians, Babylonians, and other nations of remote antiquity, had exhibited wonders in the art of building, even before the Grecians were a people.

IT muft indeed be confeffed, that though the works of the Afiatick nations were aftonifhing in point of fize and extent, yet in other refpects they were of a nature, calculated rather to give a high idea of the power and wealth of the founders, than of their fkill or tafte. We plainly fee that all their notions of grandeur were confined

---

* See the fcriptures, Homer, Herodotus, Strabo, Diodorus Siculus, Paufanias, Pliny, Juftin, Quintus Curtius.

to dimenfion; and all their ideas of elegance or beauty, to richnefs of materials, or gaudinefs of colouring. We obferve a barrennefs of fancy in their compofitions; a fimplicity and famenefs in their forms; peculiar to primitive inventions: but, even in the early works of the Egyptians, befide their prodigious dimenfions; there are evident marks of tafte and fancy; it is in them we trace the firft ornamental forms in architecture, and to their builders we are moft probably indebted for the invention of columns, bafes, capitals and entablatures. We likewife read of roofs, fupported by figures of Coloffal men and animals in the works of the Egyptians, feveral ages before the introduction of Perfians or Caryatides, in the ftructures of Greece: and of temples, adorned with ftately porticos; enriched with columns, and fculpture; and built, before there were any temples in Greece.

HENCE it may be inferred that the Grecians were not the inventors of ornamental architecture, but had that art, as well as their religion and gods, from the Egyptians: or from the Phœnicians their nearer neighbours, whofe fkill in arts is faid to have been anterior to theirs. Though both were of Egyptian origin.

DIODORUS SICULUS obferves, that the Egyptian priefts proved, both by their facred records, and alfo by other undoubted teftimonies; that not only the poets and philofophers of Greece, travelled anciently into Egypt, to collect their knowledge; but alfo their architects and fculptors, and that every thing in which the Grecians excelled, and for which they were famous; was originally carried from Egypt into Greece.

THE Phœnicians however were very early celebrated for their proficiency in the arts of defign; and there is no doubt, but the Greeks availed themfelves of their inventions.

WE are told that Hiram made two capitals for the pillars Jachin, and Boaz, in Solomon's temple; which, far as can be collected, from the accounts given of them in feveral parts of fcripture, very much refembled the Corinthian capitals, both in form and proportions; though executed fome centuries before Calimachus, is reported by Vitruvius, to have invented it at Corinth. The cherubims of Hiram too, or the Coloffal figures of men and animals, in the ftructures of the Egyptians, were prior inventions; and undoubtedly fuggefted to the Greeks, their ideas of Perfians and Caryatides.

AND though architecture is certainly indebted to the Grecians, for confiderable improvements; yet, it may with confidence be averred, that they never brought the art to its utmoft degree of excellence. The art of building, fays Leon Baptifta Alberti, " fprung up, and fpent its adolefcent ftate in Afia; after a certain time, " it flowered in Greece; and finally acquired perfect maturity in Italy; among the " Romans." And whether we call to mind, the defcriptions given by ancient writers of Nineveh, Babylon, Thebes, Memphis; the Egyptian pyramids, the fepulchres of their kings, their temples and other publick monuments: or contemplate, among the Roman works; their palaces, amphitheatres, baths, villas, bridges, maufoleums and numerous other, yet exifting, teftimonies of their fplendor; it muft candidly be confeffed, that the Grecians have been far excelled by
other

other nations, not only in the magnitude and grandeur of their ſtructures, but like‑wiſe in point of fancy, ingenuity, variety, and elegant ſelection.

How diſtant the Grecians were from perfection in proportions, in the art of profiling, and other parts of the detail; will ſoon be evident to any impartial examiner, who compares the publications of Le Roi, Stewart, Revett, and other ingenious Levantine travellers; with the antiquities of the Romans: either on the ſpot, or as they have been given in books; by Palladio, Serlio, Deſgodetz, Sandrart, Piraneſi, and other authors. The laſt of thoſe here mentioned, has publiſhed a parallel, between the faireſt monuments of Greece and Rome; which is recom‑mended to the inſpection and peruſal, of thoſe who have not yet ſeen it.

INDEED, none of the few things now exiſting in Greece, though ſo pompouſly deſcribed, and neatly repreſented, in various publications of our time; ſeem to deſerve great notice; either for dimenſion, grandeur of ſtile, rich fancy, or elegant taſte of deſign; nor do they ſeem calculated to throw new light upon the art, or to contribute towards its advancement: not even thoſe erected by Pericles or Alex‑ander; while the Grecian arts flouriſhed moſt; neither the famous lantern of Demoſthenes, nor the more famous * Parthenon; which, though not ſo conſiderable as the church of St. Martin, in St. Martin's Lane, excluſive of its elegant ſpire; had for its architects, Phidias, Callicrates, and Ictinus; was the boaſt of Athens; excited the envy and murmurs of all Greece. We find indeed, in Pliny, and other ancient writers, very pompous deſcriptions of temples, ſuch as, that of Apollo at Mi‑letus; of Ceres and Proſerpine at Eleuſes; of the Olympian Jupiter at Athens; and above all, of Diana at Epheſus; one of the ſeven wonders of the world. But if the Grecian architecture was defective in the time of Alexander, it muſt have been more ſo ſome centuries earlier: and concerning temples built in † bogs, and founded upon wool, to reſiſt earthquakes; and of which, the ſtones were ſet with ſand bags; ſome doubts may be indulged: as well as of thoſe made of ‡ wax, yet reſiſting the ardor of a Grecian Sun; or thoſe of braſs, yet catching fire and melting down.

AT firſt ſight, it may appear extraordinary, that a people ſo renowned in arms; ſo celebrated for poetry, rhetorick, and every ſort of polite learning; and who carried ſculpture farther than any of the ancient nations; ſhould be ſo deficient in architecture: yet upon farther conſideration, many reaſons will occur why it neceſſarily ſhould be ſo.——Greece, a country ſmall in itſelf, was divided into a number of little ſtates; none of them very powerful, populous, or rich: ſo that they could attempt, no very conſiderable works in architecture; having neither the ſpace, the hands, nor the treaſures that would have been neceſſary. " It muſt be " owned, ſays Monſieur D'Ablancourt, that Greece, even in the zenith of her " greatneſs, had more ambition than power: we find Athens flattering herſelf with " the conqueſt of the univerſe, yet unable to defend her own territories, againſt the " incurſions of her neighbours: and who can refrain from laughter at the Lacede‑ " monians; rivals in fame with the Athenians; yet, in deſpair, and reduced to ſue " for peace; by the loſs of four hundred men."——The lake of Mœris would have deluged all Peloponneſus, and ruined all Greece; Babylon would have covered

* Plutarch in Pericles.　　† Pliny, lib. 36, c. 14.　　‡ Pauſanias Phocid. c. 6.

H

Attica,

Attica, and more men had been employed to build that city, than there were inhabitants in all the Grecian ftates. The Egyptian labyrinth, was a hundred times larger than that of Crete; and more materials have been employed in one of the Egyptian pyramids, than were ufed in all the publick ftructures of Athens.

IF, at the fame time it be recollected, that Greece, while divided into many governments, was conftantly harraffed with domeftick wars, and from its union, always in an unfettled fituation. That, an uncommon fimplicity of manners pre-vailed among the Grecian ftates; and the ftricteft maxims of equality, were zealoufly adhered to in moft of them; it will be eafy to account for the fmall progrefs made by the Greeks in architecture. Demofthenes obferves, that the houfes of Ariftides, Miltiades, or any other of the great men of their time; were no finer than thofe of their neighbours: fuch was their moderation, and fo fteadily did they adhere to the ancient manners of their country. One of the laws of Lycurgus ordained, that the ceilings of houfes fhould only be wrought by an ax; and their gates and doors be left rough from the faw; no other tools than thefe, being permitted: which law, was fo fcrupuloufly obferved among the Lacedemonians; that when King Leo-tychidas, faw at Corinth a ceiling, of which the timbers were neatly wrought; it was fo new a fight to him, that he afked his hoft, if trees grew fquare in that country. It feems indeed, as if thefe fumptuary laws of Lycurgus, had made a general impreffion; and infpired the Greeks, rather with contempt than veneration, for fplendid ftructures: even in their beft time, they accounted it an effeminate folly, to be oftentatious in that refpect. " All the ftates of Greece, fays Plutarch, " clamoured loudly againft Pericles for decorating Athens like a vain fantaftick " woman, and adorning it with ftatues and temples, which * coft a thoufand " talents."

WHAT magnificence the Grecians difplayed in their ftructures, was confined to their publick buildings; which were chiefly temples: wherein there appears to have been nothing very furprifing, either for dimenfions; ingenuity of contrivance; or excellence of workmanfhip. Greece, almoft conftantly the theatre of war; abounded not like Italy, in magnificent villas; where the richeft productions of art were difplayed. Their publick roads were not adorned with maufoleums, to commemorate their heroes; nor the towns, with arches or bridges to celebrate their triumphs. The Grecian theatres were inconfiderable, compared with thofe of the Romans; the numachiæ and amphitheatres, unknown amongft them; as were alfo the thermini, in which the Romans affected fo much fplendor.

IN latter times indeed the Greeks, particularly the Athenians; abated of their original feverity; the orator abovementioned obferves, that in his time, there were fome private houfes more magnificent than publick edifices: but this does not appear to have been very common, and confequently could not be productive of much additional fplendor; even Alcibiades, the moft luxurious Greek of his time; for he was accufed of wearing a purple cloak, and of fleeping upon a bed with a canvas bottom; doth not feem to have been better lodged, than other Athenians; excepting, that his houfe was painted.

* The Parthenon is faid to have coft a thoufand talents; not quite fo much as was expended in onions and radifhes at the building of a pyramid: fee Diodorus Siculus.

SINCE therefore the Grecian ſtructures are neither the moſt conſiderable, moſt varied, nor moſt perfect; it follows that our knowledge ought not to be collected from them; but from ſome purer, more abundant ſource; which, in whatever relates to the ornamental part of the art, can be no other than the Roman antiquity yet remaining, in Italy; France, or elſewhere: veſtiges of buildings erected in the politeſt ages; by the wealthieſt, moſt ſplendid, and powerful people of the world. Who, after having removed to Rome, from Carthage, Sicily, Egypt and Greece; the rareſt productions of the arts of deſign; as alſo the ableſt artiſts of the times; were conſtantly employed, during many centuries, in the conſtruction of all kinds of edifices that either uſe, convenience, luxury, or ſplendor required. Pliny informs us, that the works of the Romans were much more conſiderable than thoſe of any other people; that in the courſe of thirty-five years, more than a hundred ſumptuous palaces had been erected in Rome, the moſt inconſiderable of which was fit for the reſidence of a king: and that in his own time, the time of Veſpaſian; there were a great number, much more ſplendid, than any of the hundred abovementioned. The palaces of Caligula and Nero, were in extent like towns; and enriched with every thing that the moſt exquiſite taſte, and the moſt unbounded liberality, could ſuggeſt.

THE Romans began early to cultivate architecture. Several conſiderable works were erected by their kings, and many more, during the magiſtracy of their conſuls. Julius Cæſar, was paſſionately fond of that art; and beſides the buildings erected by him in Rome; he embelliſhed with conſiderable ſtructures, ſays Suetonius, the principal cities of Italy, France, Spain, Aſia, and Greece. Auguſtus, boaſted on his death bed; that he had converted Rome into a city of marble: he not only built much himſelf, but excited his friends to follow the example; and Mecænas, his favorite and miniſter, was the patron of arts, as well as of letters.

CALIGULA and Nero, were to the utmoſt, ſplendid in their buildings. The latter, carried his paſſion for architecture, as it is ſaid, even to the extravagant exceſs of burning Rome, that he might have the pleaſure of rebuilding it with greater regularity, and magnificence; which he afterwards did.

DURING the reigns of Claudius, Veſpaſian, Titus, Domitian and Nerva, many very conſiderable publick works were erected; both at Rome, and in other parts of the Roman dominions; and Veſpaſian, not only re-edified the capitol with greater magnificence than before; but alſo all the other publick buildings of Rome; which had ſuffered by the outrages of the Vitellians. He obliged the proprietors of ruined houſes to rebuild them; and cauſed to be erected, ſeveral new edifices of great coſt and magnificence; ſuch as the temple of Peace; the largeſt covered building of antiquity: another, dedicated to Minerva; of the richeſt and moſt exquiſite workmanſhip, ever exhibited in Rome: the firſt artiſts then alive, having been employed to paint, carve, and incruſtate the ſame. He alſo built the largeſt amphitheatre in the world; capable of containing eighty thouſand ſpectators, and many other works of leſs note. His care and munificence extended themſelves in like manner, to all other parts of the Roman empire; in which he erected new cities and towns, repaired, adorned and fortified, ſuch as were old, or ruinous.

I

TITUS, his fucceffor, was fo attentive to the beauty of his metropolis; that, when a dreadful fire had deftroyed many of its temples, and publ ck buildings; he refolved to re-edify them at his own charge, with all poffible expedition: dif-pofing of the furniture and ornaments of his own palaces, to defray the expence. Death, prevented the completion of his intentions; but Domitian, finifhed what he had left undone; and alfo adorned Rome with many new ftructures; particularly with a palace, furprifing for the magnificence of its colonades, the number of its rooms, the fplendor of its baths and female apartments. His love for building was fuch; that he wifhed to be another Midas, to the end that he might indulge his paffion without control.

TRAJAN, in whofe reign the Roman empire was in its moft flourifhing ftate, cultivated all the arts of defign; and with the affiftance of the celebrated Apollodorus, his principal architect; executed many very confiderable works. He erected a bridge of ftone over the Danube, fixty feet wide, one hundred and fifty feet high, and almoft two miles in length. He alfo built feveral cities among the Dacians; embel-lifhed Rome and other parts of Italy, with many publick edifices; rebuilt Antioch, which had been almoft totally deftroyed by an earthquake; and alfo repaired many other towns in Syria, that fuffered at the fame time, by the fame calamity.

ADRIAN, whofe fkill in different branches of polite knowledge is well known; particularly in the arts of defign; embellifhed various parts of the Roman empire with fplendid and beautiful ftructures; fuch as his bridge and maufoleum at Rome; his villa near Tivoli; his wall in Britain; which extended from the river Eden in Cumberland, to the Tyne in Northumberland: many temples and other publick buildings in Gaul, in Greece, and in Africa: where he re-edified a confiderable part of Carthage. He alfo rebuilt Jerufalem; which Titus had demolifhed about fixty years before; and erected in Egypt, a ftately pillar to the memory of Pompey.

ANTONINUS PIUS re-edified a great part of Rome, Narbonne, Antioch, and Carthage: all which cities, had fuffered confiderably by fire. And it was his cuftom, whenever any damage happened to a city by an earthquake, a fire, an inundation, or other calamitous accidents; to repair it with money taken out of the publick treafury. He greatly improved the ports of Tarracina and Cayeta; built confiderable baths at Oftia; aqueducts at Antium; temples at Lavinium: and all muft be fenfible, how powerfully the example of princes, operates upon the minds of their fubjects; infpires the fame paffions, and excites to the fame purfuits.

IN fhort, architecture continued to flourifh among the Romans, though with abated luftre; till Conftantine removed the feat of empire to Byzantium: and the number of ftately ftructures, with which Rome, and the Roman dominions abounded; is almoft incredible. Their very remains, excite at this day, the aftonifhment and admiration, of every judicious beholder: in fpight of all that length of time, wars, party rage, barbarifm, cafual events, fuperftition and avarice; have done to deftroy them.

IN thefe remains, there will be found abundant materials to work upon, and form a compleat fyftem of decorative architecture. The labours of the celebrated

mafters

masters of the fifteenth, sixteenth, and seventeenth centuries, may, perhaps, be added to enrich the stock; and we may avail ourselves of their labours, to facilitate, or shorten our own; but, it should always be remembered, that though the stream may swell in its course, by the intervention of other supplies; yet it is purest at the fountain's head.   And whoever aims at being superiorly eminent in any profession, must not receive his information at second hand, from others; but mount himself to the origin and reason of things.   The man, says Michael Angelo, who follows another, always is behind; but he who boldly strikes into a different path, may climb as high as his competitor: and though the road be somewhat more rugged, yet, if his efforts are crowned with success, the reward will amply compensate, for the risque and labour of the enterprize.

An anonymous Italian writer observes, that the superiority of Raphael, may perhaps be owing, to his having been so univerfally admired and copied; that the modern sculptors never equalled the ancient, because they have done nothing but imitate them; and if, says he, all the ancient paintings hitherto discovered, are inferior to the modern; it is, perhaps owing, to our painters not having had the works of an Apelles to copy.

Nature is the supreme and true model of the imitative arts, upon which every great artist must form his idea of the profession, in which he means to excel; and the antique is to the architect, what nature is to the painter or sculptor; the source from which his chief knowledge must be collected; the model upon which his taste must be formed.

But as in nature few things are faultless, so neither must it be imagined that every ancient production in architecture, even among the Romans, was perfect; or a fit model for imitation: as blind adorers of antiquity are sometimes disposed to believe.   On the contrary, their remains are so extremely unequal, that it requires the greatest circumspection, and effort of judgement, to make a proper choice.   The Roman arts, like those of other nations; had their rife, their æra of perfection, their decline.   At Rome, as in London or Paris, there were few great architects, but many very indifferent ones; and the Romans had their connoisseurs, as we have ours; who sometimes would dictate to the artist, and cramp the fortunate sallies of his genius; force upon him and the world, their own whimsical productions; promote ignorant flatterers; discourage, even oppress, honest merit.

Vitruvius, supposed to have lived in the Augustan age, complains loudly of this hardship; and there is a remarkable instance of the vindictive spirit of an ancient connoisseur, in Adrian; who put to death the celebrated Apollodorus, for having ventured a shrewd remark upon a temple, designed by that emperor, and built under his direction.

In the constructive part of architecture, the ancients do not feem to have been great proficients.   I am inclined to believe, that many of the deformities observable in the Grecian buildings, must be ascribed to their deficiency in that particular: such as their gouty columns; their narrow intercolumniations; their disproportionate architraves; their hypetral temples, which they knew not how to cover; and their

K   temples

temples with a range of columns running in the center, to support the roof; contrary to every rule, either of beauty or convenience.

NEITHER were the Romans much more skilful: the precepts of Vitruvius and Pliny on that subject are imperfect, sometimes erroneous; and the strength or duration of their structures, is more owing to the quantity and goodness of their materials, than to any great art in putting them together. It is not therefore from any of the ancient works, that much information can be obtained in that branch of the art.

To those usually called Gothick architects, we are indebted for the first considerable improvements in construction; there is a lightness in their works, an art and boldness of execution; to which the ancients never arrived: and which the moderns comprehend and imitate with difficulty. England contains many magnificent examples of this species of architecture, equally admirable for the art with which they are built, the taste and ingenuity with which they are composed.

ONE cannot refrain from wishing, that the Gothick structures were more considered; better understood; and in higher estimation; than they hitherto seem to have been. Would our dilettanti instead of importing the gleanings of Greece; or our antiquaries, instead of publishing loose incoherent prints; encourage persons duly qualified, to undertake a correct elegant publication of our own cathedrals, and other buildings called Gothick, before they totally fall to ruin; it would be of real service to the arts of design; preserve the remembrance of an extraordinary stile of building now sinking fast into oblivion; and at the same time publish to the world the riches of Britain, in the splendor of her ancient structures.

MICHAEL ANGELO, who skilled as he was in mathematical knowledge, could have no very high opinion of the ancient construction; boasted that he would suspend the largest temple of antiquity (meaning the Pantheon) in the air: which he afterwards performed, in the cupola of St. Peter's at Rome. And Sir Christopher Wren, has conducted all parts of St. Paul's, and many others, his numerous admirable works, with so much art; that they are, and ever will be, studied and admired by all intelligent observers. To him, and to several ingenious artists and artificers since his time, we owe many great improvements in carpentry; which the English have established upon better principles, and carried to higher perfection, than any other nation.

SOME of the French architects have likewise been very skilful in construction. The mason's art in particular, has been considerably improved by that nation. And we are indebted to the French, to the Italians, and to a few of our own countrymen, for many valuable books; * in which the manner of conducting great works is taught; the necessary machines, tools, carriages, and other apparatus described; together with the properties, modes of preparing, and of employing, all kinds of materials

---

* Architettura di Andrea Palladio. Architettura Univerfale di Vincenzo Scamozzi. Archi. di Sebaftiano Serliæ. Leo. Bap. Albertis de re Edificatoria. Architecture de Philibert de Lorme. Secret d'Architecture and l'Art de Charpente d'Matheinen Jouffe. Felibien principes de l'Architecture, &c. La Pratique du trait par Defargues. Belidore Science de Ingenieurs and Architecture Hydraulique. Gautier traite des Ponts et des Chemins. Blondel Cours d'Architecture. Architecture des Voutes par Derand. De la Rue traite de la Coupe des Pierres. Evelin's Silva. Wotton's Remains. Zabaglia Opere. Price's Britifh Carpenter. Savot Archi. Françoife. Neve's Builders Dictionary. Frefier Coupe des Pierres (with the tranflations in Englifh, French, or Italian, of thofe that are tranflated.) And many others of lefs note.

used

ufed in building. They likewife have treated of the nature of foils, and the manner of laying foundations, of raifing fuperftructures, and of every other particular, having relation to the mechanick arts, connected with building.

* THESE books, the ftructures abovementioned, and many others to be found in England or elfewhere, are the fchools from which the architect muft collect the rudiments of conftruction; but practice, experience, and attentive obfervation; are requifite to render him confummately fkilled in this important part of his profeffion.

THE architect's aim being, as has been obferved, to erect handfome, ftrong, convenient, falubrious and comfortable edifices; to afcertain their value; and to build them with fafety, eafe, and frugality: the principles of his art may be ranged under four diftinct heads, which are diftribution; conftruction; decoration; and economy.

OF conftruction and decoration, it has been fhown whence his knowledge fhould be collected; and of diftribution, which comprehends all particulars relative to health, convenience, comfort, pleafure and profit; the artift may collect his general idea, from books or obfervations, made upon buildings erected for various purpofes, in different climates and ages; but it is only by practice that he can become expert, in difcovering the advantages, or defects of fituation; the nature of climates, or expofitions; the qualities of air, water, foil, and many other things neceffary to be known: and it is only by a thorough acquaintance with the cuftoms, and modes of living of his own times; and with the difpofitions, amufements, occupations, and duties, of his cotemporaries; that he can effectually learn, how to fupply their wants, or gratify their wifhes.

IN countries where general cuftom governs moft things, and where all perfons of the fame rank think, act and live, nearly after the fame manner; the diftributive part of architecture has not fo many difficulties: but wherever that is not the cafe, every new employer opens a frefh field for inveftigation; and the artift's tafk is never at an end.

THE economy of architecture is of fo complicated, fo extenfive a nature, that it is almoft impoffible for any man to know it perfectly; much more for an architect, whofe mind muft be loaded with a great variety of other knowledge. When therefore an artift has fixed his abode in any particular country, or great city; it will be beft, to limit his refearches at firft, to that place alone: informing himfelf of the different quarries, woods, kilns, fea ports or other markets from whence it is fupplied with materials for building; as alfo of the different natures and degrees of goodnefs of thefe materials, the propereft times for providing them, the beft means of tranfporting them to the places of their deftination; their value; and upon what circumftances that value depends: to the end that he may be enabled at all times, to account for the fluctuation of price, and to afcertain what they are juftly worth.

* See note, page 24.

L   THE

THE principal difficulty of this enquiry arifes; not only from the many caufes upon which the value of things and their rife or fall depends, but from the caution with which dealers and tradefmen of almoft all denominations, conceal the fecrets of their trade; and the real profits they have thereon.

His next ftep muft be to find out, all the able artifts and artificers of the place, and its environs; to form an acquaintance with them, and examine carefully, in what branches they particularly excel; how far their fkill extends; what their difpofitions, circumftances, and tempers are; with their characters and connections: that by combining thefe particulars, he may employ their abilities upon every occafion, to moft advantage, as well for them, as for himfelf.

He muft then make diligent enquiry into the ufual prices allowed for every fort of labour, or workmanfhip; according to its degree of perfection: how much time and what materials are requifite to produce given quantities thereof; what profits according to the ufage of the place, are allowed thereon to the mafter work-men; and in what manner it is meafured, or accounted for when done: that he may be entire mafter of his fubject, and enabled to judge equitably between the employer and employed, as his ftation requires. Thefe enquiries will at the firft be attended with confiderable difficulty, for the reafons beforementioned; but like propofitions in geometry, one information will facilitate another, and in the courfe of a few years practice, the artift, if he be induftrious, and fkilfully inquifitive; will have acquired a thorough acquaintance with whatever concerns his own circle: and then he may extend his enquiries to other parts. What is already known, will ferve as a clew to farther knowledge; and by degrees, he may become a very competent judge of every economical particular, in all the provinces of an extenfive kingdom.

If in this chapter, or in other parts of the work (for it may be as well to apologize at once, for all) the author has ventured to think for himfelf, and fome-times to ftart opinions, differing from thofe of other men; he begs leave to fay, that it proceeds not from the affectation of being either fingular, or dogmatical; but from conviction, that his notions are always founded in reafon, or proved by well attefted facts: and delivered with a wifh to guide the reader right. All that has been faid, refpecting the fuperiority of the Roman architecture, was written a confiderable time ago, when the Grecian had been extolled into repute; and ftructures were erecting in different parts of England, after Attick defigns. Fortu-nately, the fight of thefe firft fpecimens, excited no defires for more: after a few ineffectual ftruggles, the Roman manner obtained a compleat victory. There feemed, at that time, no farther neceffity to fight its caufe; and thefe obfervations, intended for the fecond edition of this work; were then fuppreffed. But latterly, the *Gufto Greco*, has again ventured to peep forth, and once more, threaten an invafion. What therefore was omitted in the fecond edition, it has been judged neceffary to infert in this, as a caution to ftragglers.

The Primitive Buildings &c.

The First sort of Huts.

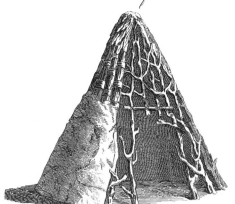

The Second sort of Huts.

The Third sort of Huts which gave birth to the Doric ORDER.

The Doric Order in its Improved State.

Origin of the Corinthian Capital.

The Doric Profile of the Temple of Theseus at Athens one of the most Antient Monuments of that Order now Existing.

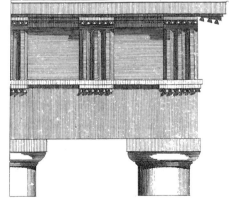

A	*Plinth*	K	*Conge*	T	*Fascia of y.e Architrave*
B	*Lower Torus*	L	*Fillet or upper Cincture*	U	*Drops*
C	*Fillet or Square*	M	*Astragal*	W	*Fillet or Senia*
D	*Scotia*	N	*Neck or Frise of y.e Capital*	X	*Triglyphs*
E	*Fillet*	O	*Fillets or Annulets*	Y	*Capital of the Triglyph*
F	*Upper Torus*	P	*Ovolo, or Echinus*	Z	*Ovolo or Quarter round*
G	*Fillet or lower Cincture*	Q	*Abacus*	1	*Mutule or Modillion Band*
H	*Conge*	R	*Inverted Cyma or Ogee*	2	*Mutules*
I	*Shaft of the Column*	S	*Fillet*	3	*Ogee*

4	*Corona or Drip*
5	*Ogee*
6	*Cavetto*
7	*Fillet*

P. Mazell sculp.

Regular Mouldings with their proper Ornaments.

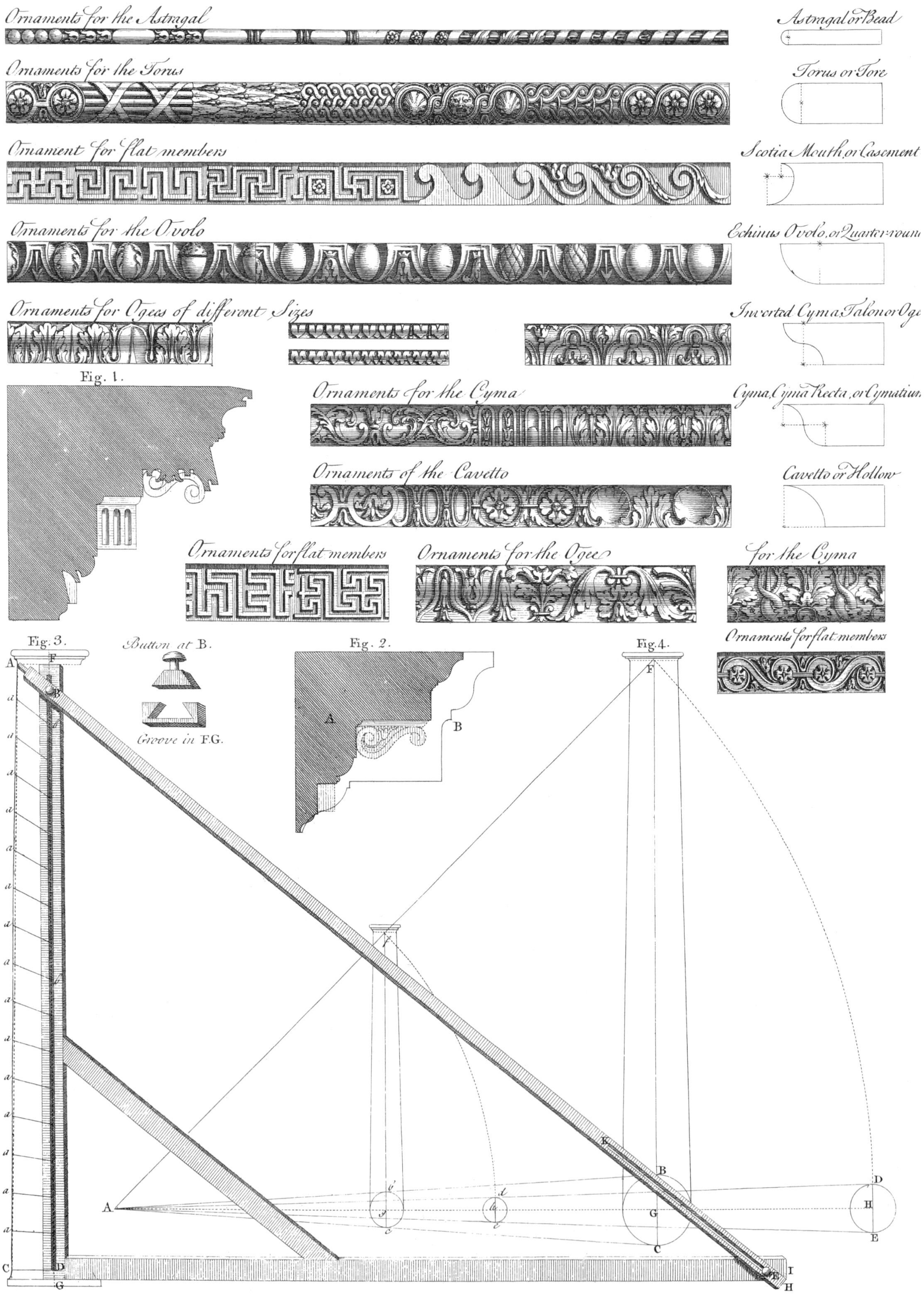

Fillet Listel or Square

Ornaments for the Astragal

Astragal or Bead

Ornaments for the Torus

Torus or Tore

Ornament for flat members

Scotia Mouth or Casement

Ornaments for the Ovolo

Echinus Ovolo, or Quarter-round

Ornaments for Ogees of different Sizes

Inverted Cyma Talon or Ogee

Fig. 1.

Ornaments for the Cyma

Cyma, Cyma Recta, or Cymatium.

Ornaments of the Cavetto

Cavetto or Hollow

Ornaments for flat members

Ornaments for the Ogee

For the Cyma

Fig. 3.

Button at B.

Groove in F.G.

Fig. 2.

Fig. 4.

Ornaments for flat members

Chambers

P. Fourdrinier Sculp.

Of the PARTS *which compofe the* ORDERS *of* ARCHITECTURE, *and of their Properties, Application, and Enrichments.*

A S in many other arts, fo in architecture, there are certain elementary forms; which, though fimple in their nature, and few in number, are the principal conftituent objects of every compofition; however complicated or extenfive it may be.

OF thefe there are in our art, two diftinct forts; the firft confifting of fuch parts, as reprefent thofe that were effentially neceffary, in the conftruction of the primitive huts: as the fhaft of the column, with the plinth of its bafe, and the abacus of its capital; reprefenting the upright trees, with the ftones ufed to raife, and to cover them. Likewife the architrave and triglyph, reprefenting the beams and joifts; the mutules, modillions, and dentils; either reprefenting the rafters, or fome other pieces of timber, employed to fupport the covering: and the corona, reprefenting the beds of materials, which compofed the covering itfelf. All thefe are properly diftinguifhed by the appellation of effential parts; and form the firft clafs. The fubfervient members, contrived for the ufe and ornament of thefe; and intended either to fupport, to fhelter, or to unite them gracefully together, which are ufually called mouldings; conftitute the fecond clafs.

THE effential parts were, moft probably, the only ones employed, even in the firft ftone buildings; as may be collected from fome ancient ftructures, yet remaining: for the architects of thofe early times, had certainly very imperfect ideas of beauty in the productions of art, and therefore contented themfelves, with barely imitating the rude model before them; but coming in time to compare the works of their own hands, with animal and vegetable productions; each fpecies of which, is compofed of a great diverfity of forms, affording an inexhauftible fund of amufement to the mind; they could not but conceive a difguft, at the frequent repetition of fquare figures in their buildings; and therefore thought of introducing certain intermediate parts; which might feem to be of fome ufe, and at the fame time be fo formed, as to give a more varied, pleafing appearance, to the whole compofition: and this, in all probability, was the origin of mouldings.

OF regular mouldings, there are * eight; which are, the ᵃ Ovolo, the ᵇ Talon, the ᶜ Cyma, the ᵈ Cavetto, the ᵉ Torus, the ᶠ Aftragal, the ᵍ Scotia, and the ʰ Fillet.

THE names of thefe are allufive to their forms; and their forms are adapted to the ufes, which they are intended to ferve. The Ovolo and Talon, being ftrong at their extremities, are fit for fupports. The Cyma and Cavetto, though improper for that purpofe, as they are weak in the extreme parts, and terminate in a point;

---

* See plate of regular mouldings.

ᵃ Ovolo, or Echinus, or quarter round.   ᶜ Cyma, cyma recta, Cymatium.   ᵉ Torus or Tore.   ᵍ Scotia, or Trochilos.
ᵇ Talon or Ogee, or reverfed Cyma.   ᵈ Cavetto, or mouth, or hollow.   ᶠ Aftragal, Bead, or Baguette.   ʰ Fillet, Liftel, Annulet.

are

are well contrived for coverings; to shelter other members: the tendency of their outline being very oppofite, to the direction of falling water; which for that reason, cannot glide along their furface, but muft neceffarily drop. The Torus and Aftragal, fhaped like ropes, are intended to bind and ftrengthen the parts on which they are employed; and the ufe of the Fillet and Scotia, is only to feparate, contraft, and ftrengthen the effect of other mouldings, to give a graceful turn to the profile, and to prevent that confufion, which would be occafioned by joining feveral convex members together.

THAT the inventors of thefe forms, meant to exprefs fomething by their diffe- rent figures, will fcarcely be denied; and that the abovementioned were their deftinations, may be deduced, not only from their figures, but from the practice of the ancients in their moft efteemed works: for if we examine the Pantheon, the three columns in the Campo Vaccino, the temple of Jupiter Tonans, the fragments of the frontifpiece of Nero, the bafilica of Antoninus, the forum of Nerva, the arches of Titus and Septimus Severus, the theatre of Marcellus; and indeed, almoft every ancient building, either at Rome, or in other parts of Italy and France, it will be found, that in all their profiles, the Cyma and the Cavetto are conftantly ufed as finifhings, and never applied where ftrength is required: that the Ovolo and Talon, are always employed as fupporters to the effential members of the compofition; fuch as the modillions, dentils, and corona: that the chief ufe of the Torus and Aftragal, is to fortify the tops and bottoms of columns, and fometimes of pedeftals, where they are frequently cut in the form of ropes: as on the Trajan column, in the temple of Concord, and on feveral fragments which I have feen both at Rome, and at Nifmes in Languedoc: and that the Scotia, is employed only to feparate the mem- bers of bafes, for which purpofe the Fillet is likewife ufed, not only in bafes, but in all kinds of profiles.

HENCE it may be inferred, that there is fomething pofitive and natural, in thefe primary forms of architecture; and confequently in the parts which they compofe: and that Palladio erred, in employing the Cavetto under the Corona, in three of his orders; and in making fuch frequent ufe through all his profiles, of the Cyma, as a fupporting member. Nor has Vignola been more judicious, in finifhing his Tufcan cornice with an Ovolo; a moulding, extremely improper for that purpofe, and productive of a very difagreeable effect: for it gives a mutilated air to the whole profile; fo much the more ftriking, as it refembles exactly that half of the Ionic cor- nice, which is under the Corona. Other architects have been guilty of the like improprieties, and are therefore equally reprehenfible.

THERE are various manners of defcribing the Contour or out-line, of mould- ings; the fimpleft however, and the beft, is to form them of * quadrants of circles, as in the annexed defigns: by which means, the different depreffions and fwellings, will be more ftrongly marked; the tranfitions be made, without any angle; and the projections be agreeable to the doctrine of Vitruvius, and the practice of the ancients: thofe of the Ovolo, Talon, Cyma, and Cavetto, being equal to their height; that of the Scotia to one third, and thofe of the curved parts of the Torus and Aftragal, to one half thereof.

* Pl. mouldings.

ON

ON particular occafions, however, it may be neceffary fometimes to increafe, and at other times to diminifh thefe projections; according to the fituation, or other circumftances attending the profile: as will hereafter appear. And whenever it fo happens; the Ovolo, Talon, Cyma, and Cavetto; may either be defcribed from the fummits of equilateral triangles, or be compofed of quadrants of the Ellypfis; of which the latter, fhould be preferred; as it produces a ftronger oppofition of light and fhade, and by that means, marks the forms more diftinctly. The Scotia may likewife be framed of ellyptical portions, or quadrants of the circle; differing more or lefs from each other, than in the annexed † defigns; by which means, its projection may either be increafed or diminifhed; but the curved part of the Torus and Aftragal, muft always be femicircular, and the increafe in their projection, be made by ftraight lines.

IN fome antiques, and likewife in various modern buildings, where the parts are far removed from the eye, or where, from the extraordinary fize of the ftructure, it has not been practicable to give to every member its due projection, recourfe has been had to artifice, in order to produce the defired effect. At St. Peter's of the Vatican, this practice is very frequent; and I have given a fection of the Cornice *, terminating the pendentives of the dome, which may ferve as a guide, in cafes where the like is neceffary.

IT will however be proper to obferve, that a frequent ufe of this expedient is to be avoided; as the artifice never fucceeds, but where, by reafon of the great diftance, it is undifcoverable: for the incifions and contortions made in the mouldings, entirely deftroy the natural beauty of their form.

CERTAIN of the modern Italians, and likewife fome of our own learned Virtuofi, who eagerly grafp at every Innovation; having obferved thefe forms in the works of Michael Angelo, and in fome of the temples of antiquity, without fufficiently confidering why they were there introduced; have very injudicioufly made ufe of them, in all their own works; by which practice, their compofitions, though having in other refpects, a certain degree of merit; are, in this particular, highly cenfurable.

AN affemblage of effential parts and mouldings, is termed a profile: and on the choice, difpofition, and proportions of thefe, depend the beauty or deformity of the compofition. The moft perfect profiles, are fuch as confift of few mouldings; varied, both in form and fize; fitly applied, with regard to their ufes; and fo diftributed, that the ftraight and curved ones, fucceed each other alternately. In every profile, there fhould be a predominant member; to which all the others ought to feem fubfervient: and made, either to fupport, to fortify, or to fhelter it, from injuries of weather: and whenever the profile is confiderable; or much complicated; the predominant, fhould always be accompanied with one or more other principal members; in form and dimenfion, calculated to attract the eye; create momentary paufes; and affift the perception of the beholder. Thefe predominant and principal members, ought always to be of the effential clafs, and generally rectangular. Thus

† Pl. of Mouldings.   * Pl. Mouldings, fig. 1.

N   in in a Cornice, the Corona predominates; the Modillions and Dentils are principals in the compofitions; the Cyma and Cavetto, cover them; the Ovolo and Talon, fupport them.

WHEN Ornaments are employed to decorate a profile, fome of the mouldings fhould always be left plain; in order to form a proper repofe: for when all are enriched, the figure of the profile is loft in confufion. In an Entablature, the corona fhould not be ornamented; nor the modillion band; nor the different fafcias of the architrave: neither fhould the plinths of columns, fillets, nor fcarcely any fquare members be carved. For generally fpeaking, they are either principal in the compofition, or ufed as boundaries to other parts; in both which cafes, their figures fhould be fimple, diftinct and unembarraffed. The Dentil Band fhould remain uncut, where the Ovolo and Talon immediately above and below it are enriched; as in the Pantheon at Rome, and at St. Paul's in London. For when the Dentils are marked; particularly if they be fmall, according to Palladio's Corinthian defign; the three members are confounded together, and being covered with ornaments, become far too rich, for the remainder of the compofition: which are defects, at all times, ftudioufly to be avoided: as a diftinct outline, and an equal diftribution of enrichments; muft on every occafion, ftrictly be attended to.

SCAMOZZI obferves, that ornaments fhould neither be too frugally employed, nor diftributed with too much profufion; their value will increafe, in proportion to the judgment and difcretion fhewn in their application. For, in effect, fays he, the ornaments of fculpture ufed in architecture, are like diamonds in a female drefs; with which it would be abfurd to cover the face, or other principal parts, either in themfelves beautiful, or appearing with greater propriety, in their natural ftate.

VARIETY in ornaments, muft not be carried to an excefs. In architecture they are only acceffories; and therefore they fhould not be too ftriking, nor capable of long detaining the attention from the main object. Thofe of the mouldings in particular, fhould be fimple, uniform, and never compofed of more than two different reprefentations upon each moulding: which ought to be cut equally deep; be formed of the fame number of parts; all nearly of the fame dimenfions; in order to produce one even uninterrupted hue throughout; that fo the eye may not be more ftrongly attracted, by any particular part, than by the whole compofition.

WHEN mouldings of the fame form and fize, are employed in one profile, they fhould be enriched with the fame kind of ornaments; by which means, the figure of the profile will be better apprehended; and the artift will avoid the imputation of a puerile minutenefs, neither much to his own credit, nor of any advantage to his works.

IT muft be obferved, that all ornaments of mouldings, are to be regularly difpofed, anfwering perpendicularly above each other; as at the three columns in the Campo Vaccino: where the middles of the modillions, dentils, eggs, and other ornaments, are all in one perpendicular line. For, nothing is more carelefs, confufed and unfeemly; than to diftribute them without any order: as they are in many of the antiques, and in moft of the buildings of this metropolis: the middle of an egg anfwers in fome places to the edge of a dentil, in fome to its middle, and in others

to

to the interval; all the reft of the ornaments being diftributed in the fame flovenly, artlefs manner. The larger parts muft regulate the fmaller; all the ornaments in the entablature are to be governed by the modillions, or mutules; and the diftribution of thefe, muft depend on the intervals of the columns; and be fo difpofed, that one of them, may come directly over the axis of each column. It is farther to be obferved, that the ornaments muft partake of the character of the order they enrich; thofe ufed in the Doric and Ionic orders, are to be of fimpler forms, and of larger bulk, than thofe employed in the Compofite or Corinthian.

WHEN Frizes or other large members are to be enriched, the ornaments may be fignificant; and ferve to indicate the deftination or ufe of the building, the rank, qualities, profeffion and achievements of the owner: but it is a foolifh practice to croud every part with arms, crefts, cyphers, and mottos; for the figures of thefe things are generally bad, or vulgar; and their introduction betrays an unbecoming vanity, in the mafter of the fabrick: Hogarth has humoroufly ridiculed this practice, by decorating a nobleman's crutch, with a coronet.

IN facred places all obfcene, grotefque, and heathenifh reprefentations ought to be avoided: for indecent fables, extravagant conceits, or inftruments and fymbols of Pagan worfhip, are very improper ornaments in ftructures confecrated to chriftian devotion.

WITH regard to the manner of executing ornaments, it is to be remembered, that as in fculpture a drapery is not eftimable, unlefs its folds are contrived to grace and indicate the parts and articulations of the body it covers; fo in architecture the moft exquifite ornaments lofe all their value, if they load, alter, or confufe the form they are defigned to enrich and adorn.

ALL ornaments of mouldings muft therefore be cut into the folid, and never be applied on their furface, as Daviliere erroneoufly teaches: becaufe it alters both their figure and proportion. The profile muft firft be finifhed plain, and afterwards be adorned; the moft prominent parts of the ornaments, being made equal with the furface of the mouldings they enrich: and great care muft be taken that the angles, or breaks, be kept perfect and untouched with fculpture; for which reafon it is cuftomary at the angles of moft mouldings, to place water leaves, or other plain leaves, the middle filament of which forms the angle, and keeps its outline entire.

THE method of the ancient fculptors, in the execution of architectonic orna-ments, was, to aim at a perfect reprefentation of the object they chofe to imitate; fo that the chefnuts, acorns, or eggs, with which the ovolo is commonly enriched, are in the antiques, cut round, and almoft entirely detached; as are likewife the berries, or beads on the aftragal: which are generally as much hollowed into the folid of the body, as the moulding projects beyond it: but the leaves, fhells, and flowers, that adorn the Cavetto, Cyma, Talon, and Torus, are kept flat, like the things they reprefent.

IN the application of their ornaments, they obferved to ufe fuch as required a confiderable relief, on mouldings that in themfelves are clumfy, as the Ovolo and Aftragal; which by means of the deep incifions made in them to form thefe enrich-

ments,

ments acquired an extraordinary lightnefs: but on more elegant parts, as the Cavetto, and Cyma, they employed thin bodies, which could be reprefented without entering too far into the folid. The ornaments of their Cornices were boldly marked, that they might be diftinguifhed from afar; but thofe of the Bafes of Columns, or of Pedeftals being nearer the eye, were more flightly expreffed; as well on that account, as becaufe it would have been improper to weaken thefe parts, and impoffible to keep them clean, had there been any deep cavities in them, to harbour duft and filth.

WHEN objects are near, and liable to clofe infpection, every part of the ornament fhould be expreffed, and well finifhed: but when they are much exalted, the detail may be flightly touched, or entirely neglected; for it is fufficient if the general form be diftinct, and the principal maffes ftrongly marked. A few rough ftrokes from the hand of a fkilful mafter, are much more effectual, than the moft elaborate finifhings of an artlefs imitator: which feldom confifting in more than fmoothing and neatly rounding off the parts, are calculated to deftroy, rather than to produce effect.

Of the ORDERS *of* ARCHITECTURE *in general.*

THE Orders of Architecture, as has been obferved, are the bafis upon which the whole decorative part of the art is chiefly built, and towards which the attention of the artift muft ever be directed, even where no orders are introduced. In them, originate moft of the forms ufed in decoration; they regulate moft of the proportions; and to their combination multiplied, varied, and arranged in a thoufand different ways, architecture is indebted, for its moft fplendid productions.

THESE orders, are different modes of building, faid, originally to have been imitated from the primitive huts; being compofed of fuch parts as were effential in their conftruction, and afterwards alfo in the temples of antiquity; which, though at firft fimple and rude, were in the courfe of time, and by the ingenuity of fucceeding architects, wrought up and improved, to fuch a pitch of perfection, that they were by way of excellence diftinguifhed by the name of orders.

OF thefe there are five *: three faid to be of Grecian origin, are called Grecian orders; being diftinguifhed by the names of Doric, Ionic, and Corinthian: they exhibit three diftinct characters of compofition; fuppofed to have been fuggefted, by the diverfity of character in the human frame. The remaining two being of Italian origin, are called Latin orders; they are diftinguifhed by the names of Tufcan and Roman, and were probably invented with a view of extending the characteriftic bounds, on one fide, ftill farther towards ftrength and fimplicity; as on the other, towards elegance and profufion of enrichments.

AT what time the orders were invented, or by whom improved to the utmoft, remains at leaft, doubtful. Of their improvement we can now only judge, from the

* Pl. Orders.

ftructures

ftructures and fragments of antiquity, built in different ages, and ftill remaining to be feen in various parts of Europe, Afia, and Africa. And of their origin little is known but from the relation of Vitruvius; the veracity of which, has been much queftioned, and is probably not much to be depended upon.

" DORUS, fays he, fon of Helenes and the nymph Optica, king of Achaia and
" of all the Peloponnefus; having formerly built a temple to Juno, in the ancient city
" of Argos; this temple, happened to be in the manner which is called Dorick;
" and was afterwards imitated in many others, built in the feveral cities of Achaia.

" ABOUT the fame time the Athenians, after having confulted the oracle of
" Apollo at Delphos, by the common confent of all Greece, fent into Afia thirteen
" colonies; each, under the command of a feparate captain: but all, under the general
" direction of Ion, fon of Xuthus and Creufa. Ion being arrived in Afia, conquered
" all Caria, and founded thirteen large cities; the inhabitants whereof, having ex-
" pelled the Carians and Leleges, called the country Ionia; in honour of Ion their
" leader: and erected temples, of which the firft, dedicated to Apollo Panionius,
" was built after the manner of thofe they had feen in Achaia, which they called
" Dorick; becaufe temples of the fame fort, had been erected in the cities of the
" Dorians.

" BUT fome time after, building a temple to Diana, different from thefe, and
" of a more delicate ftructure; being formed upon the proportions of a female body,
" as the Dorick had been on thofe of a robuft man; and adorning the capitals of
" their columns with volutes, to reprefent the curls of a woman's hair; and the fhafts
" with flutings, to exprefs the folds of her garment; they gave to this fecond
" manner of building the name of Ionick; becaufe it was invented and firft ufed
" by the Ionians.

" THE third fort of columns, which are called Corinthian; and reprefent the
" delicate figure of a young girl, owe their birth to the following accident.

* " A young woman of Corinth being dead, her nurfe placed on her tomb a
" bafket, containing certain trinkets in which fhe delighted when alive; covering
" it with a tile, to fhelter them from the weather. The bafket happened accident-
" ally to be fet on a root of the acanthus, which pufhing forth its leaves and fprigs
" in the fpring, covered the fides of it; and fome of them, longer than the reft,
" being obftructed by the angles of the tile, were forced downwards; and by
" degrees, curled into the form of volutes.

" CALLIMACHUS, a celebrated fculptor, paffing near the tomb, obferved the
" bafket; and in how graceful a manner the leaves of the acanthus had furrounded
" it: the form pleafed him exceedingly, he imitated it on the tops of fome columns,
" which he afterwards executed at Corinth; eftablifhing and regulating, by this
" model, the manner and proportions of the Corinthian order."

* Pl. Primitive Buildings.

OF the two Latin orders, the Tufcan is faid to have been invented by the inhabitants of Tufcany, before the Romans had intercourfe with the Greeks; or were acquainted with their arts: whence, it is called Tufcan. Probably however, thefe people, originally a colony of Greeks; only imitated in the beft manner they could, what they remembered in their own country: fimplifying the Dorick, either to expedite their work, or perhaps to adapt it to the abilities of their workmen.

THE fecond Latin order, though of Roman production, is but of modern adoption; the ancients never having confidered it as a diftinct order. It is a mixture of the Ionick and Corinthian, and is now diftinguifhed by the names of Roman, or Compofite.

THE ingenuity of man, has hitherto, not been able to produce a fixth order: though large premiums have been offered, and numerous attempts been made, by men of firft rate talents, to accomplifh it. Such is the fettered human imagination, fuch the fcanty ftore of its ideas, that Dorick, Ionic, and Corinthian, have ever floated uppermoft; and all that has ever been produced, amounts to nothing more, than different arrangements and combinations of their parts, with fome trifling deviations, fcarcely deferving notice; the whole generally tending more to diminifh, than to increafe the beauty of the ancient orders.

THE * fubftitution of cocks, owls, or lions heads, &c. for rofes; of trophies, cornucopias, lilies, fphinxes, or even men, women, and children, for volutes; the introduction of feathers, lyres, flower de luces, or coronets, for leaves; are more alterations, than improvements; and the fufpenfion of feftoons of flowers, or collars of knighthood, over the other enrichments of a capital; like lace on embroidery: rather tends to complicate and confufe the form, than to augment its grace, or contribute to its excellence.

THE fuppreffion of parts of the ancient orders, with a view to produce novelty; has of late years, been practifed among us, with full as little fuccefs. And though it is not wifhed to reftrain fallies of imagination, nor to difcourage genius from attepmating ot invent; yet it is apprehended, that attempts to alter the primary forms invented by the ancients; and eftablifhed, by the concurring approbation of many ages, muft ever be attended with dangerous confequences; muft always be difficult; and feldom, if ever fuccefsful. It is like coining words; which, whatever may be their value, are at firft but ill received; and muft have the fanction of time, to fecure them a current reception.

AN order, is compofed of † two principal members; the Column, and the Entablature: each of which is divided into ‡ three principal parts. Thofe of the column, are the bafe, the fhaft, and the capital. Thofe of the entablature, are the architrave, the frize, and the cornice. All thefe are again fubdivided into many fmaller parts; the difpofition, number, forms and dimenfions of which, characterize each order; and exprefs the degree of ftrength or delicacy, richnefs or fimplicity, peculiar to it.

---

* Pl. Compofite Entablatures and Capitals.   † Pl. of Primitive Buildings.   ‡ Ibid.

THE

THE fimpleft and moft folid of all, is the * Tufcan. It is compofed of few and large parts, devoid of ornaments, and is of a conftruction fo maffive, that it feems capable of fupporting the heavieft burdens; whence it is by Sir H. Wotton, compared to a fturdy labourer, dreffed in homely apparel.

THE Doric order†, next in ftrength to the Tufcan; and of a grave, robuft, mafculine afpect; is by Scamozzi, called the Herculean. Being the moft ancient of all the orders, it retains more of the ‡ ftructure of the primitive huts in its form, than any of the reft; having triglyphs in the frize, to reprefent the ends of joifts; and mutules in its cornice, to reprefent rafters, with inclined foffits, to exprefs their direction in the originals, from which they were imitated. Its column too, is often feen in ancient works, executed without a bafe, in imitation of the trees, ufed in the firft buildings, without any plinths to raife them above the ground. Freart de Chambrai fpeaking of this order, obferves, that delicate ornaments are repugnant to its characteriftic folidity; and that it fucceeds beft, in the fimple regularity of its proportions: " nofegays and garlands of flowers, fays he, grace not a Hercules, who " always appears more becomingly, with a rough club and lion's fkin. For there are " beauties of various forts, and often fo diffimilar in their natures, that thofe which " may be highly proper on one occafion, may be quite the reverfe, even ridiculoufly " abfurd, on others."

THE Ionic§, being the fecond of the Grecian orders, holds a middle ftation between the other two; and ftands in equipoife between the grave folidity of the Doric, and the elegant delicacy of the Corinthian. Among the antiques however, we find it in different dreffes; fometimes plentifully adorned, and inclining moft towards the Corinthian; fometimes more fimple, and bordering on Dorick plainnefs; all according to the fancy of the architect, or nature of the ftructure where employed. It is throughout, of a more flender conftruction than either of the afore-defcribed orders; its appearance, though fimple, is graceful and majeftic; its ornaments fhould be few; rather neat than luxuriant; and as there ought to be nothing exaggerated, or affectedly ftriking in any of its parts, it is (not unaptly) compared to a fedate matron, rather in decent than magnificent attire.

THE Corinthian‖, fays Sir Henry Wotton, is a column lafcivioufly decked, like a wanton courtezan. Its proportions are elegant in the extreme; every part of the order is divided into a great variety of members; and abundantly enriched with a diverfity of ornaments. " The ancients, fays De Chambray, aiming at the repre- " fentation of a feminine beauty, omitted nothing, either calculated to embellifh, " or capable of perfecting their work." And he obferves, " that in the many exam- " ples left of this order, fuch a profufion of different ornaments is introduced, that " they feem to have exhaufted imagination, in the contrivance of decorations for " this mafter-piece of the art. Scamozzi calls it the Virginal; and it certainly has all " the delicacy in its form, with all the gaiety, gaudinefs, and affectation in its drefs, " peculiar to young women."

---

* Pl. of Orders. † Pl. of Orders. ‡ Pl. Primitive Buildings. § Pl. of Orders. ‖ Pl. of Orders.

THE

THE Compofite order*, being properly fpeaking, only a different fpecies of the Corinthian, diftinguifhed from it merely by fome peculiarities in the capital, or other trifling deviations; retains in a great meafure the fame character, and requires no particular defcription.

To give a ftriking idea of thefe different properties, and to render the compa-rifon between the orders more eafy, I have reprefented † them all of the fame height; by which means the gradual increafe of delicacy and richnefs, is eafily perceivable; as are likewife the relations between the intercolumniations of the different orders, and the proportions which their pedeftals, impofts, archivolts, and other parts, with which they are on various occafions accompanied; bear to each other.

THE proportions of the orders were, by the ancients, formed on thofe of the human body; and confequently, it could not be their intention, to make a Corinthian column (which as Vitruvius obferves, is to reprefent the delicacy of a young girl), as thick and much taller, than a Doric one; which is defigned to reprefent the bulk and vigour of a mufcular full grown man: columns fo formed, could not be applied to accompany each other, without violating the laws, both of real and apparent folidity; as in fuch cafe, the Doric dwarf, muft be crufhed under the ftrapping Ionic, or gigantick Corinthian virago; triumphantly riding uppermoft: and reverf-ing the natural, the neceffary, predominance in the compofition.

NEVERTHELESS Vignola, Palladio, Scamozzi, Blondel, Perrault, and many others, if not all, the great modern artifts; have confidered them in this light: that is, they have made the diameters of all their orders the fame, and confequently their heights increafing: which, befides giving a wrong idea of the character of thefe different compofitions, has laid a foundation for many erroneous precepts, and falfe reafonings, to be found in different parts of their works; of which, notice will in due time be taken.

IN the opinion of Scamozzi, columns fhould not be lefs than feven of their diameters in height, nor more than ten; the former being according to him, a good proportion in the Tufcan; and the latter in the Corinthian order. The practice of the ancients in their beft works, being conformable to this precept; I have, as authorifed by the doctrine of Vitruvius, made the Tufcan column feven diameters in height, and the Doric eight; the Ionic nine, as Palladio and Vignola have done; and the Corinthian and Compofite ten: which laft meafure, is a mean between the proportions obferved in the Pantheon, and at the three columns in Camp Vaccino; both which, are efteemed moft excellent models of the Corinthian order.

THE height of the entablature, in all the orders, I have made one quarter of the height of the column; which was the common practice of the ancients; who, in all forts of entablatures, feldom exceeded or fell much fhort, of that mea-fure.

* Pl. Orders.   † Pl. Orders.

NEVERTHELESS

NEVERTHELESS Palladio, Scamozzi, Alberti, Barbaro, Cataneo, De l'Orme, and others of the modern architects; have made their entablatures much lower in the Ionic, Compofite, and Corinthian orders, than in the Tufcan or Doric. This, on fome occafions, may not only be excufable but highly proper; particularly where the intercolumniations are wide, (as in a fecond or third order;) in private houfes, or infide decorations; where lightnefs fhould be preferred to dignity, and where expence, with every impediment to the conveniency of the fabrick, are carefully to be avoided: but to fet entirely afide a proportion, which feems to have had the general approbation of the ancient artifts, is furely prefuming too far.

THE reafon alledged, in favour of this practice, is the weaknefs of the columns in the delicate orders; which renders them unfit for fupporting heavy burdens. And where the intervals are fixed, as in a fecond order; or in other places, where wide intercolumniations are either neceffary, or not to be avoided; the reafon is certainly fufficient: but, if the artift is at liberty to difpofe his columns at pleafure, the fimpleft and moft natural way of conquering the difficulty, is to employ more columns: by placing them nearer to each other, as was the cuftom of the ancients. And it muft be remembered, that though the height of the entablature in a delicate order, is made the fame as in a maffive one; yet it will not, either in reality or in appearance, be equally heavy*; for the quantity of matter in the Corinthian cornice A, is confiderably lefs than in the Tufcan cornice B; and the increafed number of parts compofing the former of thefe, will of courfe make it appear far lighter, than the latter.

WITH regard to the parts of the entablature, I have followed the method of Serlio, in his Ionic and Corinthian orders; and of Perrault, who, in all his orders, excepting the Doric, divides the whole height of the entablature into ten equal parts: three of which he gives to the architrave, three to the frize, four to the cornice. And in the Doric order, he divides the whole height of the entablature into eight parts; of which two are given to the architrave, three to the frize, and three to the cornice.

THESE meafures, deviate very little from thofe obferved in the greateft number of antiques now extant at Rome; where they have flood the teft of many ages. And their fimplicity, renders them fingularly ufeful in compofition, as they are eafily remembered, and eafily applied.

OF two manners ufed by architects, to determine the dimenfions of the mouldings, and the leffer parts that compofe an order, I have chofen the fimpleft; readieft and moft accurate; which is by the module, or femi-diameter of the column, taken at the bottom of the fhaft: and divided into thirty minutes.

THERE are indeed many, who prefer the method of meafuring by equal parts; imagining beauty to depend, on the fimplicity and accuracy of the relations, exifting between the whole body, and its members: and alledging, that dimenfions, which

* Fig. 2, Plate of Mouldings.

R   have

have evident affinities, are better remembered than thofe, whofe relations are too complicated to be immediately apprehended.

WITH regard to the former of thefe fuppofitions, it is evidently falfe: for the real relations, fubfifting between diffimilar figures, have no connection with the apparent ones. And with regard to the latter, it may or may not be the cafe, according to the degree of accuracy with which the partition is made. For inftance, in dividing the Attick bafe, (which may be numbered among the fimpleft compofitions in architecture) according to the different methods; it appears to me as eafy, to recollect the numbers 10, $7\frac{1}{2}$, 1, $4\frac{3}{4}$, 1, $5\frac{3}{4}$; as to remember that the whole height of the bafe, is to be divided into three equal parts, that two of thefe three, are to be divided into four; that three of the four, are to be divided into two; and that one of the two, is to be divided into fix; which are to be divided into three.

BUT, admitting it were eafier to remember the one than the other; it doth not feem neceffary, nor even advifable, in a fcience where a vaft diverfity of knowledge is required, to burden the memory with a thoufand trifling dimenfions. If the general proportions be known, it is all that is requifite in compofing; and when a defign is to be executed, it is eafy to have recourfe to figured drawings, or to prints. The ufe of the module is univerfal; throughout the order and all its appurtenances; it marks their relations to each other, and being fufceptible of the minuteft divifions, the dimenfions may be fpeedily determined with the utmoft accuracy; while the trouble, confufion, uncertainty, and lofs of time, in meafuring by equal parts, are very confiderable; feeing it is neceffary to form almoft as many different fcales, as there are different parts to be divided.

COLUMNS, in imitation of trees, from which they drew their origin; are tapered in their fhafts. In the antiques, the diminution is varioufly performed; fometimes beginning from the foot of the fhaft, at others from one quarter, or one third of its height; the lower part being left perfectly cylindrical. The former of thefe methods was moft in ufe amongft the ancients, and being the moft natural, feems to claim the preference; though the latter has been almoft univerfally practifed by modern artifts: from a fuppofition, perhaps, of its being more graceful: as it is more marked and ftrikingly perceptible.

THE firft architects, fays Monf. Auzoult, probably made their columns in ftraight lines, in imitation of trees; fo that their fhaft was a fruftrum of the cone: but finding this form abrupt and difagreeable, they made ufe of fome curve, which, fpringing from the extremities of the fuperior and inferior diameters of the column, fwelled beyond the fides of the cone, and by that means gave a more pleafing figure to the outline. Vitruvius, in the fecond chapter of his third book, mentions this practice; but in fo obfcure and curfory a manner, that his meaning has not been underftood; and feveral of the modern architects, intending to conform themfelves to his doctrine, have made the diameters of their columns greater in the middle, than at the foot of the fhaft. Leon Baptifta Alberti, with others of the Florentine and Roman architects, carried this practice to a very abfurd excefs; for which they have been juftly blamed: as it is neither natural, reafonable, nor beautiful.

MONSIEUR

MONSIEUR AUZOULT farther obferves, that a column, fuppofing its fhaft to be the fruftrum of a cone, may have an additional thicknefs in the middle, without being fwelled there, beyond the bulk of its inferior parts; and fuppofes the addition mentioned by Vitruvius, to fignify nothing more, than the increafe towards the middle of the column, occafioned by changing the ftraight line, which at firft was in ufe, into a curve.

THIS fuppofition, is exceedingly juft; and founded on what is obfervable in the works of antiquity; where there is no fingle inftance of a column thicker in the middle, than at the bottom, though all, or moft of them, have the fwelling hinted at by Vitruvius, all of them being terminated by curves; fome few granite columns excepted, which are bounded by ftraight lines: a proof, perhaps, of their antiquity; or of their having been wrought in the quarries of Egypt, by unfkilful workmen.

BLONDEL in his book entitled *Refolution des quatre principaux Problémes d'Archi-tecture*, teaches various manners of diminifhing columns; the beft and fimpleft of which, is by means of the inftrument invented by Nicomedes, to defcribe the firft conchoid: for this, being applied at the bottom of the fhaft, performs at one fweep, both the fwelling and the diminution; giving fuch a graceful form to the column, that it is univerfally allowed to be the moft perfect practice hitherto difcovered. The columns in the Pantheon, accounted the moft beautiful among the antiques, are traced in this manner; as appears by the exact meafures of one of them, to be found in Defgodetz's antiquities of Rome.

To give an accurate idea of the operation, it will be neceffary firft to defcribe Vignola's method of diminution, on which it is grounded. " As to this fecond " method, fays Vignola, it is a difcovery of my own; and although it be lefs " known than the former, it will be eafily comprehended by the figure. Having " therefore determined the meafures of your column, (that is to fay, the height of " the fhaft, and its inferior and fuperior diameters), * draw a line indefinitely from " C through D, perpendicular to the axis of the column:" this done, fet off the diftance C D, which is the inferior femi-diameter, from A, the extreme point of the fuperior femi-diameter; to B, a point in the axis. Then from A, through B, draw the line A B E, which will cut the indefinite line C D in E; and from this point of interfection E, draw through the axis of the column any number of rays, as E b a, on each of which, from the axis towards the circumference, fetting off the interval C D, you may find any number of points a, a, a, through which if a curve be drawn, it will defcribe the fwelling and diminution of the column.

THOUGH this method be fufficiently accurate for practice, efpecially if a confi-derable number of points be found, yet, ftrictly fpeaking, it is defective; as the curve muft either be drawn by hand, or by applying a flexible ruler to all the points; both which are liable to variations. Blondel therefore, to obviate this objection, (after having proved the curve paffing from A to C through the points a, a, to be

* Fig. 3, Pl. of Mouldings.

S

of

of the fame nature with the firſt conchoid of the ancients), employed the inſtrument of Nicomedes to defcribe it; the conſtruction of which is as follows.

HAVING determined, as above, the length of the ſhaft, with the inferior and ſuperior diameters of the column, and having likewiſe found the length of the line C D E; take three rulers, either of wood or metal, as F G, I D, and A H; of which let F G and I D be faſtened together at right angles in G. Cut a dove-tail groove in the middle of F G, from top to bottom; and at the point E on the ruler I D, (whoſe diſtance, from the middle of the groove in F G, is the fame as that of the point of interſection from the axis of the column), fix a pin; then on the ruler A H ſet off the diſtance A B, equal to C D the inferior femi-diameter of the column, and at the point B fix a button, whoſe head muſt be exactly fitted to the groove made in F G, in which it is to ſlide; and, at the other extremity of the ruler A H, cut a ſlit or channel from H to K, whoſe length muſt not be leſs than the difference of length between E B and E D, and whoſe breadth muſt be ſufficient to admit the pin fixed at E, which muſt paſs through the ſlit, that the ruler may ſlide thereon.

THE inſtrument being thus compleated; if the middle of the groove, in the ruler F G, be placed exactly over the axis of the column, it is evident that the ruler A H, in moving along the groove, will with its extremity A, defcribe the curve A a a C; which curve is the fame as that produced by Vignola's method of diminution; fuppofing it done with the utmoſt accuracy: for the interval A B, a b, is always the fame: and the point E, is the origin of an infinity of lines, of which the parts B A, b a, b a, extending from the axis to the circumference, are equal to each other, and to D C. And if the rulers be of an indefinite fize, and the pins at E and B be made to move along their refpective ruler, ſo that the intervals A B and D E may be augmented or diminiſhed at pleaſure, it is likewiſe evident, that the fame inſtrument may be thus applied to columns of any fize.

IN the remains of antiquity, the quantity of the diminution is various; but ſeldom leſs than one eighth of the inferior diameter of the column: nor more than one fixth of it. The laſt of theſe is by Vitruvius, eſteemed the moſt perfect; and Vignola has employed it in four of his orders, as I have done in all of them: there being no reafon for diminiſhing the Tuſcan column more, in proportion to its diameter, than any of the reſt; though it be the doctrine of Vitruvius, and the practice of Palladio, Vignola, Scamozzi, and almoſt all the modern architects. On the contrary, as Monſieur Perrault juſtly obferves, its diminution ought rather to be leſs than more; as it actually is in the Trajan column, being there only one ninth of the diameter. For even when the fame proportion is obferved through all the orders; the abſolute quantity of the diminution in the Tuſcan order, fuppofing the columns of the fame height, exceeds that in the Corinthian, in the ratio of ten to feven; and if, according to the common practice, the Tuſcan column be leſs by one quarter at the top, than at its foot; the difference between the diminution in the Tuſcan and in the Corinthian columns, will be as fifteen to feven; and in the Tuſcan and Doric nearly as fifteen to nine: ſo that notwithſtanding there is a very confiderable difference between the lower diameters of a Tuſcan and of a Doric column, both being of the fame height, yet the diameters at their top will be nearly equal; and confequently the Tuſcan column, will in reality be no ſtronger than the Doric one, which is contrary to the character of the order.

VITRUVIUS

VITRUVIUS allots different degrees of diminution, to columns of different heights; giving to thofe of fifteen foot, one fixth of their diameter; to fuch as are from twenty to thirty foot, one feventh; and when they are from forty to fifty foot high, one eighth only: obferving, that as the eye is eafily deceived in confidering diftant objects, which always feem lefs than they really are; it is neceffary to remedy the deception, by an increafe of their dimenfions: otherwife the work will appear ill-conftructed and difagreeable to the eye.

MOST of the modern architects have taught the fame doctrine: but Perrault in his notes, both on this paffage, and on the fecond chapter of the fixth book, endeavours to prove the abfurdity thereof. In fact, it is on moft occafions, if not on all, an evident error; which Vitruvius and his followers have probably been led into, through neglect of combining circumftances. For, if the validity of Perrault's arguments be not affented to, and it is required to judge according to the rigour of optical laws; it muft be remembered, that the proper point of view, for a column of fifty foot high, is not the fame as for one of fifteen: but on the contrary more diftant, in the fame proportion, as the column is higher: and that confequently, the apparent relation between the lower and upper diameters of the column will be the fame, whatever be its fize. For, if we fuppofe * A to be a point of view, whofe refpective diftance from each of the columns f g, F G, is equal to the refpective heights of each, the triangles f A g, F A G, will be fimilar; and A f, or A h, which is the fame, will be to A g, as A F, or its equal A H, is to A G: therefore if d e, be in reality to b c, as D E is to B C, it will likewife be apparently fo; for the angle d A e, will then be to the angle b A c, as the angle D A E, is to the angle B A C; and if the real relations differ, the apparent ones will likewife differ.

I HAVE fuppofed the eye of the fpectator, to be in a line perpendicular to the foot of the fhaft; but if the columns be proportionably raifed to any height above the eye, the argument will ftill remain in force; as the point of view muft of courfe be proportionably more diftant: and even when columns are placed immediately on the ground, which feldom or ever is the cafe, the alteration occafioned by that fituation, is too trifling to deferve notice.

WHEN therefore a certain degree of diminution, which by experience is found pleafing, has been fixed upon, there will be no neceffity for changing it, whatever be the height of the column; provided, the point of view is not limited: but in clofe places, where the fpectator is not at liberty to chufe a proper diftance for his point of fight, the architect, if he inclines to be fcrupuloufly accurate, may vary. Though it is in reality, a matter of no importance; as the nearnefs of the object, will render the image thereof indiftinct; and confequently, any fmall alteration imperceptible.

SCAMOZZI, who efteems it an effential property of the delicate orders, to exceed the maffive ones in height; has applied the above cited precept of Vitruvius,

---

* Fig. 4, Pl. of Mouldings.

T

to the different orders: having diminifhed the Tufcan column one quarter of its diameter; the Doric one fifth; the Ionic one fixth; the Roman one feventh; and the Corinthian one eighth. In the foregoing part of this chapter, I have fhewn the fallacy of his notion, with refpect to the heights of his orders, and likewife endeavoured to prove the error of diminifhing the Tufcan column, more than any of the others; fo that it will be needlefs, to fay any thing farther on thefe fubjects now; for as the cafe is fimilar, the fame arguments may be employed in confutation thereof.

My intention being to give an exact idea of the orders of the ancients, I have reprefented them under fuch figures and proportions, as appear to have been moft in ufe in the efteemed works of the Romans; who, in the opinion of Leon Bap. Alberti, and other eminent writers, carried architecture to its perfection. It muft not however be imagined that the fame general proportions will on all occafions fucceed. They are chiefly collected from the temples, and other public ftructures of antiquity, and may by us be employed in churches, palaces, and other buildings of magnificence: where majefty and grandeur of manner, fhould be extended to their utmoft limits; and where the whole compofition being generally large, the parts require an extraordinary degree of boldnefs, to make them diftinctly perceptible, from the proper general points of view. But in lefs confiderable edifices, and under various circumftances of which I fhall hereafter give a detail, more elegant proportions may often be preferable.

Of the TUSCAN ORDER.

AMONG the antiques, there are no remains of a regular Tufcan order; the doctrine of Vitruvius upon that fubject, is obfcure; and the profiles of Palladio, Scamozzi, Serlio, De l'Orme, and Vignola, are all, more or lefs imperfect.

Of the two defigns left us by Palladio, that taken from the defcription of Vitruvius, is unpleafingly ruftic. The other again is too rich, and injudicioufly compofed. That of Scamozzi is yet richer, and much too like the Doric. Serlio's is heavy; and Vignola's, though fuperior to the others, is defective in the cornice, which is clumfey, compared with the reft of the order; ill proportioned in its parts, and incorrectly profiled: as it finifhes with a fupporting moulding, which has nothing to fupport; and confequently muft excite the idea of a mutilation: the more ftriking, as the general outline of the compofition, refembles exactly the bed moulds of the Ionic cornice; fuppofing the dentil band left uncut, as is often the cafe.

In the defign here annexed, I have chiefly imitated Vignola's, who in this order has been almoft univerfally followed. Even Inigo Jones, who was fo clofe an adherer to Palladio; has employed Vignola's profile, in his York ftairs, and others, his buildings. But, as the cornice appears to me, far inferior to the reft of the compofition, I have not fcrupled to reject it; and to fubftitute in its place, that of Scamozzi;

with

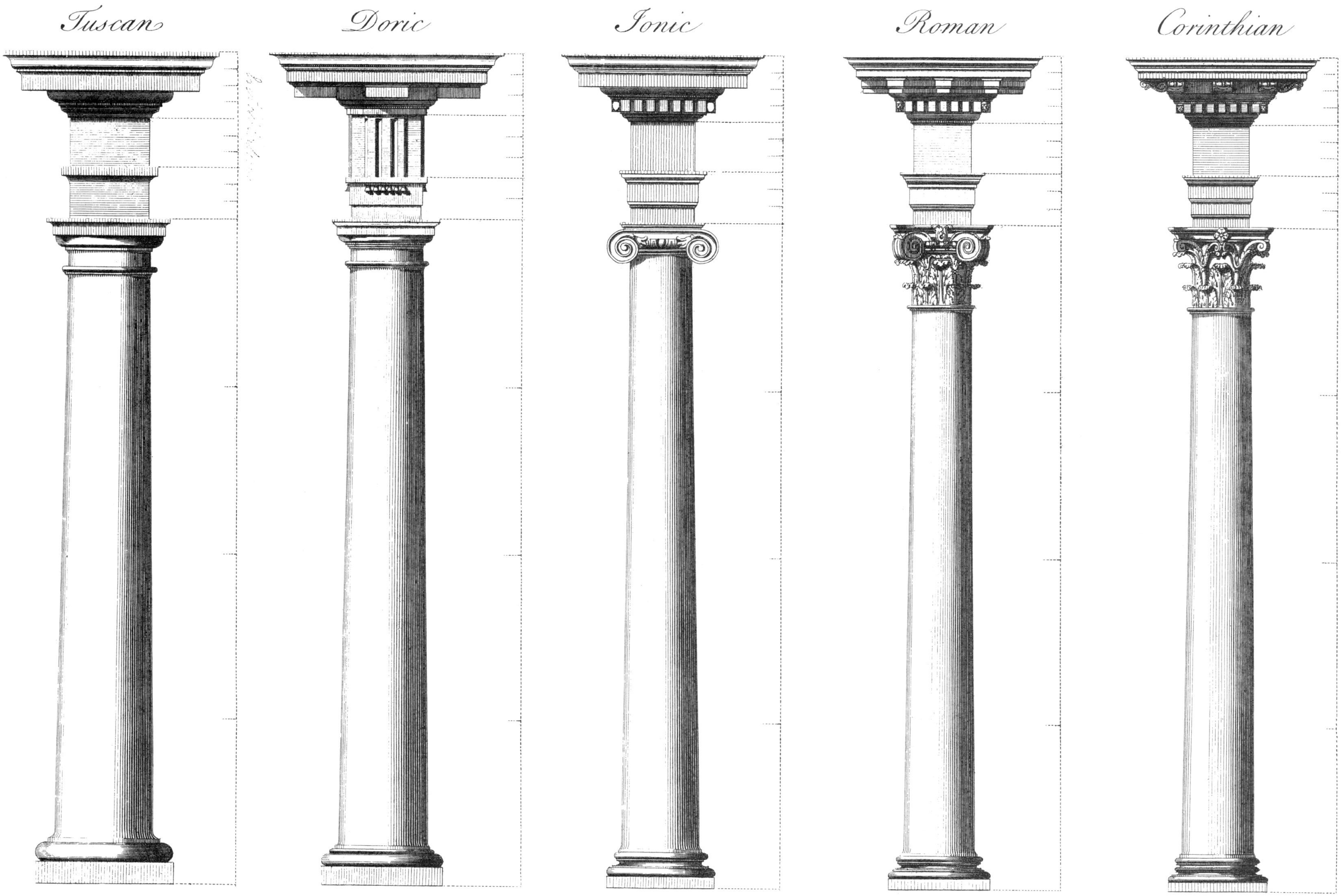

Corinthian

Roman

Ionic

Doric

Tuscan

The Orders of the Antients.

Fourdrinier Sculp.

T. Crunden delin.

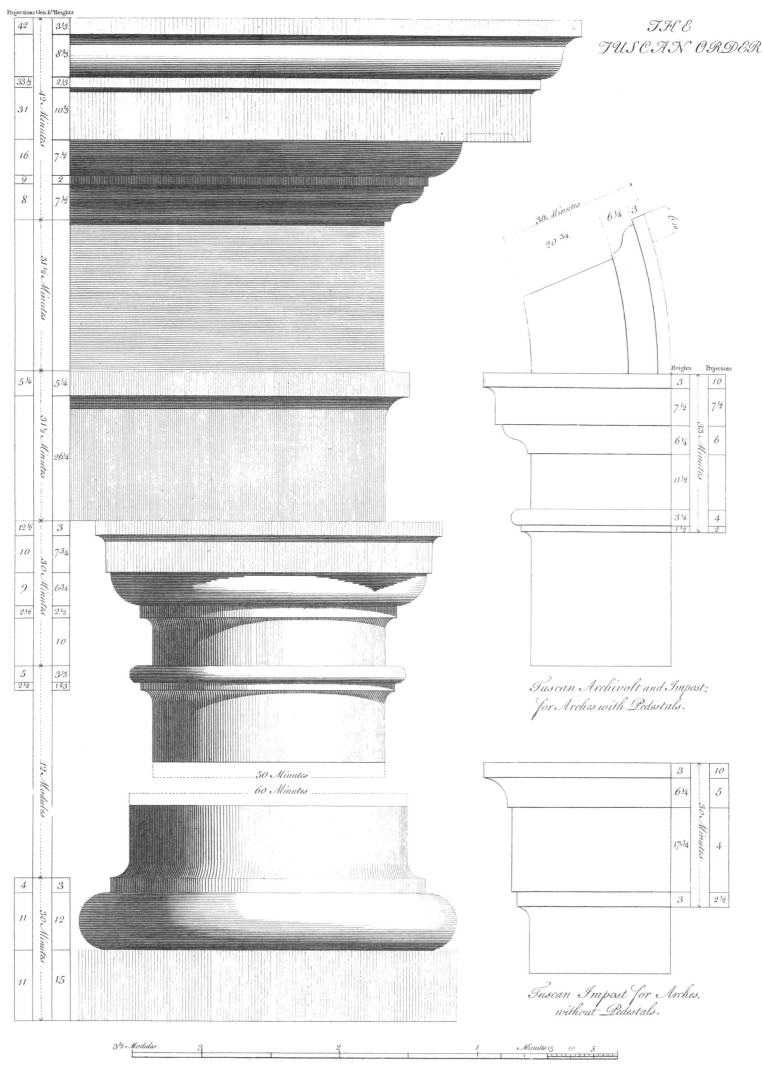

THE
TUSCAN ORDER

Tuscan Archivolt and Impost;
for Arches with Pedestals.

Tuscan Impost for Arches,
without Pedestals.

W. Chambers   T. Patton Sculp.

with fuch alterations as were evidently neceffary, to render it perfect — Conformable to the doctrine of Vitruvius, and to the almoft general practice of the moderns, I have given to the height of the column, fourteen modules, or feven diameters; and to that of the whole entablature, three and a half modules; which being divided into ten equal parts, three of them are for the height of the architrave, three for that of the frize, and the remaining four, for the cornice. The capital is in height, one module; the bafe, including the lower cincture of the fhaft, is alfo one module; and the fhaft, with its upper cincture and aftragal, twelve modules. Thefe are the general meafures of the order.

WITH refpect to the particular dimenfions of the minuter parts, they may be collected from the defign; whereon the heights and projections of each member, are figured; the latter of thefe being counted from perpendiculars, raifed at the extremities of the inferior and fuperior diameters of the fhaft: a method, preferable to that of De Chambray and Defgodetz, who count from the axis of the column; becaufe, the relations between the heights and projections of the parts, are more readily difcoverable: and, whenever a cornice or entablature, is to be executed without a column, which frequently happens, it requires no additional time or labour, as the trouble of deducting from each dimenfion, the femi-diameter of the column is faved.

SCAMOZZI, that his bafes might be of the fame height in all the orders, has given to the Tufcan one, exclufive of the cincture, half a diameter. But I have rather chofen to imitate Vignola and Palladio, who in this order have deviated from the general rule: for as the Tufcan bafe is compofed of two members only, inftead of fix, which conftitute the other bafes, it becomes much too clumfey, when the fame general proportion is obferved.

THE Tufcan order admits of no ornaments of any kind: on the contrary, it is fometimes cuftomary to reprefent on the fhaft of its column, ruftic cinctures; as at the palace Pitti in Florence; that of the Luxembourg in Paris; York Stairs in London; and many other buildings of note. This practice though frequent, and to be found in the works of many celebrated architects, is not always excufable; and fhould be indulged with caution; as it hides the natural figure of the column, alters its proportions, and affects the fimplicity of the whole compofition. There are few examples of thefe bandages in the remains of antiquity; and, in general, it will be advifeable to avoid them in all large defigns, referving the ruftic work for the intercolumniations, where it may be employed with great propriety, to produce an oppofition; which will help to render the afpect of the whole compofition, diftinct and ftriking.

BUT in fmaller works, of which the parts, being few, are eafily comprehended, they may be fometimes tolerated; fometimes even recommended; as they ferve to diverfify the forms, are productive of ftrong contrafts, and contribute very confiderably to the mafculine, bold afpect of the compofition. Le Clerc thinks them proper in gates of citadels and prifons, of which the entrances fhould be terrifick; and they are likewife fit for gates to gardens, or parks, for grottos, fountains, and baths; where elegance of form, and neatnefs of workmanfhip, would be out of character. De l'Orme, who was exceeding fond of thefe cinctures, has employed

U   them

them in feveral parts of the Thuilleries covered with arms, cyphers, and other enrichments: but this feems abfurd, for they can never be confidered in any other light, than as parts, which to avoid expence and trouble, were left unfinifhed. We likewife find in different parts of the Louvre, vermiculated ruftics, of which the tracts reprefent flowers de luce, and other regular figures: a practice, ftill more unnatural than the forementioned; though Monfieur Daviler, very gravely tells us, that it fhould always be done with propriety; and exprefs a relation to the owner of the ftructure: that is, the figures fhould reprefent his arms, his creft, motto, cypher, and fo forth: as if worms were draughtfmen, and underftood heraldry.

IN the plates of defigns for gates, doors and windows, and likewife in thofe of different compofitions, at the end of the book; are given feveral defigns of ruftick columns, and other ruftick work; all collected from buildings of note, in different parts of Europe: and for the manner of executing them, as it cannot well be defcribed, the ftudent is referred to various parts of Somerfet Place, to the Horfe Guards, the Treafury, the Doric entrance of the King's Mews, the gate of Burlington Houfe, &c. in all which, the different kinds of ruftication, are managed with tafte, and command of the chiffel.

DE CHAMBRAY, in the introduction to his parallel of ancient and modern architecture, treats the Tufcan order with great contempt; and banifhes it to the country: as unworthy a place, either in temples or palaces. But, in the fecond part of the fame work, he is more indulgent; for tho he rejects the entablature, the column is taken into favour, " and compared to a queen, feated on a throne; fur-
" rounded with all the treafures of fame, and diftributing honours to her minions;
" while other columns only feem to be fervants and flaves of the buildings they
" fupport."

THE remainder of this paffage, too long to be here inferted at full length; is calculated to degrade and totally to exclude from buildings, the Tufcan order: but by a different mode of employing, and dreffing the column, to exalt its confequence; increafe its majefty and beauty; fo as to ftand an advantageous comparifon with any of the reft; he therefore wifhes, in imitation of the ancient architects, to confecrate the Tufcan column, to the commemoration of great men, and their glorious actions; inftancing Trajan's column, one of the proudeft monuments of Roman fplendor, which is of that order; was erected by the fenate and people of Rome, in acknow-ledgment of his fervices, and has contributed more to immortalize that emperor, than the united pens of all hiftorians. He farther inftances the Antonine column, likewife erected at Rome on a fimilar occafion, in honour of Antoninus Pius: and another of the fame fort at Conftantinople, raifed to the emperor Theodofius, after his victory over the Scythians: both which, prove by their refemblance to the Trajan column, that this fort of appropriation recommended by him; had paffed into a rule, among the ancient mafters of the art.

I SHALL not here difpute the juftnefs of Mr. De Chambray's remarks; but may venture to affirm, that not only the Tufcan column, but the whole order, as repre-fented in the annexed defign, (which, being in fact the production of Vignola and Scamozzi, I may praife without the imputation of vanity,) is extremely beautiful, a

ufeful,

ufeful, even neceffary gradation in the art; and for its purpofes, inferior to none of the reft.

THE Tufcan, order as it conveys ideas of ftrength and ruftic fimplicity, is very proper for rural purpofes; and may be employed in farm houfes, in barns and fheds for implements of hufbandry, in ftables, maneges and dog-kennels, in green houfes, grottos and fountains, in gates of parks and gardens, and generally wherever magnificence is not required, and expence is to be avoided. Serlio recommends the ufe thereof in prifons, arfenals, treafuries, fea ports and gates of fortified places; and Le Clerc obferves, that though the Tufcan order as treated by Vitruvius, by Palladio, and fome others, ought to be entirely rejected; yet according to the compofition of Vignola, there is a beauty in its fimplicity, which recommends it to notice; and entitles it to a place, both in private and public buildings: as, in colonades and porticos, furrounding fquares or markets; in granaries or ftorehoufes; and even in royal palaces: to adorn the lower apartments, offices, ftables and other places, where ftrength and fimplicity are required; and where richer, or more delicate orders would be improper.

IN conformity to the doctrine and practice before-mentioned, feven diameters or fourteen modules, have been given to the height of the Tufcan column; a proportion, very proper for rural or military works, where an appearance of extraordinary folidity is required: but in town buildings, intended for civil purpofes; or in interior decorations; the height of the column, may be fourteen and a half, or even fifteen modules, as Scamozzi makes it; which augmentation, may be entirely in the fhaft, without changing any meafures either of the bafe or capital. Nor need the entablature be altered; for, as it is compofed of few parts, it will be fufficiently bold; although its height be fomewhat lefs, than one quarter of the height of the column.

Of the D O R I C   O R D E R.

IN the parallel, are given three profiles of the Doric order: one of which is taken from the theatre of Marcellus, and the other two, are copied by Pietro Ligorio, from various fragments of antiquity, in and near Rome. Vignola's fecond Doric profile, bears a near refemblance to the moft beautiful of thefe, and was not improbably collected from the fame antique, which Ligorio copied: though it muft be owned, that Vignola has, in his compofition, far exceeded the original: having omitted the many trivial, infignificant mouldings, with which that is over-loaded; and in various other refpects, improved both its form and proportions.

THIS profile of Vignola's, being compofed in a greater ftile, and in a manner more characteriftic of the order, than any other, I have chofen for my model; having, in the general form and proportions, ftrictly adhered to the original; though in particular members I have not fcrupled to vary, when obfervation taught me they might be improved.

VIGNOLA, as appears by the preface to his rules; fuppofed, that the graceful and pleafing afpect of Architectonic objects, was occafioned by the harmony and fimplicity of the relations exifting between their parts; and in compofing his profiles, he conftantly regulates his meafures, by thefe fimple affinities; imagining the deviations from them in his antique models, to proceed, rather from the inaccurate execution of the workmen, than from any premeditated defign in the contriver. To this notion may be afcribed, many little defects in the proportions of his mouldings, and minuter members; which, though trifling in themfelves, are yet, from the fmallnefs of the parts where they happen to be, of confequence; and eafily perceivable, by a judicious eye. Thefe I have therefore endeavoured to correct, not only in this, but in others of his orders; which, from their conformity to the beft antiques, I have in the courfe of this work, chofen to imitate.

IT has already been obferved, that the real relations, fubfifting between diffimilar figures, have no connection with the apparent: the form, and fituation, of the object viewed, ever altering the affinity; and it is a truth, too evident to require demonftration. No one will deny, for inftance, that the ovolo in the annexed Doric cornice*, viewed in its proper elevation, will appear much larger than the capital of the triglyph, under and contiguous to it; though they are in reality, nearly of the fame dimenfions: and, if the fame ovolo were placed as much below the level of the fpectator's eye, as it is in the prefent cafe above; it is likewife evident, that it would appear confiderably lower, than any flat member of the fame height. Thefe things being fo, a ftrict attachment to harmonic relations, feems entirely out of the queftion; fince, what is really in perfect harmony, may in appearance produce the moft jarring difcord.

PERFECT proportion, in architecture, if confidered only with regard to the relations between the different objects in a compofition; and, as it merely relates to the pleafure of the fight; feems to confift in this: that thofe parts which are either principal or effential, fhould be contrived to catch the eye fucceffively, from the moft confiderable, to the leaft, according to their degrees of importance in the compofition; and imprefs their images on the mind, before it is affected by any of the fubfervient members: yet, that thefe fhould be fo conditioned, as not to be entirely abforbed, but be capable of raifing diftinct ideas likewife; and fuch, as may be adequate to the purpofes, for which thefe parts are defigned.

THE different figures and fituations of the parts may, in fome degree, contribute toward this effect: for fimple forms will operate more fpeedily than thofe that are complicated; and fuch as project, will be fooner perceived, than fuch as are more retired: but dimenfion feems to be the predominant quality; or that which acts moft powerfully on the fenfe: and this, it is apprehended, can only be difcovered by experience; at leaft to any degree of accuracy. When therefore a number of parts, arranged in a particular manner, and under particular dimenfions, excites, in the generality of judicious fpectators, a pleafing fenfation; it will be prudent on every occafion, where the fame circumftances fubfift, to obferve exactly

* Pl. Doric Order.

the

THE
DORIC ORDER.

Soffit of the Corona & Mutules

Doric Base

50 Minutes
60 Minutes

| 1 | 2 | 3 | 4 Modules |
5 10 15   30 Minutes

W. Chambers Delin.

E. Rooker Sculp.

Doric Entablature. Imitated from the Theatre of Marcellus.

Doric Entablature of Palladio, as Executed in the Basilica at Vicenza.

Soffit   18 Min.

Soffit   14¾ Min.

J. Gandon Delin.

Ja. Patton sculp.

the fame arrangement and proportions; notwithftanding they may in themfelves appear irregular, and unconnected.

In compofing the orders and other decorations, which are contained in the prefent publication, this method has conftantly been obferved; the author having himfelf, with that view, meafured with the utmoft accuracy, and not without fome danger; many ancient and modern celebrated buildings, both at Rome and in other parts of Europe; ftrictly copying fuch things as appeared to be perfect; and carefully correcting others, which feemed in any degree, faulty: relying therein not alone on his own judgment, in doubtful cafes; but much on the opinion and advice, of feveral learned, ingenious artifts of different nations; with whom he had the advantage of being intimately connected, when abroad.

Sensible he is, that the extraordinary degree of accuracy, which has been aimed at in thefe compofitions, is of little confequence to the generality of fpecta-tors; who fee in the grofs, and feel by the lump. Neverthelefs, as in poefy, mufic, painting, and indeed in all arts, there are delicacies, which, though they efcape the vulgar notice, afford uncommon pleafure to perfons of enlightened conception; fo in architecture, this kind of perfection, is the fource of fecondary pleafures; lefs forcible perhaps, but not always lefs delightful than the firft: thefe may be compa-red, to thofe excited by the energy or graces of language in poetry; by the fhakes, fwells, inflections, and other artifices of the inftrument, or voice in mufic; which give fentiment and expreffion to the performance. Or in painting, by a judicious choice, and artful difpofition of the objects; a nice difcrimination of the paffions; an elegant tafte of defign, and a fpirited, mafterly touch of the pencil. To all but local colour, and general refemblance, the unfkilful are commonly blind; but the correct eye, and ripened judgment, derive their chief pleafure, from that, which the igno-rant rarely perceive, and feldom or ever tafte.

It may perhaps, be objected, that the proportions here eftablifhed, though proper and good on one occafion, may on many others be defective. But this objection will, I flatter myfelf, have little weight; when it is remembered, that the fituation of capitals and entablatures, with refpect to the order of which they are parts, is conftantly the fame: and the points of view more or lefs diftant, according to the fize or elevation of the order. And that confequently, the apparent magni-tudes of all their parts, will always have, very nearly, the fame proportion to each other; even though they fhould be exalted to a fecond or third ftory.

With regard to bafes indeed, their being placed on pedeftals, or immediately on the ground, will occafion fome little difference in their appearance; and when they are raifed to a fecond ftory, their figure and apparent proportions will be confiderably altered. Neverthelefs it doth not feem neceffary, in either of thefe cafes, to vary their dimenfions: for in the former of the two, the alteration would be trifling; and in the latter, the object being far removed from the eye, the fpectator will rather be occupied in confidering the general mafs, than in examining its parts; which, on account of their diftance, cannot be diftinctly perceptible.

The height of the Doric column, including its capital and bafe, is fixteen modules; and the height of the entablature, four modules; the latter of which being
Y
divided

divided into eight parts, two of them are given to the architrave, three to the frize, and the remaining three to the cornice.

IN moſt of the antiques, the Doric column is executed without a baſe: Vitruvius likewiſe makes it without one; the baſe, according to that author, having been firſt employed in the Ionic order, to imitate the ſandal or covering of a woman's foot. Scamozzi blames this practice; and moſt of the moderns have been of his opinion; the greateſt part of them having employed the Attic baſe in this order. Monſieur De Chambray, however, whoſe blind attachment to the antique is, on many occaſions, ſufficiently evident; argues vehemently againſt this practice: which, as the order is formed upon the model of a ſtrong man, who is conſtantly repreſented bare-footed; is, according to him, very improper: and " though, ſays he, " the cuſtom of employing a baſe, in contempt of all ancient authority, has by " ſome unaccountable and falſe notions of beauty, prevailed; yet I doubt not but " the purer eye, when appriſed of this error, will eaſily be undeceived; and as " what is merely plauſible will, when examined, appear to be falſe; ſo apparent " beauties, when not founded in reaſon, will of courſe be deemed extravagant."

LE CLERC'S remarks on this paſſage, are very judicious; and as they may ſerve to deſtroy a notion, which ſoon after our Athenian diſcoveries, about thirty years ago, was much too prevalent among us; and might, perhaps, in ſome future hour of extravagance, prevail again; I ſhall, for the benefit of ſuch as are unacquainted with the original, tranſlate the whole paſſage. " In the moſt ancient " monuments of this order, ſays he, the columns are without baſes; for which it " is difficult to aſſign any ſatisfactory reaſon. Monſieur De Chambray, in his " parallel, is of the ſame opinion with Vitruvius, and maintains that the Doric " column, being compoſed upon the model of a naked, ſtrong, and muſcular man, " reſembling a Hercules, ſhould have no baſe; pretending that the baſe to a column, " is the ſame as a ſhoe to a man. But I muſt own, I cannot conſider a column " without a baſe, in comparing it to a man; but I am at the ſame time ſtruck with " the idea of a perſon without feet, rather than without ſhoes: for which reaſon I " am inclinable to believe; either, that the architects of antiquity had not yet thought " of employing baſes to their columns, or that they omitted them, in order to leave " the pavement clear; the angles and projection of baſes, being ſtumbling blocks to " paſſengers, and ſo much the more troubleſome, as the architects of thoſe times, " frequently placed their columns very near each other: ſo that had they been " made with baſes, the paſſages between them would have been extremely narrow " and inconvenient: and it was doubtleſs for the ſame reaſon, that Vitruvius made " the plinth of his Tuſcan column round; that order, according to his conſtruction, " being particularly adapted to ſervile and commercial purpoſes; where conveniency " is preferable to beauty. However this be, perſons of good taſte will grant, that " a baſe not only gives a graceful turn to the column, but is likewiſe of real uſe; " ſerving to keep it firm on its plan: and that if columns without baſes are now ſet " aſide, it is a mark of the wiſdom of our architects, rather than an indication of " their being governed by prejudice, as ſome adorers of antiquity would inſinuate."

IN imitation of Palladio, and all the modern architects except Vignola; I have made uſe of the Attic baſe in this order: and it certainly is the moſt beautiful of any; though for variety's ſake, when the Doric and Ionic orders are employed together,

together, the bafe invented by Vignola, of which a profile is annexed, may fometimes be ufed.   Bernini has employed it in the colonades of St. Peter's, and it has been fuc-cefsfully applied in many other buildings.

THE ancients fometimes made the fhaft of the Doric column prifmatic, as appears by a paffage in the fourth book of Vitruvius; and at other times they adorned it with a particular kind of fhallow flutings, defcribed from the center of a fquare, no interval or fillet being left between them.   Of this fort, there are now fome columns to be feen in the temples of Peftum, near Naples; in different parts of Sicily; and in the church of St. Peter in Catenis, at Rome.   The firft of thefe manners has not, I believe, been imitated by any of the modern mafters; nor is the fecond very frequent: Scamozzi blames it for its want of folidity, the projecting angles between the flutings being eafily broken, and, if the material be foft, very fubject to moulder.

VITRUVIUS gives to the height of the Doric capital one module; and all the moderns, except Alberti, have followed his example.   Neverthelefs, as it is of the fame kind with the Tufcan, they fhould both bear nearly the fame proportion to the heights of their refpective columns; and confequently, the Doric capital ought to be more than one module, which it accordingly is, both at the Colifeum, and in the theatre of Marcellus: being in the former of thefe buildings, upwards of thirty-eight minutes, and in the latter thirty-three minutes high.

IN the defign here offered, I have made the height of the whole capital thirty-two minutes, and in the form and dimenfions of the particular members, I have deviated but little, from the profile of the theatre of Marcellus.   The frize, or neck, is enriched with hufks and rofes, as in Palladio's defign, and as it has been executed by Sangallo, at the Farnefe Palace in Rome, and by Cigoli, in the Cortile of the Strozzi at Florence, as well as in feveral buildings of note in this metropolis.   The projection of thefe hufks and flowers, muft not exceed that of the upper cincture of the column.

THE architrave is one module in height, and compofed only of one fafcia and a fillet, as at the theatre of Marcellus: the drops are conical, as they are in all the antiques; not pyramidal, as they are improperly made by moft of our Englifh workmen: they are fuppofed to reprefent drops of water draining from the triglyph, and confequently they fhould be cones, or parts of cones, not pyramids.

THE frize and the cornice, are each of them one module and a half in height: the metope is fquare, and enriched with a bull's fcull, adorned with garlands of beads, in imitation of thofe on the temple of Jupiter Tonans, at the foot of the Capitol.   In fome antique fragments, and in a greater number of modern buildings, the metopes are alternately enriched with thefe ox-fculls, and with pateras; but they may be filled with any other ornaments, of good forms; and frequently with greater propriety.   Thus, in military ftructures, heads of Medufa, or of the Furies, thunderbolts, and other fymbols of horror, may be introduced: likewife helmets, daggers, garlands of laurel or oak, and crowns of various kinds; fuch as thofe ufed among the Romans, and given as rewards for different military achievements: but fpears, fwords, quivers, bows, cuiraffes, fhields, and the like; muft be avoided:

Z   becaufe

becaufe the real dimenfions of thefe things, are too confiderable to find admittance in fuch fmall compartments: and reprefentations in miniature, always carry with them an idea of triviality, carefully to be avoided in architecture; as in all other arts. In facred buildings, cherubs, chalices, and garlands of palm or olive, may be employed; likewife doves, or other fymbols of moral virtues. And in private houfes, crefts or badges of dignity, may fometimes be fuffered: though feldom; and indeed never, when they are of fuch ftiff, infipid forms, as ftars, garters, modern crowns, coronets, mitres, truncheons, and fimilar gracelefs objects: the ill effects of which may be feen at the Treafury, in St. James's Park, and in many other places.

Too much variety in the ornaments of the metopes, muft be avoided; left the unity of the compofition fhould be deftroyed. It is beft, never to introduce more than two different reprefentations; which fhould not confift of above one, or at moft two objects each; of fimple forms, and not overcharged with ornaments. In the difpofition of thefe, care muft be taken to place them with fymmetry; thofe on the right, in correfpondence with thofe on the left. Wherefore, when a triglyph happens to be in the middle of a front, it becomes neceffary to couple the middle ones, by filling the two metopes, on each fide of the central triglyph, with the fame fort of ornaments; as is done at the gate of Burlington Houfe in Piccadilly; diftributing the reft alternately, throughout the compofition, as ufual. It is like-wife to be obferved, that ornaments in metopes, are not to project fo much as they do at Bow Church, or at General Wade's Houfe in Burlington Gardens; where, from their great relief, they are far more ftriking than the triglyphs; which ought to predominate: as being effential, and principal parts in the compofition. Palladio in his Bafilica of Vicenza, has given to the moft elevated parts of the ox-fculls and pateras, with which the metopes are filled; very little more projection, than that of the triglyph; and in this, he has copied the ancients; who feldom or never, gave more projection to any ornament, than that of the frame or border, in which it was inclofed: as appears by thofe inimitable fragments in the Villa Medici, and many others in different parts of Rome, and elfewhere. The channels of the triglyph on their plan, commonly form a right angle; but, to give them more effect, a narrow fquare groove may be cut in the inner angle, from top to bottom; and quite into the folid of the frize.

In the cornice, I have deviated very little from my original. Le Clerc, who in his Doric profile, has imitated that of Vignola; makes the mutules as broad as the capital of the triglyph: Mr. Gibbs has followed his example; and they have been executed in that manner, on a couple of doors to houfes, on the north fide of Lincoln's-Inn Fields. But Vignola's method is preferable, who makes them no broader than the triglyph; as it is more fightly, and more conformable to the car-penter's art: in which, the width of the rafter, never exceeds the width of the beam or joift, it ftands upon. The ornaments of the foffit, are nearly the fame as thofe of Vignola. They fhould be entirely funk up, wrought in the folid of the corona, and never drop down lower than its foffit. There is no neceffity for cutting them deep: in moft of Palladio's buildings, they do not enter above two minutes, into the corona; and that is quite fufficient.

VIGNOLA'S

VIGNOLA's other Doric profile, is in imitation of that of the theatre of Marcellus; in it he has very judicioufly pointed out, and in fome meafure, corrected the faults of the original: but reverence for the antique, has made him rather too fparing of his amendments. I have given a defign of this profile*, with fuch farther corrections as appeared neceffary; the moft confiderable of them, confifting in the enlargement of the dentils; which are neither in the antique model, nor in Vignola's profile, fufficiently confpicuous, to hold their due place in the compofition.

AT the theatre of Marcellus, the ornaments of the foffit are not in a horizontal pofition, but hang down towards the front of the corona; which, as it appears by Vitruvius, was a common practice among the ancients; and done to imitate the inclination of the rafters. Palladio, and Vignola, have both adopted this particularity; which, Davilere fuppofes to have been firft ufed, in order to make the projection of the entablature, appear more confiderable. To me it has an exceeding difagreeable appearance; the whole foffit feems in a falling ftate: and fo far is it from producing the effect which Davilere fuppofes, that it actually makes, as it evidently muft, the projection feem lefs than in reality it is.

VIGNOLA's two Doric entablatures, fays Davilere, are both of them fo elegantly compofed, that it is fcarcely poffible to determine, which of them ought to have the preference. The firft, which is entirely antique, is the lighteft; and confequently propereft for interior decorations, or objects intended for near infpection; the other, compofed by Vignola himfelf, from various fragments of antiquity, being bolder, and confifting of larger parts, feems better calculated for outfide works; and places where the point of view is either diftant, or unlimited. On polygonal plans, however, the mutule cornice muft be avoided; becaufe the foffits of the angular mutules, would form irregular and very difagreeable figures: neither fhould it be employed in concaves of fmall dimenfions, for the fame reafon; nor in places where frequent breaks are requifite; it being extremely difficult, often impoffible, to prevent the mutules from penetrating, and mutilating each other, in various unfightly manners. And wherever this cornice is ufed on a convex furface, the fides of the mutules muft be made parallel; for it would be both difagreeable and unnatural, to fee them broader, and confequently heavier in front, than where they fpring out of the mutule band.

PALLADIO's Doric entablature, is likewife very beautiful: I mean as it is executed in the Bafilica of Vicenza, where it differs widely from the profile in his book†, and is far preferable thereto. In the fame plate with Vignola's dentil entablature, there is a defign of it, accurately copied from that building; which may ferve as one inftance of many, to fhew, how little the meafures of his book are to be relied upon.

OF all the entablatures, the Doric is moft difficult to diftribute; on account of the large intervals, between the centers of the triglyphs; which neither admit of increafe, or diminution, without injuring the fymmetry, and regular beauty of

---

* Pl. Doric Entablatures.   † Pl. Doric Entablatures.

the

the compofition. Thefe conftantly confine the compofer to intercolumniations, divifible by two modules and a half; entirely exclude coupled columns; and produce fpaces, which, in general, are either too wide or too narrow, for his purpofes.

To obviate thefe difficulties, the triglyphs have often been omitted, and the entablature made plain; as at the Colifeum in Rome, the colonades of St. Peter's, of the Vatican; and in many other buildings, both at home and abroad. This indeed, is an eafy expedient: but while it robs the order of its principal charaɛteriftick diftinɛtion, leaves it poor, and very little fuperior to the Tufcan, the remedy feems defperate, and fhould never be employed, but as a laft refource.

THE ancients employed the Doric, in temples dedicated to Minerva, to Mars, and to Hercules; whofe grave and manly difpofitions, fuited well with the charaɛter of this order. Serlio, fays it is proper for churches dedicated to Jefus Chrift, to St. Paul, St. Peter; or any other Saints, remarkable for their fortitude, in expofing their lives, and fuffering for the Chriftian faith. Le Clerc, recommends the ufe of it, in all kinds of military buildings; as arfenals, gates of fortified places, guard rooms, and fimilar ftruɛtures. It may likewife be employed in the houfes of generals, or other martial men; in maufoleums ereɛted to their memory, or in triumphal bridges and arches, built to celebrate their viɛtories.

I HAVE made the height of the Doric column, fixteen modules; which, in buildings where majefty, or grandeur are required, is a proper proportion: but in others, it may be fomewhat more flender. Thus, Vitruvius makes the Doric column in porticos, higher by half a diameter, than in temples; and moft of the modern architeɛts, have on fome occafions, followed his example. In private houfes therefore, it may be $16\frac{1}{3}$, $16\frac{1}{2}$, or $16\frac{2}{3}$ modules high; in interior decorations, even feventeen modules, and fometimes perhaps a trifle more: which increafe in the height, may be added entirely to the fhaft, as in the Tufcan order; without changing either the bafe, or capital. The entablature too, may remain unaltered, in all the aforefaid cafes; for it will be fufficiently bold, without alteration.

Of the IONIC ORDER.

A MONGST the ancients, the form of the Ionic profile, appears to have been more pofitively determined, than that of any other order; for in all the antiques at Rome, (the temple of Concord excepted,) it is exaɛtly the fame; and conformable to the defcription Vitruvius has given thereof.

THE modern artifts, have likewife been more unanimous in their opinions upon the fubjeɛt; all of them, excepting Palladio and his imitators, having employed the dentil cornice, and the other parts of the profile, nearly as they are found in the Colifeum, the temple of Fortune, and the theatre of Marcellus.

IN Palladio's works, we meet with three different Ionic entablatures; all of them very beautiful. The firft is the true antique, which he has made ufe of at the

palace

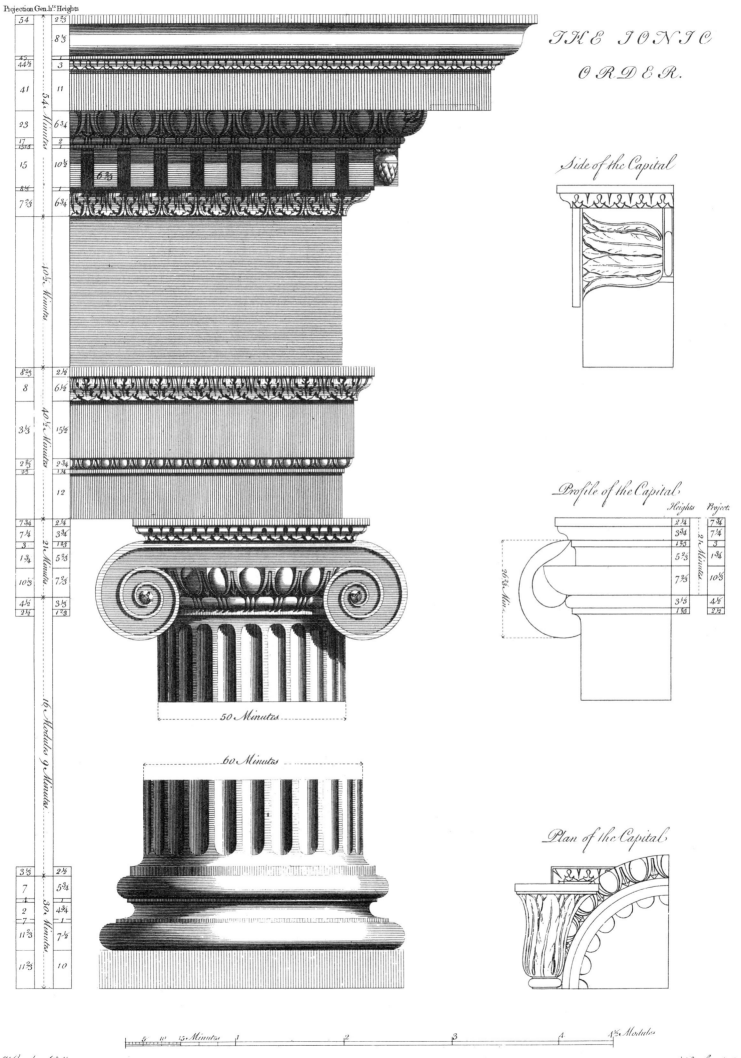

THE IONIC ORDER.

Side of the Capital

Profile of the Capital

Plan of the Capital

50 Minutes

60 Minutes

W. Chambers Delin.

E. Rooker Sculp.

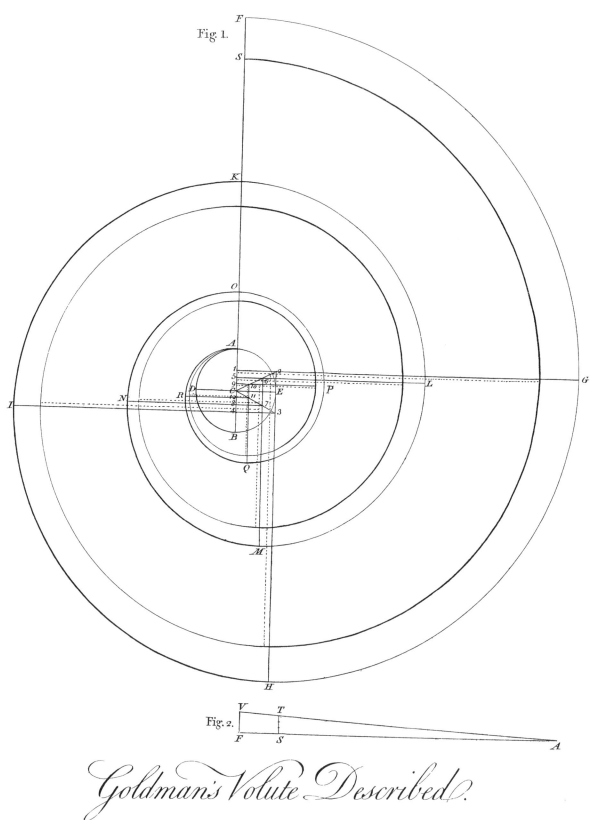

Fig. 1.

Fig. 2.

Goldman's Volute Described.

Fig. 1.   Draw the Cathetus F C whose length must be half a Module, and from the point C describe the Eye of the Volute A E B D, of which the Diameter is to be 3⅓ minutes, divide it into four equal Sectors by the Diameters A B, D E, Bisect the Radii C A, C B in 1 and 4, and on the line 1. 4 Construct a Square 1.2.3.4, from the Centre C to the Angles 2.3 draw y̓ Diagonals C. 2 C. 3. and divide the side of the Square 1,4 into Six equal parts at 5. 9. C 12.8. then through the points 5. 9. 12. 8 draw the lines 5. 6. 9. 10. 12. 11. 8. 7. parallel to the Diameter E D which will cut the Diagonals in 6 7 10 11. and y̓ points 1. 2. 3. 4. 5. 6. 7. 8. 9. 10. 11. 12. will be the Centres of the Volute. From the first Centre 1 with the Interval 1. F. describe y̓ Quadrant F G, from the second Centre 2 with the Interval 2 G describe the Quadrant G H, and continuing the same opperation from all the twelve Centres, the Contour of the Volute will be Completed. ———————

Fig. 2.   The Centres for describing the fillet are found in this manner, Construct a Triangle of which y̓ side A F is equal to the part of the Cathetus contained between A F, and the side F V equal to C 1, on the side A F place y̓ distance F S from F towards A, equal to F S the breadth of the fillet, and through the point S draw the line S T, which will be to C 1 in the same proportion as A S is to A F, place this line on each side of the Centre C on the Diameter of the Eye A B, divide it into three equal parts, and through the points of division draw lines parallel to the Diameter E D, which will cut the Diagonals C. 2, C. 3, and you will have twelve new Centres, from whence the interior Contour of y̓ fillet may be describ'd, in the same manner as the exterior one was from the first Centres. ———————

palace of the Porti; and in feveral doors and windows, of the Thieni, and Valmarano palaces, in Vicenza. The fecond, is a very judicious imitation of the entablature in the temple of Concord; and is executed by him, in the upper arcade of the Bafilica, in the fame city. The third, which is an invention of his own; being the fame with that in his book; he has employed with fome fmall difference, at the Chiericato palace, at the rotunda of Marchefe Capra, and in various others of his buildings in the Vicentine, or at Venice.

In the firft plate of the Ionic order, there is a defign of the antique profile, collected by me, from different antiquities at Rome. The height of the column is eighteen modules, and that of the entablature, four modules and a half; or one quarter of the height of the column, as in the other orders: which is a trifle lefs, than in any of the regular antique Ionics. The bafe is Attic, as in all the antiques; and the fhaft of the column may either be plain, or fluted, with twenty-four, or with twenty flutings only, as at the temple of Fortune: of which, the plan fhould be a little more than femi-circular, as it is at the temple of Jupiter Tonans, and at the forum of Nerva; becaufe then they are more diftinctly marked. The fillet, or interval between the flutes, fhould not be broader than one third of their width; nor narrower than one quarter thereof. The ornaments of the capital, are to correfpond with the flutes of the fhaft; and there muft be an ove or a dart, above the middle of each flute. The volutes are to be traced according to Goldman's method, which is the beft. I have given a defign of it, with an exact defcription upon the plate. Perrault prefers De l'Orme's method of defcribing it; yet certainly, it is not fo perfect: for in Goldman's, the circular portions that compofe the volute, have their radii, at their junction, in the fame ftraight line; fo that they meet, without forming an angle: whereas, in that of De l'Orme, the radii never coincide; and confequently no two of the curves can join, without forming an angle. The fpace, in De l'Orme's volute, between the firft quadrants, in the firft and fecond revolution, is of the fame breadth throughout; both the quadrants being defcribed from the fame center: but in Goldman's, the fpace between the revolutions, diminifhes regularly from the very firft. Moreover, De l'Orme has given no directions for defcribing the inner fpiral, which determines the breadth of the fillet; and which, in his defign, is nearly of the fame breadth from firft to laft; but Goldman has taught the manner of defcribing it, fo as to diminifh gradually, with the fame accuracy as the outward fpiral.

Palladio's volute, differing but little from that of De l'Orme, has nearly the fame defects: and though Mr. Gibbs has in fome meafure, amended it, yet, his likewife, is faulty in the breadth of the fillet; which is equal through the greateft part of the firft revolution.

Vignola and Scamozzi, Serlio, Alberti, and others have, in their architraves, imitated thofe of the theatre of Marcellus, and of the Colifeum; having compofed them of three fafcias, diftinguifhed from each other, only by fmall projections. This, has but an indifferent effect; the feparations fo faintly marked, are not fufficiently ftriking; and the architrave is left too deftitute of ornaments, for the reft of the profile: a defect moft ftriking, whenever the mouldings of the profile are enriched.

                                   On

ON the other hand, Palladio's and De l'Orme's architraves, appear too rich; being likewife compofed of three fafcias, feparated by mouldings: I have therefore in this particular, chofen to imitate the profile of the temple of Antoninus and Fauftina; where there are only two fafcias, feparated from each other by a moulding.

THE three parts of the entablature, bear the fame proportion to each other in this, as in the Tufcan order: the frize is plain, as being moft fuitable to the fimplicity of the reft of the compofition; and the cornice is almoft an exact copy from Vignola's defign, in which there is a purity of form, a grandeur of ftile, and clofe conformity to the moft approved antiques, not to be found in the profiles of his competitors.

IF it be required to reduce this entablature, to two ninths of the height of the column, (which, on moft occafions, is a proportion preferable to that of one quarter; particularly, where the eye has been habituated to contemplate diminutive objects), it may eafily be done; by making the module for the entablature, lefs by one ninth, than the femi-diameter of the column; afterwards dividing it as ufual, and obferving the fame dimenfions as are figured in the defign. The diftribution of the dentil band will, in fuch cafe, anfwer pretty nearly in all the regular intercolumniations; and in the outer angle, there will be a dentil, as there is in the temple of Fortune, at Rome.

IN interior decorations, where much delicacy is required, the height of the entablature may be reduced even to one fifth of the column; by obferving the fame method, and making the module, only four fifths of the femi-diameter.

OF Palladio's profiles, that, imitated from the temple of Concord, appears to me the beft: it's height is equal to one fifth of the height of the column. The defign which I have given of it, is clofely copied from the Bafilica, at Vicenza: but it will be more perfect, if the frize be made flat, and it's height augmented, fo as to equal that of the architrave; by which means, the proportion of the entablature to the column, will be better: for the relation of one to five, is, generally fpeaking, too fmall. In the cornice it will likewife be well to add, between the corona and fillet, under the cyma, an oge; of the fame dimenfion, with that over the modillions. Thus, all the parts will be equally rich, and the upper cyma be better fupported. This, Scamozzi has done in his profile: though in other refpects, his Ionic entablature may be confidered as a copy, from Palladio: the fillet, being thus fuftained by the oge, may be diminifhed a trifle.

PALLADIO's other profile, I have copied from the rotunda of Capra; it's height is likewife one fifth of the column. The frize, as in the former defign, is low and fwelled: but it will be better to raife it to the fame height with the architrave, and keep it upright as before directed; for the fwell gives it a clumfy form, and appearing a continuity of the fame undulations, which compofe the architrave and cornice; ferves to render the outline of the whole entablature confufed, and much too abundant in curves. The frize, when fo formed, conveys the idea of a piece of timber, ufed without being hewn; as was the practice of ruder

times

times among the Greeks, and cannot with propriety be introduced in a finifhed work.

IN the antique, there are few examples of thefe fwelled frizes; Palladio probably took his hint, from the temple of Bacchus, near Rome; where the fwelled frize has been ufed in a Compofite order: or perhaps, from the Bafilica of Antoninus, where it has been employed in a Corinthian: with little fuccefs at the laft, and with much lefs, at the firft of thefe places; for as the columns are there infulated, and the profile is marked at the four angles, the deformity becomes fo much the more confpicuous: and, notwithftanding Palladio's partiality to this form of frize, which fo frequently recurs in moft of his works; it feldom or never can be introduced with fuccefs, but on doors or windows, where the profile of the architrave is not marked under it: there indeed, the fwell forms a good contraft with the upright jambs; and has the farther advantage of contracting the fpread of the cornice; which, in narrow intercolumniations, is very convenient; and in moft cafes, may prevent the licentious practice, of making the frize and cornice no wider than the aperture of the door or window, and fupporting them on each fide with a fort of fcroll; as at the Sorbonne in Paris, and at the Manfion Houfe in this city.

PALLADIO, in both thefe profiles, has enriched the foffit of the corona with rofes; which are here omitted, as in moft cafes they ought to be. However when the column is fluted, and the reft of the compofition much adorned, they may, and fhould be introduced; care being taken to proportion the pannels, and other parts furrounding them, in the fame manner, as if the order were Corinthian or Compofite.

THE antique Ionic capital, differs from any of the others: its front and fide faces are not alike. This particularity, occafions great difficulty, wherever there are breaks in the entablature; or where the decoration is continued in flank, as well as in front: for either, all the capitals in the flank muft have the balufter fide outward, or the angular capitals will have a different appearance from the reft; neither of which is admiffible. The architect of the temple of Fortune at Rome, has fallen upon an expedient, which in fome degree, remedies the defect. In that building, the corner capitals have their angular volutes in an oblique pofition, inclining equally to the front and fide, and offering volute faces both ways. Wherever perfons are violently attached to the antique, or furioufly bent on rejecting all modern inventions, however excellent; this is the only mean to gratify them: but when fuch is not the cafe, the angular capital invented by Scamozzi, or imitated and improved by him, from the temple of Concord, or borrowed from fome modern compofitions extant in his time, ought to be employed; for the diftorted figure of the antique capital, with one volute ftraight and the other twifted, is very perceptible, and far from being pleafing to the eye.

ANNEXED is a defign of Scamozzi's capital, and another of a very beautiful one, executed in St. Peter's of the Vatican; probably compofed by Michael Angelo. Similar capitals may alfo be feen in the church of the Roman college, and in various other buildings at Rome.

IN

IN this order, I have employed the Attic bafe. Of the antique bafe defcribed by Vitruvius, and ufed by Vignola and Philibert De l'Orme, in their Ionic orders, and by Sir Chriftopher Wren, in fome parts of St. Paul's; I think there is no example among the antiques; and being univerfally efteemed a very imperfect production, I have not even given a defign of it.

As the Doric order, is particularly affected in churches or temples, dedicated to male faints; fo the Ionic, is principally ufed in fuch as are confecrated to females, of the matronal ftate. It is likewife employed in courts of juftice, in libraries, colleges, feminaries, and other ftructures having relation to arts or letters; in private houfes, and in palaces; to adorn the women's apartments; and, fays Le Clerc, in all places dedicated to peace and tranquillity. The ancients employed it in temples facred to Juno, to Bacchus, to Diana, and other deities whofe difpofitions held a medium, between the fevere and the effeminate.

Of the COMPOSITE ORDER.

STRICTLY fpeaking, the ancients had but four orders; the Compofite was not confidered by them as a diftinct production: Vitruvius exprefsly tells us, book IV. chap. 1, that on Corinthian columns, other capitals of various kinds were employed; which neverthelefs ought not to change the names of the columns, becaufe their proportions remained ftill the fame.

THE moderns, however, have ranked the Compofite with the four orders mentioned by Vitruvius; having among the great number of different Compofite capitals, to be met with in the remains of antiquity, chofen for their model, that which has been ufed in the triumphal arches, in the temple of Bacchus, and at the baths of Dioclefian: rather, I believe, as agreeing moft with the defcription of Vitruvius, (who obferves that thefe capitals were compofed of the Ionic, Doric, and Corinthian,) than from any preference in point of beauty to many others.

NEITHER doth it appear, that the ancients affected any particular form of entablature to this order: fometimes they made the cornice entirely plain, as in the temple of Bacchus; at others, enriched with dentils, and differing very little from the Ionic, as in the arch of Septimus Severus; and in the arch of Titus, there are both dentils and modillions; the whole form of the profile, being the fame with that of the Corinthian; as it is executed in moft of the antiques, at Rome and elfewhere.

THE modern architects, have varied more in this, than in any other of the orders. Abandoned, as De Chambray obferves, by their guide Vitruvius; and left entirely at large, they have all taken different paths: each following the bent of his own particular fancy. Among them, Serlio has been leaft fuccefsful; having chofen for the model of his entablature, that of the fourth order of the Colifeum: a

compofition

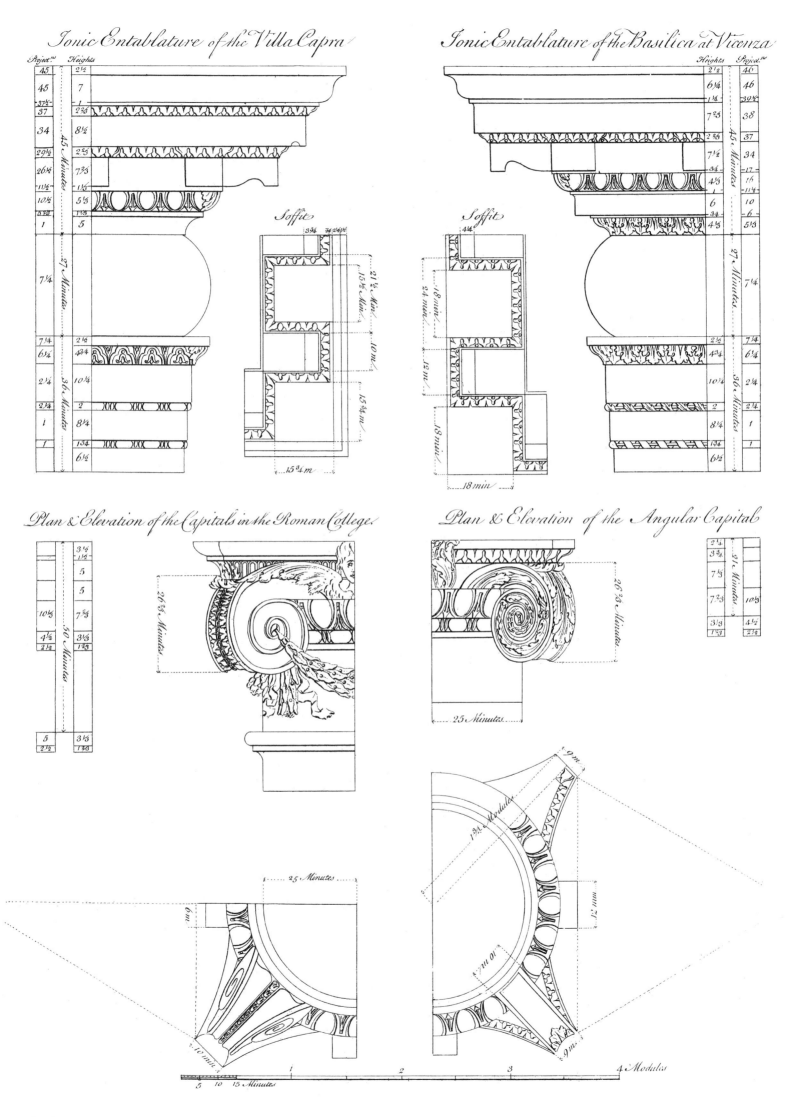

Ionic Entablature of the Villa Capra

Soffit

Ionic Entablature of the Basilica at Vicenza

Soffit

Plan & Elevation of the Capitals in the Roman College

Plan & Elevation of the Angular Capital

W. Chambers.

I. Potter Sculp.

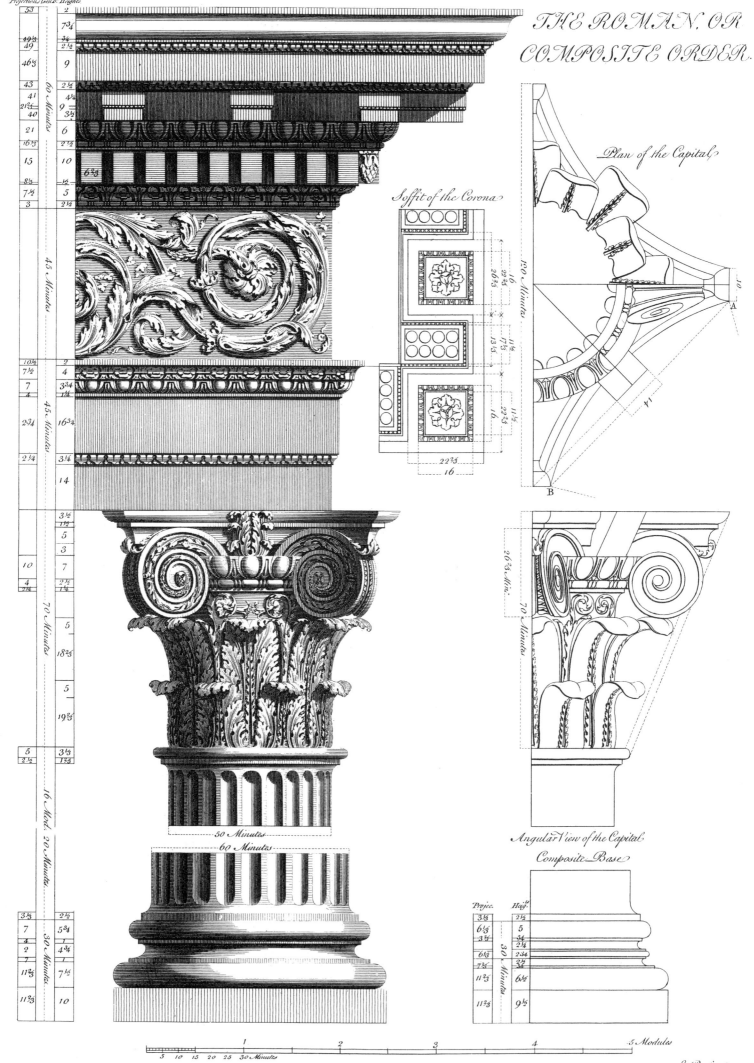

THE ROMAN. OR
COMPOSITE ORDER.

Plan of the Capital

Soffit of the Corona

Angular View of the Capital

Composite Base

50 Minutes

60 Minutes

1   2   3   4   5 Modules

5 10 15 20 25 30 Minutes

W. Chambers Del.

E. Rooker Sculp.

compofition too clumfy, even for a Tufcan order. De l'Orme, however, has followed his example; and miftaken the columns of the fourth order of the Colifeum, which are Corinthian, for Compofite.

PALLADIO in his profile, has imitated the cornice of the frontifpiece of 'Nero; and corrected its defects with much judgment. His architrave is likewife taken from the fame building: but he has omitted its beautiful frize, and fubftituted in its place a fwelled one, fimilar to that of the Bafilica of Antoninus. His whole entablature is too low; being only one fifth of the column: and it is remarkable, that, though he has made the column more delicate, than in the Corinthian order, yet his entablature is made far more maffive; being compofed of fewer and much larger parts. In the defign given on the fecond plate of the Compofite order, Palladio's meafures have been clofely obferved: but if the frize were augmented, fo as to raife the entablature to two ninths of the column; made upright, and enriched with ornaments; it would be more perfect: and might be employed with fuccefs, in works of large dimenfions, which require to be feen from a confiderable diftance. But for interior decorations, or in places where much delicacy is required; the compofition is fomewhat too maffive.

PALLADIO's capital and bafe, are imitations from the arch of Titus. The latter of them is defigned without a plinth, as it is executed in the temple of Vefta, at Tivoli; and joined to the cornice of the pedeftal, by a flope: which not only has a bad effect, but is in itfelf defective; becaufe the bafe is thus divefted of its principal member, and rendered difproportionate.

VIGNOLA's Compofite, has nothing in it remarkable. The architrave differs but little, from that of the frontifpiece of Nero; and the cornice is nearly the fame, with that of his Ionic order: the principal difference confifting in the tranfpofition of fome mouldings, and enlargement of the dentils; both which feem rather altera- tions for the worfe, than improvements.

SCAMOZZI's entablature being like Palladio's, only one fifth of the column, and much divided, has a trifling appearance: the cornice however is, upon the whole, well compofed; and in a great meafure, imitated from that of the third order of the Colifeum; the capital is much like Palladio's, and the bafe is Attic enriched with aftragals, as at the Bafilica of Antoninus.

THE defign which I have given in the firft plate of the Compofite order, is an invention of my own; in which I have attempted to avoid the faults, and unite the perfections, of thofe abovementioned: how far with fuccefs, is left to the reader's determination: and at any rate, recourfe may ftill be had to Palladio, Scamozzi, or Vignola, as heretofore. The height of the column is twenty modules, that of the entablature, five: the bafe is Attic, and its meafures are the fame, as in the Doric or Ionic orders; but as the module is lefs, all its parts are of courfe propor- tionably more delicate. The fhaft is enriched with flutings, which may either be to the number of twenty, or of twenty-four, as on the Ionic column: for there is no reafon why in different orders, their number fhould either be augmented or diminifhed; the module being lefs, the flutes will likewife be lefs, and correfpond exactly with the character of the reft of the compofition.

THE capital is of the kind, which all the moderns have employed in this order; being enriched with leaves of the acanthus, as all the antique capitals of this fort are. With regard to the method of tracing it, few directions will fuffice: for the defigns are exactly drawn and figured. The curvatures of the abacus, are defcribed from the fummits of equilateral triangles: the projection of the volutes, is determined by a line drawn from the extremity of the aftragal, to the extremity of a horn of the abacus; and the projection of the leaves, is determined by another line drawn parallel to that; from the fillet under the aftragal.

THE manner of executing both thefe, and all other enriched capitals in this city, is generally fpeaking, bad. I do not, however, mean to accufe our Englifh workmen of incapacity, many of them are excellent; and in neatnefs of execution, out-do, perhaps, thofe of any other country: but, fometimes from the parfimony of their employers, and in fome degree perhaps, for want of thorough fkill and facility in defign, their performances are often infipid, without intention or effect, and by no means expreffive, either of the tafte or intelligence of the performer.

MANY, even of our greateft architects, have too much neglected the detail; having employed their attention wholly, on the general difpofition of their compofitions. This neglect, though authorifed by great examples, ought by no means to be imitated: it is the bufinefs of the architect, to attend to the minuteft objects, as well as to the moft confiderable. If the entire execution of the fabrick be left to his direction, the faults that are committed, will of courfe be ftated to his account: and therefore it will be prudent in him to felect the ableft workmen, and to furnifh them with proper models, and precife inftructions; in which he will fhew the extent of his capacity, and diftinguifh himfelf from the common herd of thofe, who, without due qualifications, affume the title of architects. The moft mafterly difpofition, incorrectly executed, can only be confidered as a fketch in painting; or as an excellent piece of mufic, miferably murdered by village fidlers, equally deftitute of tafte and powers of execution.

CARE muft be taken in Compofite, as well as in Corinthian capitals, that the feet of the lower leaves, do not project beyond the upper part of the fhaft of the column, as at St. Carlo in the Corfo at Rome, and at the Banqueting-Houfe in London; for nothing can be uglier: neither are thefe leaves as they mount, to bend forwards, as in many of the antiques, and in fome modern buildings; becaufe they then hide a confiderable part of the upper row of leaves, and give a ftunted, difagreeable form, to the whole capital. The different divifions of the acanthus leaf, and bunches of olive or parfley, which compofe the total of each leaf; muft be firmly marked, and maffed in a very diftinct manner: the ftems that fpring from between the upper leaves, are to be kept low upon the vafe of the capital, while rifing between the leaves; then fpring gradually forwards, to form the different volutes: and the ornaments, which fometimes are ufed to adorn the fides of the angular volutes; are never to project beyond the fillets, between which they are confined. Thefe are all the directions that well can be given in writing; but thofe who would excel in ornamental works of this kind, or any other; muft confult the foliages and flowers of nature; the buildings, ancient or modern, in which they have been executed with care and judgment. The Ionic, Compofite, and Corinthian

inthian capitals, to be feen in various parts of Somerfet Place; were copied from models, executed under my direction at Rome; and imitated, both in point of forms and manner of workmanfhip, from the choicest antique originals. They may ferve as guides to fuch, as have had no opportunity of examining the buildings, from which thefe models were collected.

THE parts of the entablature, bear the fame proportion to each other, as in the Ionic and Tufcan orders. The architrave is nearly of the fame form with thofe of Palladio and Vignola, and that of the Bafilica of Antoninus. The frize is enriched with foliages, in imitation of thofe on the frize of Nero's frontifpiece; of which the moft prominent parts, fhould never project more than doth the uppermoft moulding of the architrave under them.

THE cornice is imitated from Scamozzi, and differs from the Corinthian, only in the modillions; which are fquare, and compofed of two fafcias. The foffit of the intervals between the dentils, muft be hollowed upwards behind the little fillet in front, as they are in moft of the antiques; which occafions a dark fhade, that marks the dentil more diftinctly. And the fame method muft be obferved in the Ionic and Corinthian orders, for the fame reafon. The rofes, in the foffit of the corona, are not to project beyond its horizontal furface; and care muft be taken not to vary them fo much as at St. Peter's of the Vatican, becaufe the unity of the compofition fuffers thereby: the modillions or dentils, might with almoft as much propriety be varied. It will be proper therefore, in fmall compofitions, to make them all alike, as they are in moft of the antiques; that fo, they may not ftrike, nor occupy the attention of the beholder as objects for diftinct contemplation, but as parts, of one great whole. In larger compofitions, they may be of two kinds, but fimilar in out-line and dimenfion; which occafions more variety, yet without confufion: for then, the images fucceed each other fo rapidly, and are from their fimilitude, fo inftantaneoufly comprehended; that the third impreffion takes place, before the firft is in any degree obliterated: fo that nearly the fame effect is produced, as by a continued fucceffion of the fame object.

BUT though this variety be practifed, and is to a certain degree, allowable in fmall objects, which the eye perufes at a glance; or in fuch, as being merely acceffory, may or may not be introduced, and do not affect the general out-line, or bent of the compofition; yet, it is by no means to be tolerated in columns, and other principal or effential parts; which, from the number of their conftituent points, are not conveyed to the mind at once, either with eafe or perfect clearnefs; and therefore, if varied, cannot fail of exciting confufed ideas.

IN the fourth book of Palladio, we find, among other ancient temples, one, of which the portico confifts of four Corinthian columns, and two pilafters. The pilafters are fluted in a perpendicular direction; two of the columns are fluted fpirally; and the other two have the fhafts covered with laurel leaves: a variety, abfurd as unpleafing; which totally deftroys the general effect of the compofition, and conveys no idea, but that of a ftructure made up of difcordant fragments, as they happened to come in the builder's way.

THE Romans ufed the Compofite order, more frequently in their triumphal arches, than in any other buildings; meaning, as Serlio fuppofes, to exprefs their dominion over thofe nations, that invented the orders of which this is compofed. It may, fays Le Clerc, be ufed with propriety, wherever elegance and magnificence are to be united; but it is more particularly adapted to buildings, defigned to commemorate fignal events, or celebrate the virtues and atchievements of conquerors, and legiflators: becaufe the capitals, and other ornaments may be compofed of emblems, and of allufive reprefentations; agreeable to the cuftom of the ancients: as appears, by very many fragments of capitals, and other members of architecture, fcattered about, in different parts of Rome, and elfewhere. Some of thefe, are reprefented in the fecond plate of the Compofite order; and more may be found in the works of Montano, Le Clerc, Piranefi, and others, of whofe works the reader will find a catalogue, in the *ABECEDARIO pittòrico*.

THE Compofite entablature may be reduced to two ninths of the column, (which to avoid fractions, I fhall call four modules and a half,) by making the module only nine tenths of the femi-diameter, and obferving the fame meafures, as are figured in the defign; and there then will be a dentil in the outward angle, as in the Ionic order. It may likewife, if required, be reduced to one fifth, by making the module four fifths of the femi-diameter. Though, in cafes where it may be necef- fary to diminifh fo much, it will always be better to employ the Ionic cornice: which, being compofed of fewer parts, will ftill retain an air of grandeur, notwithftanding the fmallnefs of the general mafs.

MOST authors give to the Compofite order the laft place, as being laft invented, and a compound; which of courfe, ought to be preceded by all the fimples. I have however followed Scamozzi's arrangement; his appearing to me, the moft natural: for his orders fucceed each other, according to their degree of ftrength, and in the progreffion, that muft abfolutely be obferved, whenever they are to be employed together.

Of the CORINTHIAN ORDER.

THE three columns in the Campo Vaccino, fuppofed remains of the temple of Jupiter Stator; are generally allowed to be, the moft perfect models of the Corinthian order amongft the antiques at Rome. Palladio in his fourth book, where he gives the whole profile at large; acknowledges that he never had feen any work better executed, or more delicately finifhed; that its parts are beautifully formed, well proportioned, and fkilfully combined; all which laft qualities, are certainly fignified, by his *Beniffimo Intefi*.

WITH thefe favorable fentiments, it is extraordinary, that in his defign of the Corinthian order, he fhould fo very confiderably deviate from this excellent original, as fcarcely to leave the fmalleft fhadow of refemblance.

VIGNOLA,

Composite Entablatures & Capitals.

A. Palladio

J. B. da Vignola

Soffit

Soffit

Flora

Mars

Apollo

French Order

Venus

Jupiter

W. Chambers.

P. Mazell sculp.

THE CORINTHIAN ORDER

Projections. Genl. Hights.

Soffit of the Corona

Plan of ÿ Capital

Angular View of the Capital

Corinthian Base

Projec.ns   Hts

50 Minutes
60 Minutes

Wm Chambers Delin.

E. Rooker sculp.

1   2   3   4   5   Modules

5 10 15   30 Minutes

VIGNOLA, in his Corinthian profile, has chiefly imitated the abovementioned fragment, and the interior order of the Pantheon, another very perfect model. His compofition is uncommonly beautiful, and without difpute, fuperior to that of any other mafter: he, having artfully collected all the perfections of his originals, and formed a whole, far preferable to either of them.

THE defign which I have given, differs but little from that of Vignola. The column is twenty modules high, and the entablature five; which proportions, are a medium between thofe of the Pantheon, and of the three columns. The bafe of the column, may be either Attic or Corinthian: both are beautiful. Palladio and Scamozzi have employed the Attic bafe enriched with aftragals; but fo frequent a repetition of the fame femi-circular forms in junction, has a very indifferent effect; as may be obferved at the church of St. Martin in the Fields, at the Bank, and in various other buildings of this city: in which, the profiles and forms of Palladio, good, bad, or indifferent, have indifcriminately been employed.

IF the entablature be enriched, the fhaft of the column fhould be fluted; provided it be not compofed of variegated marble: for a diverfity of colours renders even fmooth furfaces confufed, and ornaments of fculpture only ferve to make the confufion greater. The flutings may be filled to one third of their height, with cablings, as on the infide order of the Pantheon; which ftrengthen the lower part of the column, and make it lefs liable to damage. But when the columns are not within reach, nor fubject to be hurt by paffengers, the cables are better omitted: as the general hue of the fhaft will then be the fame throughout, and feem of a piece; which, when a part of the flute is filled, and the other part left empty, is not the cafe: for the fhaft then appears divided, and is lefs calculated to produce a great effect.

IN fome very rich buildings, the cablings are compofed of reeds, hufks, fpiral-twifted ribbands, flowers, and various other ornaments. At the Thuilleries in Paris, there are fome Ionic columns exquifitely wrought in this manner; one of them by Jean Gougeon's own hand, and the reft under his immediate infpection.

IT is however, far better to referve fuch niceties for interior decorations. In exterior compofitions, whatever doth not contribute to the forcible effect of the whole ftructure, is in a great meafure ufelefs, fometimes even detrimental; and an expence, which might more judicioufly be employed, where it would be more attentively confidered. In general, it may be laid down as a maxim, that exceffive ornaments, though they may, and often do, increafe the magnificence of a building, almoft always deftroy, more or lefs, the grandeur of its effect. Parts in themfelves large, formed and difpofed to receive broad maffes, or ftrong oppofitions of light and fhade, muft neceffarily excite great ideas: but when thefe parts are broken into a number of fmall divifions, and their furfaces fo varied, as to catch a thoufand fpotty impreffions of light, demi-tints, and darknefs, the whole, will of courfe, form a confufed appearance of trifling objects, which divide the attention, and are utterly incapable of exciting any powerful emotions whatever.

THE

THE capital is enriched with olive leaves, as are almoft all the antiques at Rome, of this order; the acanthus being feldom employed, but in the Compofite. De Cordemoy, however, prefers the acanthus; and obferves that the flexible fprigs, which accompany the leaves of that plant, may more naturally be fuppofed to form the contour of the volutes, than the ftiff branches of a laurel, or an olive tree. " Strange it is, fays he, that we foon ceafe to efteem what is natural: nature and " reafon muft always be violated, and thus a confufed jumble of little pointed leaves " of an olive, or a laurel, is preferred to the fimple and graceful outline of the " acanthus."

DE CORDEMOY's obfervation is, ftrictly fpeaking, juft; yet to variety, fome-thing muft be facrificed, fome liberties taken; and both the ancient as well as modern fculptors, have, by uniting feveral olive, laurel, or parfley leaves together, to form diftinct bunches; feparated by filaments between which they feem to grow; contrived to compofe leaves: different in appearance from the acanthus indeed, yet, neither more confufed, nor lefs graceful than that.

WITH refpect to the manner of tracing and working this capital, the defigns with what has been faid on the fame fubject in the Compofite order, will ferve as a fufficient explanation.

THE divifions of the entablature bear the fame proportion to each other, as in the Tufcan, Ionic, and Compofite orders. The frize is enriched with a bafs relief, compofed from various fragments in the Villa Medici at Rome. The parts and ornaments of the cornice, are all regularly difpofed, and perpendicularly over each other: the coffers in the foffit of the corona are fquare, and the borders round them equal on all fides; as they are in the arch of Titus, and as Palladio has made them: a precaution neglected by Vignola, notwithftanding his ufual regu-larity.

THE ancients frequently employed the Ionic entablature in the Corinthian order, as appears by many of their buildings; and fometimes, according to Vitru-vius, even the Doric: though of the latter practice, there is not now, that I know of, any example extant. The fame author obferves, that the Greeks in their works, never employed the dentils under the modillions; becaufe the rafters, which are reprefented by the dentils, could never in reality be placed under the beams or joifts, which are reprefented by the modillions. However this may be, we are certain that the Romans were not fo very fcupulous; for in their moft efteemed works, fuch as the temple of Jupiter Stator, the forum of Nerva, the temple of Jupiter Tonans, and feveral others; we find the dentils placed under the modillions. Thefe examples will fufficiently authorife the fame practice. The origin or reafon of things of this nature, are remote; and known to but few: while the general effect of a compofition, is obvious to all. If deviating therefore, from what is little known, and lefs felt; will eminently contribute towards the perfection of that which all fee, and all approve; it cannot juftly be cenfured.

THIS liberty, however, of deviating from the origin or reafon of things, was by the ancients; and muft by us, be exercifed with great caution: as it opens a
wide

wide door to whim and extravagance, and leaves a latitude to the compofer, which often betrays, and hurries him into ridiculous abfurdities. Bernini, fometimes quitted the beaten road with judgment; but Boromini, firft his fcholar, and at length his rival; in attempting to conquer by novelty, and quitting the ancient rules, was fubmerged in an ocean of extravagance. Thus, fays the author of his life, from being among the firft men of his time for abilities and extent of genius, Boromini funk to a level with the laft, by a ridiculous application of his talents.

I DO not know who firft introduced among us, the favorite ornament of feftoons ftanding up like arches, inftead of hanging down as nature directs; nor do I recollect the name of him, who in the church of St. Romolo at Florence, has for the fake of variety, placed the capitals at the feet of his columns: but felect thefe facts, as abfurd inftances among others, of the length to which innovators may carry any fyftem unreftrained by rules, and fubject to no other laws, than the crude momentary effufions of a vitiated fancy. Things evidently abfurd, no time nor authority, can fanctify.

WHEN the modillion cornice is employed on large concave furfaces, the fides of the modillions and coffers of the foffit, fhould tend towards the center of the curve; as in the Pantheon: but when the concave is fmall, it will be better to direct them towards the oppofite point in the circumference, that the contraction may be lefs perceptible, and the parts dependent thereon, fuffer lefs deviation from their natural form. The fame rules muft be obferved with regard to dentils, to the abacus and bafes of columns or pilafters, and likewife to the flanks of the pilafter itfelf. But on a convex furface, the fides of all thefe fhould be parallel to each other, for it would be unnatural, and very difagreeable to fee them narroweft where they fpring out of the cornice, diverging as they advance forwards, forming fharp angles, and a fort of mutilated triangular plan, with enlarged folids, and diminifhed intervals: all calculated to deftroy, the ufual proportions and beauty of the compofition.

THE Corinthian entablature may be reduced to two ninths, or one fifth of the height of the column, by the fame rules as are given in the Ionic and Compofite orders: but where it becomes neceffary, or is judged expedient, to make the entablature fo fmall as one fifth, it will, I apprehend, be beft to fubftitute the Ionic entablature, as Palladio has done in the Periftyle of his Olympic Theatre at Vicenza, and in many others of his buildings: or elfe, to retrench the dentils of the cornice, as in one of Serlio's, and in Scamozzi's profiles; the part of the cornice under the modillion-band, remaining then compofed of only the ovolo and ogee, feparated by a fillet: as in the temples of Trevi and Scifi in Umbria, mentioned in Palladio's fourth book.

THE Corinthian order is proper for all buildings, where elegance, gaiety, and magnificence are required. The ancients employed it in temples dedicated to Venus, to Flora, Proferpine, and the nymphs of fountains; becaufe the flowers, foliage, and volutes, with which it is adorned, feemed well adapted to the delicacy and elegance of fuch deities. Being the moft fplendid of all the orders, it is extremely proper for the decoration of palaces, public fquares, or galleries and arcades, furrounding them; for churches dedicated to the Virgin Mary, or to other

G g

virgin

virgin faints: and on account of its rich, gay, and graceful appearance, it may with propriety be ufed in theatres, in ball or banquetting rooms, and in all places confecrated to feftive mirth, or convivial recreation.

Of   P I L A S T E R S.

PILASTERS are, I believe, a Roman invention, and certainly an improvement. The Greeks employed antæ in their temples, to receive the architraves where they entered upon the walls of the cell. Thefe, tho they were in one direc- tion of equal diameter with the columns of the front, were in flank, extravagantly thin in proportion to their height; and neither their bafes nor capitals, bore any refemblance to thofe of the columns they accompanied. The Roman artifts, difgufted probably, with the meager afpect of thefe antæ, and the want of accord in their bafes and capitals, fubftituted pilafters in their places; which, being proportioned and decorated in the fame manner with the columns, are certainly more feemly, and preferve the unity of the compofition much better.

PILASTERS differ from columns in their plan only; which is fquare, as that of the column is round. Their bafes, capitals, and entablatures, have the fame parts, with all the fame heights and projections, as thofe of columns, and they are diftinguifhed in the fame manner, by the names of Tufcan, Doric, Ionic, Compofite, and Corinthian.

OF the two, the column is, doubtlefs, moft perfect. Neverthelefs, there are occafions, in which pilafters may be employed with great propriety; and fome, where they are, on various accounts, even preferable to columns.

I AM not ignorant, that feveral authors are of a different opinion: a certain French Jefuit in particular; who fome thirty years ago, firft publifhed an effay on architecture, which from its plaufibility, force and elegance of diction, went through feveral editions; and operated very powerfully on the fuperficial part of European connoiffeurs. He inveighs vehemently againft pilafters, as againft almoft every other architectonic form but fuch, as were imitated by the firft builders in ftone, from the primitive wooden huts: as if, in the whole catalogue of arts, architecture fhould be the only one, confined to its priftine fimplicity, and fecluded from any deviation or improvement whatever.

To pilafters, the effayift objects, becaufe they are, in his opinion, nothing better than bad reprefentations of columns. Their angles (fays he) indicate the formal ftiffnefs of art, and are a ftriking deviation from the fimplicity of nature; their projections, fharp and inconvenient, offend and confine the eye; and their furfaces without roundnefs, give to the whole order a flat air: they are not fufcep- tible of diminution, one of the moft pleafing properties of columns; they are never neceffary, and to fum up the whole, he hates them: his averfion was firft innate, but has fince been confirmed, by the ftudy of architecture.

CONCERNING

CONCERNING the reverend father's inborn averfion, much need not be faid; and feveral others of his objections, as they confift more of words than meaning, feem not to require any refutation; but, to affert that pilafters are not fufceptible of diminution, fhews very little acquaintance either with books of architecture, or with buildings: there are many inftances in the remains of antiquity, of their being diminifhed, particularly when accompanying columns; they are fo in the temple of Mars the avenger, in the frontifpiece of Nero, in the portico of Septimus Severus, and in the arch of Conftantine, all at Rome. Scamozzi always gave to his pilafters, the fame diminution as to his columns: Palladio has diminifhed them in the church of the Redentore at Venice, and in many others of his buildings; as Inigo Jones has likewife done in many of his; particularly at the Banquetting-Houfe at Whitehall.

AND if we go back to the origin of things, and confider pilafters, either as reprefenting the ends of partition walls, or trunks of trees, reduced to the diameter of the round trunks which they accompany, but left fquare for greater ftrength; the reafon for diminifhing them will, in either cafe, be ftrong and evident.

IT is likewife an error to affert, that pilafters are never neceffary; but that columns will at all times, anfwer the fame end: for, at the angles of all buildings, they are evidently neceffary, both for folidity and beauty; becaufe the angular fup-port, having a greater weight to bear than any of the reft, ought to be fo much the ftronger; fo that its diameter muft either be increafed, or its plan altered from a circle to a fquare; the latter of which is certainly the moft reafonable expedient, on feveral accounts; but chiefly as it obviates a very ftriking defect; occafioned by employing columns at the angles of a building; which is, that the angle of the entablature is left hanging in the air without any fupport: a fight very difagreeable in fome oblique views, and in itfelf very unfolid.

IT is indeed cuftomary in porches, and other detached compofitions, to employ columns at the angles; and it is judicious fo to do: for of two defects, the leaft is to be preferred. And although father Laugier, the writer whofe objections I have juft now cited, could fee no reafon for rejecting detached pilafters, when engaged ones were fuffered; yet there is a very fubftantial reafon, which is, that a detached pilafter in fome oblique views, appears thicker than it does in front, nearly in the ratio of feven to five; and confequently if, when feen in front, it appears well proportioned in itfelf, and with regard to the columns it accompanies; it never can appear fo, when viewed upon the angle; as may be obferved in the colonades of the great court at Burlington-Houfe in Piccadilly, and at the porch of St. George's Church, near Hanover-Square.

ENGAGED pilafters are employed in churches, galleries, halls, and other inte-rior decorations, to fave room: for as they feldom project beyond the folid of the walls, more than one quarter of their diameter, they do not occupy near fo much fpace, even as engaged columns. They are likewife employed in exterior decora-tions; fometimes alone, inftead of columns, on account of their being lefs expenfive; as at the Duke of Queenfbury's Houfe in Burlington-Gardens; General Wade's Houfe in the fame place; and in many other buildings here in London. At other

H h   times,

times, they accompany columns; being placed behind them to fupport the fpringing of the architraves, as in the Pantheon at Rome; and in the porch of St. Martin in the Fields, Weftminfter: or on the fame line with them, to fortify the angles; as in the portico of Septimus Severus at Rome, and in the church of St. Laurence of the Jewry in London. Blondel fays, they may likewife be employed inftead of columns, detached to form periftyles and porticos: but there is no inftance of this, that I remember, in all the remains of antiquity; neither has any modern architect, I believe, been fo deftitute of tafte, as to put it in practice.

WHEN pilafters are ufed alone, as principal in the compofition; they fhould project one quarter of their diameter beyond the walls, as Scamozzi teaches, and as they do at the Banquetting-Houfe, Whitehall; which gives them a fufficient boldnefs, and, in the Corinthian and Compofite orders, is likewife moft regular; becaufe the ftems of the volutes, and the fmall leaves in flank of the capital, are then cut exactly through their middles: but if the cornice of the windows fhould be continued in the inter-pilafter, as is fometimes ufual; or if there fhould be a cornice, to mark the feparation between the principal and fecond ftory, as at the Manfion-Houfe of London; or large impofts of arches; the projection muft in fuch cafes, be increafed; provided it is not otherwife fufficient to ftop the moft prominent parts of thefe decorations; it being very difagreeable, to fee feveral of the uppermoft mouldings of an impoft or cornice, cut away perpendicularly, in order to make room for the pilafter, while the cornice or impoft on each fide, projects confiderably beyond it; as has been done at St. Peter's of the Vatican, as well as in feveral other buildings of Rome, and other towns of Italy. Mutilations, are on all occafions, ftudioufly to be avoided, as being deftructive of perfection; and ftrong indications, either of inattention or ignorance in the compofer.

WHEN pilafters are placed behind columns, and very near them, they need not project above one eighth of their diameter, or even lefs; excepting there fhould be impofts, or continued cornices in the inter-pilafter: in which cafe, what has been faid above, muft be attended to: but if they be far behind the columns, as in porticos, porches, and periftyles, they fhould project one fixth of their diameter at leaft; and when they are on a line with columns, their projection is to be regulated by that of the columns; and confequently, it never can be lefs than a femi-diameter, even when the columns are engaged as much as poffible. This extraordinary projection, however, will occafion no very great deformity; as the largeft apparent breadth of the pilafter will exceed the leaft, only in the ratio of eleven to ten, or thereabouts. But if columns be detached, the angular pilafter fhould always be coupled with a column, to hide its inner flank; as in the portico of Burlington-Houfe: becaufe the pilafters will otherwife appear difproportionate, when feen from the point of view proper for the whole building; efpecially, if the fabrick be fmall, and the point of view near.

IT is fometimes cuftomary to execute pilafters without any diminution: in the antiques, there are feveral inftances thereof, as well as of the contrary practice; and Palladio, Vignola, Inigo Jones, and many of the greateft architects, have frequently done fo. Neverthelefs it is certain, that diminifhed pilafters are, on many accounts, much preferable. There is more variety in their form; their capitals are better proportioned, both in the whole, and in their parts, particularly in the Compofite

and

and Corinthian orders; and the irregularities occafioned by the paffage of the architraves, from diminifhed columns, to undiminifhed pilafters, are thereby avoided; as are likewife the difficulties of regularly diftributing, the modillions and other parts of the entablature, either when the pilafters are alone, or accompanied with columns.

ANOTHER difagreeable effect of undiminifhed pilafters, is likewife obviated by rejecting them: indeed, I am at a lofs to account for it; and, as it is diametrically oppofite to a received law in optics, I imagined it might be the refult of fome defect in my own fight; till by enquiry, I found others were affected in the fame manner. It is this; the top of the fhaft always appears broader than the bottom; as any one may obferve, by cafting a glance on the pilafters of St. Paul's; of St. George's, Hanover-Square; or any others that are not diminifhed. The author of *l'Efprit des Beaux Arts*, accounts for a fimilar effect, in a manner more fubtle, I believe, than true. He makes it to be the refult of a nice comparifon, between the real and the apparent diftance; which, to me feems to have little, or rather no fhare at all in it. An ingenious * writer of our own country obferves, that the fenfes ftrongly affected in fome one manner, cannot quickly change their tenor, or adapt themfelves to other things; but continue in their old channel, until the ftrength of the firft mover decays: this being admitted, it is not improbable, that the capital, which is immediately above the fhaft; being confiderably broader, and certainly the firft attractive object; may have an influence on the apparent upper breadth of the fhaft, and occafion the effect abovementioned. Perhaps too, the light may in fome meafure contribute thereto, it being ftronger at the foot of the fhaft, than towards its top.

THE fhafts of pilafters are fometimes adorned with flutings, in the fame manner as thofe of columns; the plan of which may be a trifle above a femi-circle: and they muft be to the number of feven on each face. which makes them nearly of the fame fize with thofe of the columns. The interval between them muft be either one third, or one fourth of the flute in breadth; and when the pilafter is placed on the pavement, or liable to be broken by the touch of paffengers, the angle may be rounded off, in the form of an aftragal; between which and the adjoining flute, there muft be a fillet, or interval, of the fame fize with the reft; as in the porch of the Pantheon at Rome.

THE flutes may, like thofe of columns, be filled with cablings to one third of their height; either plain and fhaped like an aftragal, or enriched, according as the reft of the compofition is fimple, or much adorned. Scamozzi is of opinion, that there fhould be no flutings on the fides of engaged pilafters, but only in front: and whenever cornices or impofts are continued home to the pilafter, this fhould particularly be attended to; that the different mouldings of thefe members, by entering into the cavities of the flutes, may not be cut off in irregular and difagreeable forms. But if the flanks of the pilafter are entirely free, it may be as well to enrich them in the fame manner as the front, provided the flutes can be fo diftributed, as to have a fillet or interval adjoining to the wall; which is always neceffary, to mark the true fhape of the pilafter diftinctly.

* See Burke's Enquiry into the Origin of our Ideas of the Sublime and Beautiful.

THE capitals of Tufcan or Doric pilafters, are profiled in the fame manner as thofe of the refpective columns: but in the capitals of the other orders, there are fome trifling differences to be obferved. In the antique Ionic capital, the extraordinary projection of the ovolo makes it neceffary, either to bend it inwards confiderably towards the extremities, that it may pafs behind the volutes; or, inftead of keeping the volutes flat in front, as they commonly are in the antique; to twift them outwards, till they give room for the paffage of the ovolo. Le Clerc thinks the latter of thefe expedients, the beft; and, that the artifice may not be too ftriking, the projection of the ovolo may be confiderably diminifhed, as in the annexed defign*; which, as the moulding can be feen in front only, will occafion no difagreeable effect.

THE fame difficulty fubfifts, with regard to the paffage of the ovolo behind the angular Ionic volutes: Le Clerc therefore advifes to open, or fpread the volutes fufficiently, to leave room for the ovolo to pafs behind them, as in the defign †annexed; which may eafily be done, if the projection of the ovolo is diminifhed. Inigo Jones has in the Banquetting-Houfe, made the two fides of the volutes parallel to each other, according to Scamozzi's manner; and at the fame time has continued the ovolo in a ftraight line under them: fo that the volutes have an enormous projection, which added to the other faults of thefe capitals, renders the whole compofition unufually defective, and exceedingly ugly.

WHAT has been faid, with regard to the paffage of the ovolo behind the volutes in the Ionic order, is likewife to be remembered in the Compofite: and in the Corinthian, the lip, or edge of the vafe or bafket, may be bent a little inwards, towards its extremities; by which means, it will eafily pafs behind the volutes. The leaves in the Corinthian and Compofite capitals, muft not project beyond the top of the fhaft, as they do at St. Carlo in the Corfo at Rome, and at the Banquetting-Houfe, Whitehall: but the diameter of the capital, muft be exactly the fame as that of the top of the fhaft. And to make out the thicknefs of the fmall-bottom leaves, their edges may be bent a trifle outwards; and the large angular leaves may be directed inwards, in their approach towards them; as in the annexed defign‡: and as they are executed in the church of the Roman College at Rome. Where the fmall leaves have a confiderable thicknefs, though the diameter of the capital is exactly the fame as that of the fhaft. In each front of the Compofite or Corinthian pilafter-capital, there muft be two fmall leaves, with one entire, and two half large ones: they muft be either of olive, acanthus, parfley, or laurel; maffed, divided, and wrought in the fame manner as thofe of the columns are; the only difference being, that they will be fomewhat broader.

THE employing half, or other parts of pilafters, that meet, and as it were penetrate each other, in inward or outward angles, fhould as much as poffible be avoided; becaufe it generally occafions feveral irregularities in the entablatures, and fometimes in the capitals alfo. Particular care muft be taken, never to introduce more than one of thefe breaks in the fame place; for more can never be neceffary. In many of the churches at Rome, we fee half a dozen of them together; which

---

* Pl. of Pilafters, fig. 2.   † Pl. of Pilafters, fig. 1.   ‡ Pl. of Pilafters, fig. 3.

produces

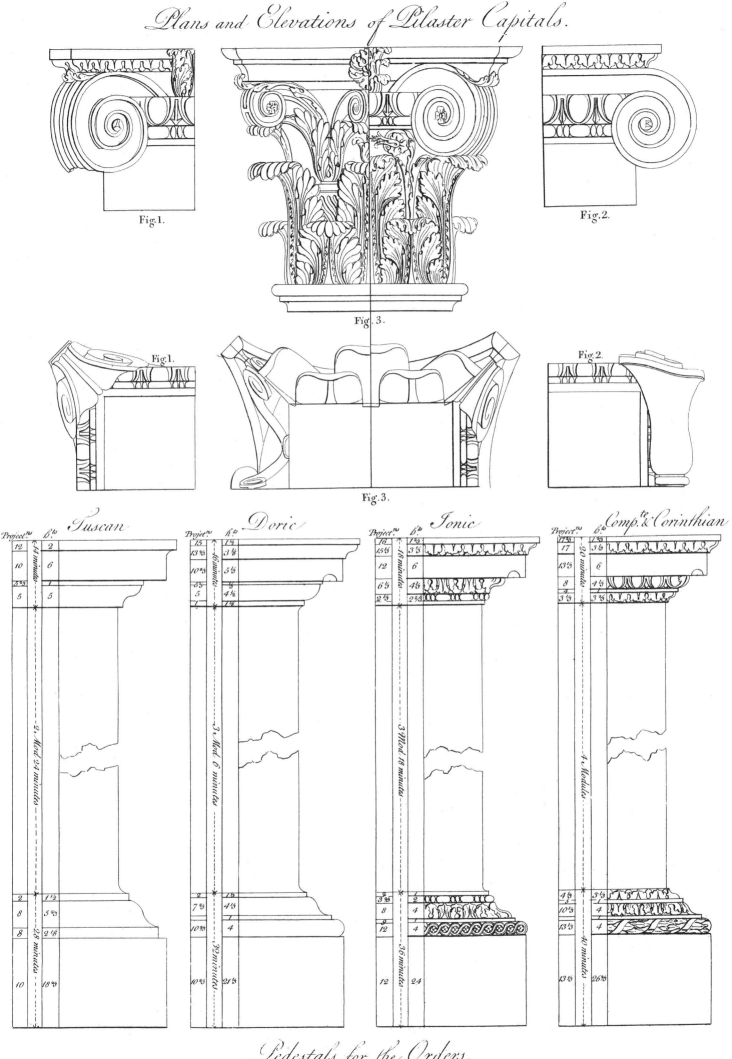

Plans and Elevations of Pilaster Capitals.

Fig. 1.

Fig. 2.

Fig. 3.

Fig. 1.

Fig. 2.

Fig. 3.

Tuscan

Doric

Ionic

Comp.^te & Corinthian

Pedestals for the Orders.

W. Chambers.

P. Mazell Sculp.

1

2

3

4

5

6

7

8

9

10

11

12

produces a long feries of undulated capitals and bafes, and a number of mutilated parts in the entablature: than which, nothing can be more confufed or difagreeable.

INSTEAD of pilafters, it is fometimes cuftomary to employ columns, that penetrate each other in the inward angle. There are feveral inftances of this at Paris, particularly about the Louvre; but it is a practice univerfally condemned, and the bad effect thereof may be feen on the front of the Royal Exchange towards Cornhill, and within the Banquetting-Houfe at Whitehall.

Of PERSIANS and CARYATIDES.

BESIDES columns and pilafters, it is fometimes cuftomary to employ reprefentations of the human figure, to fupport entablatures in buildings. The male figures are called Perfians, Telamones, or Atlantides; and the females Carians, or Caryatides. The origin of this cuftom, Vitruvius tells us, is as follows.

THE inhabitants of **Caria**, a city of the Peloponnefus, having joined the Perfians in a war againft the reft of the Greeks; and that war, being terminated by the defeat of the Perfians, the Greeks commenced hoftilities againft the Caryates, took their city, demolifhed it, and putting all the males to the fword; carried the females into captivity: and to treat them with ftill greater ignominy, they forbad the ladies to diveft themfelves of their robes, or any of their ornaments; that fo, they might not only be once led in triumph, but in a manner, fuffer the mortification of a triumph all their lives after; by appearing conftantly in the fame drefs, as on the triumphal day. And further, as an everlafting teftimony of the punifhment inflicted on the Caryates, and to inform pofterity what had been the nature of their chaftifement; the architects of that time, inftead of columns, employed the reprefentations of thefe women, to fupport the entablatures of their public buildings.

THE Lacedemonians did the fame thing after the battle of Platea; erecting, with the fpoils taken from the enemy, a gallery; which they called Perfian: wherein ftatues, in the form of captive Perfians, with their ufual dreffes, fupported the arches; intending thereby to punifh that nation in fuch a manner, as its pride had merited; and to leave pofterity, a monument of the valour and victories of the Lacedemonians.

THE introduction of figures of men and animals to fupport burthens in buildings, or otherwife; had certainly an earlier origin, than that afcribed to it by Vitruvius. It feems to have been a very early and favourite idea, among feveral people of the remoteft antiquity. Homer mentions the practice in the feventh book of the Odyffey, and I think, in one or more other places of his poems. Hiram's molten fea, was fupported by twelve bulls; and on the walls of the oracle he placed alternate cherubims and palm trees, fupporting wreaths of flowers, and probably

K k

the

the ceiling. In the fepulchre of King Ofymanduas, which, as Diodorus Siculus relates, was ten furlongs in circuit; there was a ftone hall, forming a fpace of four hundred feet every way, of which the roof inftead of pillars, was fupported by animals, each of a fingle ftone, and twenty-four feet high; being carved in the ancient Egyptian manner. The roof was alfo entirely of ftone, compofed of ftones twelve feet fquare; the whole being coloured to reprefent an azure fky, befpangled with ftars. Of the number or natures of thefe animals, nothing is faid; but if the whole fpace was covered, more than one thoufand would have been requifite to fupport the roof; and more than a thoufand ftones to form it. In feveral Indian buildings too, fuppofed to be of great antiquity; may be obferved figures of men and animals fupporting the roofs, after the manner defcribed in the fepulchre of Ofymanduas; particularly in that cut in the folid rock near Bombay, ufually called the Elephanta.

AMONG the antiquities at Rome, there are various fragments of male figures, which, from their attitudes, and fome ornaments about them, may be conjectured to have ferved as fupports to the entablatures of buildings: but there are no remains of any female ftatues of that kind, excepting the three Graces fupporting an urn, in the Villa Borghefi. Pliny makes mention of fome by the hand of Praxiteles, which in his time, were in the library of Afinius Pollio at Rome: and of other female figures in the Pantheon, where, although the ftructure was enriched with feveral works of Diogenes the Athenian, they were held in much efteem: they feem to have been cut in baffo or alto relievo, to have been placed over the columns, and were probably, as Fontana conjectures, employed to adorn the Attic; and fupport its cornice.

AMONG the antiquities of Athens, publifhed by Mr. Le Roy, there are five Caryatides fupporting an entablature, contiguous to the temple of Erectheus. They bear a confiderable refemblance to thofe celebrated ones of Jean Goujon, in the Swifs Guard Room of the Louvre at Paris; of one of which, there is a reprefentation, fig. 8, plate of Caryatides. Speaking of thefe figures, Monfieur Le Roy expreffes himfelf in the following manner. " The hiftory of the Caryatick " order, fays he, is fo curious, that almoft all authors have quoted it; but though " we are well informed of its origin, yet we have hitherto learnt nothing of the " proportions obferved therein by the ancients; Vitruvius is filent upon the fubject, " there is no monument of that order at Rome, and the only ancient example " perhaps, exifting in Europe, which is that here given; has hitherto remained " unnoticed. The four figures ftanding in front, refemble each other entirely, " excepting, that the two to the right have the right leg foremoft, and the two to " the left, the left leg; in order to fymmetrife more perfectly. They are crowned " with capitals, upon which is placed the entablature; remarkable, by a fuppreffion " of the frize; a peculiarity which the ancients, perhaps, ufually practifed to " characterize this order.

" THE general mafs of the entablature is very high; it exceeds a third of the " height of the figures: and it would be difficult to afcribe a reafon for this excefs, " were it not confidered that a full dreffed woman, which thefe reprefent, forms a " fhape more in the proportion of a very fhort Doric column, than of an elegant " Ionic one; which probably induced the architect to enlarge his entablature, to

prevent

" prevent its appearing too flight for the figures. Be this as it may, the profile of
" the entablature is very perfect. The dentils in the cornice fhew it to be Ionic;
" and there are on the upper fafcia, an ornament confifting of little rounds, like
" nail heads, which has not been introduced in any of the other orders.

" BUT that which is moft excellent in this building, is doubtlefs the Carya-
" tides themfelves. There are now only five left of the fix originally there; they
" are of a beautiful defign, with drapery in the ftile of that of the Flora, in the
" Farnefian Palace at Rome."

I PERFECTLY agree with Mr. Le Roy, as to the beauty of the figures, but
whatever might have been the architect's inducement to enlarge his entablature,
he certainly has done it to a monftrous excefs: it feems calculated to crufh the
figures to atoms, and all that, in my humble idea, can either be faid of the profile
of the cornice, or the clumfy capitals on which the entablature ftands, is, that far
from deferving to be admired, they would fcarcely be tolerated any where, but in
a traveller's book: and it feems very extraordinary that Monfieur Le Roy, who
is himfelf a man of excellent tafte; fhould applaud, what in his own judgment he
muft condemn.

JEAN GOUGEON, in his beautiful compofition at the Louvre, abovementioned,
has far furpaffed this Greek fpecimen of the Caryatick order. His figures, which
are twelve feet high, and of exquifite workmanfhip, ftand on bafes one fixth of
that height; on their heads are capitals of the Doric order, of which, the fhape
and proportion ferve to decorate, but not to over-load the head; the capitals fupport
a tribune, forming the entablature; which confifts of architrave, frize, and cornice.
It is richly decorated, of the Ionic order; and meafures one quarter of the height
of the figures, including the bafes on which they ftand. By introducing thefe bafes,
the fculptor has artfully contrived to diminifh the height, and confequently the
bulk of his figures; and by a regular divifion of his entablature, he has rendered it
light, at the fame time that it is truly proportioned to the figures by which it is
fupported.

IT is not cuftomary now, as formerly, fays Le Clerc, to reprefent Caryatides,
with attributes of flavery and fervitude. Such characters are too injurious to the
Fair. On the contrary, they are at prefent, confidered as the richeft, moft valued
ornaments of buildings; and reprefented under the figures of Prudence, Wifdom,
Juftice, Temperance, &c.

FREART DE CHAMBRAY, blames this practice; which he confiders as the
effect of inadvertency, in the architects who firft introduced it: obferving, that if
they had fufficiently reflected on the text of Vitruvius, with regard to the origin of
Caryatides, they would have perceived the impropriety of employing the reprefentations of faints and angels, loaded like flaves, with cornices, and other heavy
burdens; and likewife, that of employing the Caryatick order promifcuoufly, in all
forts of buildings; particularly in facred ftructures, which are the houfes of God,
and afylums of mercy; where vengeance and flavery ought never to appear.

ON the other hand Blondel obferves, that, though this remark be juft, if the origin of thefe ornaments be rigoroufly attended to; yet to ferve in any fhape in the houfe of God, and in particular at the altar; has always appeared in the minds of the prophets, and faints, fo glorious and great; that not only men, but angels, ought to efteem it a happinefs: and that confequently it can be no indication of difrefpect, to employ their reprefentations, in offices which they themfelves would execute with pleafure.

THE ancients, fays the fame author, made frequent ufe of Caryatick and Perfian figures, and delighted in diverfifying them in a thoufand manners. The modern artifts have followed their example; and there is a great variety of compofitions of this kind, to be met with in different parts of Europe: of fome of which, defigns are exhibited in the annexed plate; and others may be invented, and adapted to different purpofes with great propriety; provided the figures introduced be analogous to the fubject, as Mr. Ware obferves; and feem at leaft, a neceffary part in the compofition. Thus, fays Le Clerc, if they are employed to fupport the covering of a throne, they may be reprefented under the figures and fymbols of heroic virtues; if to adorn a facred building, they muft have an affinity to religion; and when they are placed in banquetting rooms, ball rooms, or other apartments of recreation; they muft be of kinds proper to infpire mirth, and promote feftivity.

IN compofing them, particular care muft be taken to avoid indecent attitudes, diftorted features, and all kinds of monftrous or horrid productions; of which there are fuch frequent inftances, in the works of our northern predeceffors. On the contrary, the attitudes muft be fimple and graceful; the countenances, though varied, always pleafing, and ftrongly marked with the expreffion peculiar to the occafion, or the object reprefented. There muft be no variety in the general form or outline, of the different figures employed in the fame compofition, and but little flutter in the draperies; which ought to fit clofe to the bodies of the figures, with folds contrived to exprefs diftinctly, both their action and fhape. Le Clerc obferves that they fhould always have their legs clofe together, and the arms clofe to the body or head; that fo they may have, as much as poffible, the fhape of columns, whofe office they are to perform: and it may be added, that for the fame reafon, their attitudes fhould be as nearly perpendicular, as can conveniently be, without giving a ftiff conftrained air to the figures.

The fame author obferves, that Caryatides ought always to be of a moderate fize; left, being too large, they fhould appear hideous in the eyes of the fair fex: and indeed, as thefe figures are generally reprefented in endearing offices, and under the forms of amiable and benevolent beings, the caution feems very proper. It will therefore be judicious, never to make them much larger than the human ftature.

BUT male figures may, on the contrary, be of any fize; the larger the better: as they will then be fitter to ftrike with awe and aftonifhment. There are few nobler thoughts, in the remains of antiquity, than Inigo Jones's Perfian Court; the effect of which, if properly executed, would have been furprifing and great in the higheft degree.

MALE

MALE figures may be introduced with propriety in arſenals, or galleries of armour, in guard rooms, and other military places; where they ſhould repreſent the figures of captives, or elſe of martial virtues; ſuch as Strength, Valour, Wiſdom, Prudence, Fortitude, and the like. Their entablature muſt be Doric, and bear the ſame proportion to them, as to columns of the ſame height: and the proper enta-blatures for Caryatides will be either Ionic, or Corinthian, according as the character of the figures is more or leſs delicate.

PERSIAN or Caryatick figures, ought never to be employed to ſupport the ſame entablature with columns: for figures of men or women, as high as columns, are conſiderably more bulky; and when they are of an uncommon ſize, convey an idea of greatneſs, that entirely deſtroys the effect of the columns, by making them appear very trifling. Neither ſhould they be placed upon columns, as they are in the court of the Old Louvre at Paris, for the ſame reaſons.

PALLADIO, ſenſible of this inconvenience, yet willing to introduce a ſpecimen of Perſian figures, has in the Valmarano Palace at Vicenza, divided the large Compoſite pilaſters which decorate the front, into five parts; three of which he has given to a diminutive Corinthian order, ſqueezed into the inter-pilaſters, and feebly ſuſtaining the extremities of the fabrick; while the remaining two parts are, at the angles, occupied by figures on pedeſtals, as diminutive as the aforeſaid Corinthian order, and introduced with as little propriety; more eſpecially as they are made to ſupport the ends of an enormous, bulky Compoſite entablature, of which the height ſurpaſſes two thirds of that of the figures themſelves.

IT is ſometimes cuſtomary to employ terms, inſtead of Caryatides or Perſians, to ſupport the entablatures of gates, monuments, chimney-pieces, and ſuch like compoſitions. Theſe figures owe their origin to the ſtones, uſed by the ancients to mark the limits of each particular perſon's poſſeſſions. Numa Pompilius, to render theſe inviolable, and prevent encroachments, erected the Terminus into a deity, inſtituted feſtivals and ſacrifices to his honour, and built a temple on the Tarpeian Mount which he dedicated to him, and in which he was repreſented under the figure of a ſtone.

IN proceſs of time, however, the God Terminus was repreſented with a human head, placed on a poſt or ſtone, ſhaped like an inverted obeliſk; which being on particular ſolemnities, adorned with garlands; compoſed altogether, a very pleaſing form: to the imitation of which, may with great probability be attributed, the introduction of theſe ornaments into building: where they have been varied into a great diverſity of ſhapes. I have occaſionally, in the courſe of this work, given ſome deſigns of them; and many others may be invented, and adapted to the particular purpoſes, for which they ſhall be intended.

IN conſideration of their origin, the Termini are proper ornaments in gardens, and in fields; where the upper part of them may repreſent Jupiter, who in the remoter ages of antiquity, was protector of boundaries: or ſome of the rural deities; as Pan, Flora, Pomona, Vertumnus, Ceres, Priapus, Faunus, Sylvanus, Nymphs and Satyrs. Mr. Ware recommends the uſe of them as boundaries to counties,

    where

where they may be enriched with ornaments allufive to the produce, manufacture, and commerce of each refpective county.

THE three firſt figures, in the annexed plate of Perſians and Caryatides, are copied from Candelabre's, in St. Peter's of the Vatican. They are caſt from models of Michael Angelo Buonaroti, and repaired either by himſelf, or doubtleſs under his direction: for the workmanſhip is very perfect. Figure 2, may be employed in buildings; but the others are properer for the angles of coved ceilings, or other ſuch ornamental works, being not unlike ſome introduced by the Caracchi, in the Farneſian ceilings at Rome. No. 4, is a copy of one of the figures that ſurround the choir, in the cathedral of Milan; which are the work of Andrea Biffi, a celebrated Milaneſe ſculptor. No. 5, is executed in the Judgment-Hall, of the Stadt-Houſe of Amſterdam, by Artus Quellinus. No. 6, is an admired work of Michael Angelo, now in the Villa Ludoviſi at Rome. No. 7, is in part by the ſame hand, and executed from the waiſt upwards, in the monument of Pope Julius the ſecond, in the church of St. Pietro, in the Vincoli at Rome. No. 8, is one of thoſe executed by Jean Gougeon, in the Swiſs Guard-Room of the Old Louvre, at Paris; as has before been mentioned. No. 9 and 10, are taken from paintings of Daniel da Volterra, in the church of the Trinta del Monte at Rome. No. 11, is a figure in baſſo relievo, on the Goldſmiths arch at Rome; and No. 12, is copied from an original deſign of Polidore da Caravaggio, now in my poſſeſſion.

Of P E D E S T A L S.

MOST writers conſider the pedeſtal as a neceſſary part of the order, without which, it is not eſteemed complete. It is indeed a matter of ſmall importance, whether it be conſidered in that light, or as a diſtinct compoſition: neverthelefs, ſeeing that in the particular deſcription, given by Vitruvius, of the Doric, Corinthian, and Tuſcan orders, no notice is taken of any pedeſtal; and that, in the Ionic order, he only mentions it as a neceſſary part in the conſtruction of a temple, without ſignifying that it belongs to the order, or aſſigning any particular proportions for it, as he doth for the parts of the column and the entablature—I have judged it more regular to treat of the pedeſtal as a ſeparate body; having no more connection with the order, than as an attic, a baſement, or any other part with which it may, on ſome occaſions, be accompanied.

A PEDESTAL like a column or an entablature, is compoſed of three principal parts; which are the baſe, the dye, and the cornice. The dye is always nearly of the ſame figure; being conſtantly either a cube, or a parallelopiped; but the baſe and cornice are varied, and adorned with more or fewer mouldings, according to the ſimplicity or richneſs of the compoſition in which the pedeſtal is employed. Hence pedeſtals are, like columns, diſtinguiſhed by the names of Tuſcan, Doric, Ionic, Compoſite, and Corinthian.

SOME authors are very averſe to pedeſtals, and compare a column raiſed on a pedeſtal, to a man mounted on ſtilts; imagining that they were firſt
introduced

introduced merely through neceffity, and for want of columns of a fufficient length.

It is indeed true, that the ancients often made ufe of artifices to lengthen their columns; as appears by fome that are in the Baptiftery of Conftantine at Rome; the fhafts of which, being too fhort for the building, were lengthened and joined to their bafes, by an undulated fweep, adorned with acanthus leaves. And the fame expedient has been made ufe of in fome fragments, which were difcovered a few years ago at Nimes, contiguous to the temple of Diana. Neverthelefs it doth not feem proper to comprehend pedeftals, in the number of thefe artifices; fince there are many occafions on which they are evidently neceffary; and fome, in which the order, were it not fo raifed, would lofe much of its beautiful appearance. Thus, within our churches, if the columns fupporting the vault were placed immediately on the ground, the feats would hide their bafes, and a good part of their fhafts; and, in the theatres of the ancients, if the columns of the fcene had been placed immediately on the ftage, the actors would have hid a confiderable part of them from the audience. For which reafon, it was ufual to raife them on very high pedeftals; as was likewife cuftomary in their triumphal arches. And in moft of their temples, the columns were placed on a bafement, or continued pedeftal: that fo, the whole order might be expofed to view, notwithftanding the crouds of people with which thefe places were frequently furrounded. And the fame reafon will authorife the fame practice in our churches, theatres, courts of juftice, or other publick buildings, where crouds frequently affemble.

In interior decorations, (where generally fpeaking, grandeur of ftile is not to be aimed at,) a pedeftal diminifhes the parts of the order, which otherwife might appear too clumfy; and has the farther advantage of placing the columns in a more favourable view, by raifing their bafe nearer to the level of the fpectator's eye. And in a fecond order of arcades, there is no avoiding pedeftals; as without them, it is impoffible to give the arches any tolerable proportion.

Sometimes too, the fituation makes it neceffary to employ pedeftals: an inftance of which there is in the Luxembourg Palace at Paris: where the body of the building ftanding on higher ground than the wings, the architect was obliged to raife the firft order of the wings on a pedeftal, to bring it upon a level with that of the body, or *corps de logis* of the building, which ftands immediately upon the pavement.

These inftances, will fufficiently fhew the neceffity of admitting pedeftals in decorations of architecture. With regard to the proportion, which their height ought to bear, to that of the columns they are to fupport, it is by no means fixed: the ancients, and moderns too, having in their works varied greatly in this refpect; and adapted their proportions to the occafion, or to the refpective purpofes for which the pedeftals were intended. Thus, in the amphitheatres of the ancients, the pedeftals in the fuperior orders were generally low; becaufe in the apertures of the arches, they ferved as rails to inclofe the portico, and therefore were, for the conveniency of leaning over, made no higher than was neceffary to prevent accidents: and the cafe is the fame in moft of our modern houfes; where the height of the pedeftals in the fuperior orders, is generally determined by the cills of

the

the windows. The ancients, in their theatres, made the pedeſtals in the firſt order of their ſcene, high; for the reaſon mentioned in the beginning of this chapter: but the pedeſtals in the ſuperior orders were very low; their chief uſe being to raiſe the columns ſo, as to prevent any part of them from being hid, by the projection of the cornice below them. And thus, on different occaſions, they uſed different proportions; being chiefly guided by neceſſity in their choice. The moderns have followed their example; as will appear to any one who examines the works of Palladio, of Vignola, of Michael Angelo, Scamozzi, and many other famous architects.

NEVERTHELESS, writers on architecture have always thought it incumbent upon them, to fix a certain determinate proportion for the pedeſtal, as well as for the parts of the order. It would be uſeleſs to enumerate in this place, their different opinions: but I muſt beg leave to obſerve, that Vignola's method is the only true one. His pedeſtals, are in all the orders of the ſame height; being one third of the column: and as their bulk increaſes or diminiſhes of courſe, in the ſame degree as the diameters of their reſpective columns do, the character of the order is always preſerved; which according to any other method is impoſſible.

IN the deſigns which I have given of arches with pedeſtals, the pedeſtals are all of the ſame height; each of them being three tenths of the height of their reſpective columns. But it is not neceſſary to adhere always to this proportion: they may be higher or lower, as the occaſion ſhall require. It is, however, to be obſerved, that, when pedeſtals are profiled under each column, and the dye is much leſs than a ſquare in height, the pedeſtal has a clumſy appearance; and when a pedeſtal of the ſame kind exceeds one third of the height of the column, it has a lean, unſolid, tottering aſpect. But if they are continued without any breaks, this need not be attended to; though indeed, there are very few occaſions in which pedeſtals higher than one third of the column, ought to be ſuffered; as they leſſen too much the parts of the order, and become themſelves too principal in the compoſition.

WITH regard to the diviſions of the pedeſtal, if the whole height be divided into nine parts, one of them may be given to the height of the cornice, two to the baſe, and the remaining ſix to the dye; or if the pedeſtal is lower than ordinary, its height may be divided into eight parts only, of which one may be given to the cornice, two to the baſe, and five to the dye; as Palladio has done in his Corinthian order; and Perrault in all the orders.

THE plan of the dye is always made equal to that of the plinth of the column; the projection of the cornice may be equal to its height; and the baſe, being divided into three parts, two of them will be for the height of the plinth, and one for the mouldings, of which the projection muſt be ſomewhat leſs than the projection of the cornice; that ſo, the whole baſe may be covered and ſheltered by it: a precaution which Scamozzi has obſerved in all his deſigns, though Palladio has neglected it in the greateſt part of his; the palace of the Porti, and one or two other buildings in the Vicentine excepted.

THESE

THESE meafures are common to all pedeftals; and in the annexed plate there are defigns of proper ones for each order; in which the forms and dimenfions of the minuter parts, are accurately drawn and figured.

IT is fometimes cuftomary to adorn dyes of pedeftals with projecting tablets, or with pannels funk in, and furrounded with mouldings. The former of thefe practices ought feldom to be admitted, as thefe tablets alter the general figure of the pedeftal, and when they project much, give it a heavy appearance. And the latter fhould be referved for very large pedeftals only, of fuch kinds as thofe fup-porting the Trajan and Antonine columns at Rome, and the Monument in London; where they may be filled with infcriptions, or adorned with bas-reliefs, analogous to the occafion on which the column was erected. Even in the largeft buildings, pedeftals are commonly too fmall to admit of fuch ornaments, which only ferve to give them an unfolid, trifling appearance, and contribute to complicate, without improving, the compofition.

WITH regard to the application of pedeftals, it muft be obferved, that when columns are entirely detached and at a confiderable diftance from the wall, as when they are employed to form porches, periftyles, or porticos, they fhould never be placed on detached pedeftals, as they are in fome of Scamozzi's defigns, in the temple of Scifi, mentioned by Palladio; and at Lord Archer's Houfe, now Lowe's Hotel, in Covent Garden: for then they may indeed be compared to men mounted on ftilts, as they have a very weak and tottering appearance. In compofitions of this kind, it is generally beft to place the columns immediately upon the pavement; which may either be raifed on a continued folid bafement, or be afcended to by a flight of fronting fteps, as at St. Paul's, and at St. George's, Bloomfbury: but if it be abfolutely neceffary to have a fence in the intercolumniations; (as in the cafe of bridges, and other buildings on the water; or in a fecond order;) the columns may then, in very large buildings, be raifed on a continued plinth, as in the upper order of the weftern porch of St. Paul's, which, in fuch cafe will be fufficiently high: and in fmaller buildings, wherever it may not be convenient nor proper to place the balluftrade between the fhafts; the columns may be raifed on a continued pedeftal; as they are in Palladio's defign for Signior Cornaro's Houfe at Piombino, and at the Villa Arfieri, near Vicenza; another beautiful building of the fame mafter.

THE bafe and cornice of thefe pedeftals, muft run in a ftraight line on the outfide throughout: but the dyes are made no broader than the plinths of the columns; the intervals between them being filled with balluftres: which is both really and apparently lighter, than if the whole pedeftal were a continued folid.

IT will be fuperfluous to caution our Englifh architects againft employing triangular, circular, or polygonal pedeftals in their buildings; or fuch as are fwelled, and have their dye in the form of a balluftre, or are furrounded with cinctures: fuch extravagances, though frequent in fome foreign countries, are feldom to be met with in England, and are now laid afide, wherever good tafte prevails.

IN

I<small>N</small> my defigns of pedeftals*, I have reprefented them under the proportions obferved by me in arches with pedeftals; but when it is neceffary to vary the general height, the meafures of the particular members may eafily be determined, by dividing the whole height in the Tufcan order into $4\frac{1}{5}$ parts, in the Doric into $4\frac{4}{5}$, in the Ionic into $5\frac{2}{5}$, and in the Compofite or Corinthian into fix parts, making ufe of one of thefe parts as the module, and determining the heights and projections of the different members, according to the figures marked in the defigns.

Of the APPLICATION of the ORDERS of ARCHITECTURE.

A<small>MONG</small> the ancients, the ufe of the orders was very frequent: many parts of their cities were provided with fpacious porticos; their temples were furrounded with colonades; and their theatres, baths, bafilicas, triumphal arches, maufoleums, bridges, and other public buildings, were profufely enriched with columns; as were likewife the courts, veftibules, and halls of their private villas and houfes.

I<small>N</small> imitation of the ancients, the moderns, have made the orders of architecture the principal ornaments of their ftructures. We find them employed in almoft every building of confequence; where they are fometimes merely ornamental, but at others, they are of real ufe as well as ornament; ferving to fupport the covering, or any other burdens placed upon them. On fome occafions, they are employed alone: the whole compofition confifting only of one or more ranges of columns with their entablature. At other times the intervals between the columns are filled up, and adorned with arches, doors, windows, niches, ftatues, bas-reliefs, and other fimilar inventions: the columns are either placed immediately on the pavement, or raifed on plinths, pedeftals, or bafements; either engaged in the walls of the building, or ftanding detached, near, or at fome diftance from them; and frequently, different orders are placed one above the other, or intermixed with each other on the fame level. In all thefe, and in all other cafes, in which the orders are introduced; particular meafures, rules, and precautions are to be obferved, of which, I fhall endeavour to give a full detail, in the following chapters.

Of INTERCOLUMNIATIONS.

C<small>OLUMNS</small> are either engaged, or infulated: and when infulated, they are either placed very near the walls, or at fome confiderable diftance from them.

* See Pl. of Pilafters.

W<small>ITH</small>

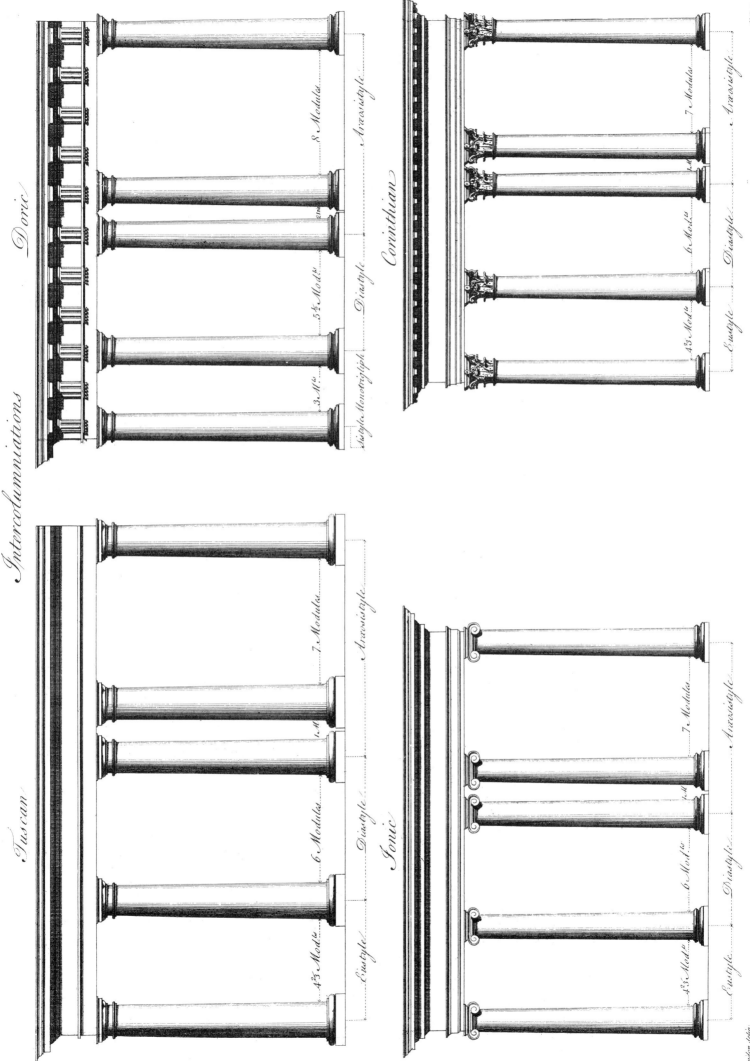

Intercolumniations

W<small>ITH</small> regard to engaged columns, or fuch as are near the walls of a building, the intercolumniations are not limited; but depend on the width of the arches, windows, niches, or other objects and their decorations, placed within them. But columns that are entirely detached, and perform alone the office of fupporting the entablature; as in periftyles, porches, and galleries, muft be near each other; both for the fake of real and apparent folidity.

T<small>HE</small> ancients had feveral manners of fpacing their columns, which are defcribed by Vitruvius in his third and fourth books. Thofe practifed in the Ionic and Corinthian orders, were the * Pycnoftyle, of which the interval was equal to one diameter and a half of the column; the Syftyle interval, of two diameters; the Euftyle, of two diameters and one quarter; the Diaftyle, of three diameters; and the Aræoftyle, of four. In the Doric order they ufed other intercolumniations, regulating them by the triglyphs, of which one was always to be placed directly over the middle of each column: fo that they were either fyftyle monotriglyph, of one diameter and a half; diaftyle, of two diameters and three quarters; or aræoftyle, of four diameters; and the Tufcan intervals were exceedingly wide, fome of them being above feven diameters: which, as the architraves were of wood, was practicable.

A<small>MONG</small> thefe different intercolumniations, the pycnoftyle and fyftyle are too narrow: and though Mr. Perrault imagines, from their frequency in the remains of antiquity, that the ancients delighted more in them, than in any of the others, yet, I believe, their ufe muft be afcribed rather to neceffity than to choice. For as the architraves were compofed of fingle ftones or blocks of marble, extending from the axis of one column to that of another, it would have been difficult to find blocks of a fufficient length for diaftyle intervals, in large buildings.

W<small>ITH</small> regard to the aræoftyle and Tufcan intercolumniations, they are by much too wide either for beauty or ftrength, and can only be ufed in ruftic ftructures, where the architraves are of wood, and where convenience or economy takes place of all other confiderations. Nor is the diaftyle fufficiently folid in large compofitions. The euftyle therefore, being a medium between the narrow and wide intervals, and at the fame time being both fpacious and folid, has been preferred by the ancients as well as moderns, to any of the reft.

V<small>ITRUVIUS</small>, in the fecond chapter of his third book, fays, that the thicknefs of the column fhould be augmented, when the intercolumniation is enlarged; fo that if, in a pycnoftyle, the diameter is one tenth of the height, it fhould in an aræoftyle, be one eighth: for if, fays he, in an aræoftyle, the thicknefs of the columns do not exceed a ninth or tenth part of their height, they will appear too flender and delicate; whereas if, in a pycnoftyle, the diameter of the column be equal to one eighth of its height, it will appear gouty, and difagreeable to the eye.

* See Pl. of Intercolumniations.

T<small>HE</small>

THE intention of Vitruvius was good; but the means by which he attempts to compaſs it, are inſufficient. His deſign was to ſtrengthen the ſupports, in proportion ·as the intervals between them were enlarged; yet, according to the method propoſed by him, this cannot be effected: ſince one neceſſary conſequence of augmenting the diameter of the column, is enlarging the intercolumniation proportionably. Palladio and Scamozzi, have however, admitted this precept as literally juſt; and by their manner of applying it, have been guilty of a very conſiderable abſurdity.

IT is evident that Vitruvius, intended the five intercolumniations mentioned in his third book, merely for the Ionic and Corinthian orders; the latter of which, according to him, differed from the former, only in its capital. For, in the ſecond and ſeventh chapters of his fourth book, he eſtabliſhes other intervals for the Doric and Tuſcan orders. Nevertheleſs, they have employed theſe intercolumniations in different orders. Palladio, has uſed the ſyſtyle in the . Corinthian, and the aræoſtyle in the Tuſcan; by which means the Corinthian periſtyle, of which the character ſhould be extreme delicacy and lightneſs, becomes twice as ſtrong and material as the Tuſcan; of which the diſtinguiſhing characteriſtic ought to be extreme ſolidity: and Scamozzi has fallen into the ſame error, though not to ſo great an exceſs; his Tuſcan intercolumniation being only diaſtyle.

IT may perhaps be alledged, in favour of this precept of Vitruvius, that, by following his doctrine, the ſolidity of the column is increaſed or diminiſhed in a greater degree, than the breadth of the interval; the difference of the latter, between columns of eight or ten diameters in height, being only as eighty to one hundred; whereas that of the former is as ſixty-four to one hundred. But the apparent magnitudes of cylindrical bodies viewed in a vertical poſition, are to each other, nearly in the ſame ratio as their diameters, not as their ſolid contents: and as the bulk of the architrave and other parts of the entablature, vary exactly in the ſame proportion as that of the column does, the real ſtrength of the ſtructure is not in the leaſt affected by it.

VIGNOLA has obſerved nearly one and the ſame proportion in all his intercolumniations: which practice, though condemned by ſeveral eminent writers, is certainly preferable to any other; as it anſwers perfectly the intention of Vitruvius, preſerves the character of each order, and maintains in all of them an equal degree of real ſolidity.

SETTING therefore aſide the pycnoſtyle and ſyſtyle diſpoſitions, on account of their want of ſpace; and the aræoſtyle, for its deficiency in point of ſtrength; it may be eſtabliſhed, that the diaſtyle intercolumniation, and the euſtyle, (of which the latter ought, on moſt occaſions, to have the preference,) may be employed without diſtinction, in all the orders, excepting the Doric; in which the moſt perfect interval is the ditriglyph; neither the monotriglyph, nor the aræoſtyle, being to be admitted, but in caſes of neceſſity.

IT

It is however to be obferved, that if the meafures of Vitruvius be fcrupuloufly adhered to, with regard to the euftyle interval, the modillions in the Corinthian and Compofite cornices, and the dentils in the Ionic, will not come regularly over the middle of each column. The ancients, generally fpeaking, were indifferent about thefe little accuracies: but the moderns, taking example by fome of the chafteft remains of antiquity, have with reafon, ftrictly attended to them. A trifling alteration will remedy this defect, and being attended with no inconveniency, it may without hefitation be allowed. I fhall therefore, in imitation of Vignola, inftead of two diameters and a quarter, give two diameters and one third to the euftyle intercolumniation; not only in the Ionic, Corinthian, and Compofite orders, but likewife in the Tufcan: for I would endeavour to fimplify the art, and avoid an unneceffary increafe of rules, in a fcience already too much encumbered with them.

SOMETIMES, on account of the windows, doors, niches, or other decorations, which correfpond with the intercolumniations in the periftyle or gallery; it is not poffible to make the intervals fo narrow as euftyle, or even as diaftyle: wherefore the moderns, authorifed by fome few examples of antiquity, where grouped columns are employed; have invented a manner of difpofing them, by Perrault called Aræofyftyle; which admits of a larger interval, without any detriment to the apparent folidity of the building. This kind of difpofition is compofed of two fyftyle intercolumniations; the column that feparates them, being approached towards one of thofe at the extremities; fufficient room being only left between them, for the projection of the capitals: fo that, the great fpace is three diameters and a half wide; and the fmall one, only half a diameter.

THIS manner has been applied with fuccefs on the porch of St. Paul's in London, and on the principal front of the Old Louvre in Paris: the decorations of the niches in the laft of thefe buildings, having required fuch wide intercolumniations, that they could never have been tolerated without coupled columns.

MR. BLONDEL in his *Cours d'Architecture*, employs feveral chapters of his firft book, part 3, to prove the abfurdity of the aræofyftyle difpofition. His principal objections are its want of real folidity; its great expence, (fince near double the quantity of columns are required, that would be fufficient in the diaftyle;) and the irregularities which it occafions in the Doric, Corinthian, and Compofite entablatures.

THESE objections are too confiderable not to deferve attention; and it will always be beft to avoid the grouping of columns. Neverthelefs, if on any occafion, either to humour the fancy of fome capricious patron, or to conquer fome other infurmountable difficulty, it fhould be found neceffary to introduce them, they may doubtlefs be employed; care however, being taken, to ufe fuch precautions as will render the irregularities, occafioned by this difpofition, leaft ftriking and difagreeable.

Q q   IN

IN the Tuſcan, or Ionic orders, no precautions will be found neceſſary; the entablature in the former of theſe being entirely plain, and in the latter only enriched with dentils, which admit of a regular diſtribution, in all intervals diviſible by thirds of modules. But in the Corinthian and Compoſite, it muſt be obſerved, that if the modillions are regularly diſpoſed, and ſpaced according to their juſt meaſures, they will neither anſwer in the large or little intercolumniation, ſo as to have one of them over the middle of each column.

To remedy this defeꝗ, Perrault, the architeꝗ of the periſtyle of the Louvre, has enlarged both the modillions and the ſpaces between them; the diſtance from one center to another, in the broad intervals, being one module, thirteen minutes; and in the narrow ones, one module, fifteen minutes. This method, though tolerable in that building, where the dentil-band is not cut, and the angles are terminated by undiminiſhed pilaſters, will not anſwer in moſt other caſes: for, either the whole cornice muſt be enlarged, and all its proportions changed, or the modillions will not fall regularly over the dentils; the coffers in the ſoffit will be oblong inſtead of ſquare; and the ſpace between the laſt modillion and that over the angular column, will be leſs by far than any of the others: all which are irregularities too great to be tolerated.

THE ſimpleſt and beſt manner of proceeding, is to obſerve a regular diſtribution in the entablature, without any alteration in its meaſures; beginning at the two extremities of the building: by which method the modillions will anſwer to the middle of every other column, and be ſo near the middle of the intermediate ones, that the difference will not eaſily be perceivable. The only inconvenience ariſing from this praꝗice is, that the three central intercolumniations of the compoſition will be broader, by one third of a module, than is neceſſary for eleven modillions: but this is a very trifling difference, eaſily divided, and rendered imperceptible, if the extent be any thing conſiderable.

IN the Doric order, grouped columns are not ſo eaſily managed; and though they have been employed in many conſiderable buildings, and by eminent archi-teꝗs, yet, in very few of them, have they been properly treated. At the church of St. Gervais, and ſeveral other buildings in Paris, the metope between the coupled columns is much broader than any of the others; at the Minims near the *Place Royale*, that the metope might be ſquare, the baſes of the columns are made to penetrate each other; at the caſtle of Vincennes, the height of the frize is conſiderably augmented for the ſame reaſon: and Scamozzi, wherever he joins together two Doric columns, or pilaſters, omits the baſe of one of them, ſubſtituting a plinth in its place; that ſo the interval may not be too broad to admit of a regular metope.

NONE of theſe methods are good, nor equal to that which Palladio has prac-tiſed at the palace of Count Chiericato, and in the Baſilica at Vicenza. In the latter of theſe, the interval between the coupled columns is twenty-one minutes only: ſo that the diſtance, from the axis of one column to that of the other, is

two

two modules, twenty-one minutes; or fix minutes more than is fufficient, for a regular metope and two half triglyphs. In order to hide this excefs, each of the triglyphs is thirty-one minutes broad, their centers are each of them removed one minute within the axis of the column, and the metope, is three minutes broader than the others. A difference fo trifling, that it cannot be perceived without great difficulty: more efpecially as the next metopes to the wide one, become, by the removal of the triglyphs abovementioned, each one minute wider than the reft in the compofition.

WHEN, therefore, grouping of columns cannot be avoided in the Doric order; the Attic bafe of Palladio muft be employed, on account of its fmall projection; the great interval muft be aræoftyle, and the fmall one, twenty-one minutes, which leaves a fpace of one minute between the plinths of the coupled columns.

IN periftyles, galleries, or porticos, all the intercolumniations muft be equal: but in a logia, or a porch, the middle interval may be broader than the others, by a triglyph; a couple of modillions; or three or four dentils: unlefs, the columns at the angles, be either coupled; or grouped with pilafters; in which cafes, all the other intervals, fhould be of the fame dimenfion. For when they are of different widths, as at the Sorbonne; and the College Mazarin in Paris; it creates confu-fion, and the unity of the compofition fuffers thereby.

BLONDEL obferves, that, when periftyles or colonades are compofed of more than one row of columns, as are thofe of the piazza of St. Peter's at Rome; they fhould neither be of circular nor polygonal figures, but continued, as much as poffible, in ftraight lines: becaufe in either of the former cafes, the regular difpofition of the columns, is only perceivable from the center of the figure; the whole appearing, from all other points, a difagreeable heap of confufion. This remark is very juft; I have frequently obferved and regretted, the bad effect of a circular difpofition in the abovementioned magnificent ftructure; where the four ranges of columns of which the colonades are compofed, offer nothing but confufion to the fpectator's eye from every point of view.

THE fame inconveniency, though in a fmaller degree, fubfifts with regard to engaged pilafters, or half columns; placed behind the detached columns, of fingle, circular, oval, or polygonal periftyles; as may be feen in thofe of Burlington-Houfe. Wherefore, in buildings of that kind, it will perhaps be beft, to decorate the back-wall of the periftyle with windows or niches only.

WHEN buildings are to be executed on a fmall fcale, as is frequently the cafe of temples, and of other inventions, ufed for the ornament of gardens; it will be found neceffary to make the intercolumniations, or at leaft the central one, broader, in proportion to the diameter of the columns, than ufual; for when the columns are placed nearer each other than three feet, there is not room for a fat perfon to pafs between them.

Of ARCADES *and* ARCHES.

ARCHES, though not fo magnificent as colonades; are ftronger, more folid, and lefs expenfive. They are proper for triumphal entrances, gates of cities, of palaces, of gardens, and of parks; for arcades or porticos round public fquares, markets, or large courts: and in general, for all apertures that require an extraordinary width. In Bologna, and fome other cities of Italy, the ftreets are on each fide, bordered with arcades, like thofe of Covent-Garden and the Royal Exchange; which add greatly to their magnificence. In hot or rainy climates, thefe arcades are exceedingly convenient to paffengers, affording them both fhade and fhelter; but on the other hand, they are a great nuifance to the inhabitants, as they darken their apartments, hinder a free circulation of air, and ferve to harbour idle and noify vagabonds, who croud their entrances, and difturb their quiet. At Rome, the courts of the Vatican, thofe of Monte Cavallo, of the Borghefe, and of many other palaces, are likewife furrounded with arcades, where the equipages and domefticks attend under cover: fome of them being fufficiently fpacious, to admit two or three coaches abreaft. Such conveniences would be very ufeful in this metropolis; particularly, contiguous to the Court, to the Houfes of Parliament, to churches, to all places of publick amufement, and even to moft town habitations of the nobility and principal gentry, where numerous fine equipages and valuable horfes ftand half the night, expofed to all weathers. But the fcarcity and prodigious value of ground in the fafhionable or commercial parts of the town, render them, in general, inattainable.

THERE are various manners of decorating arches: fometimes their piers are rufticated; at others they are adorned with pilafters, columns, terms, or Caryatides; and on fome occafions, they are made fufficiently broad to admit niches, or windows. The circular part of the aperture is either furrounded with ruftic arch ftones, or with an archivolt, enriched with mouldings; which in the center, is generally interrupted by a key ftone in form of a confole, a mafk, or fome other proper ornament of fculpture; ferving, at the fame time, as a key to the arch, and as a feemingly neceffary fupport to the architrave of the order. Sometimes the archivolt, fprings from an impoft placed at the top of the pier, and at others from columns with their regular entablature or architrave cornice, placed on each fide of the arch; and there are fome inftances of arcades without any piers; the arches being turned from fingle or coupled columns; fometimes with, fometimes without entablatures: as in the temple of Faunus at Rome, and at the Royal Exchange in London; which, however is a practice, feldom to be imitated; being neither folid nor handfome.

WHEN arches are large, the key ftone fhould never be omitted, but cut into the form of a confole, and carried clofe up under the foffit of the architrave; which, by reafon of its extraordinary length of bearing, requires a fupport in the middle. And if the columns that adorn the piers, are detached, as in the triumphal arches

at

at Rome, it is neceffary to break the entablature over them; making its projection in the interval no more, than if there were no columns at all: for, though the architrave might be made fufficiently folid, yet it would be difagreeable to fee fo great a length of entablature hanging in the air, without any prop or apparent fupport.

It is, however, to be remembered, that thefe breaks in entablatures fhould be very fparingly employed, never indeed, but to avoid fome confiderable inconve- uience or deformity: for they are unnatural, render the columns or other fupports, apparently ufelefs, deftroy in a great meafure, the fimplicity of the compofition, and can feldom be contrived without fome mutilations, or ftriking irregularities, in the capitals and cornices of the orders, as may be obferved in feveral parts of the infide of St. Paul's in this city, and in many other places.

The impofts of arches fhould never be omitted; at leaft, if they are, a plat-band ought to fupply their place. And when columns are employed without pedeftals in arcades, they fhould always be raifed on plinths; which will ferve to keep them dry and clean, prevent their bafes from being broken, and improve the proportions of the arches; particularly in the Doric order, where the inter- columniations being governed by the triglyphs, are rather too wide for a well proportioned arch. In all arches it is to be obferved, that the circular part muft not fpring immediately from the impoft, but take its rife at fuch a diftance above it, as may be neceffary to have the whole curve feen at the proper point of view. When archivolts are employed without a key, or confole, in their middle, the fame diftance muft be preferved between the top of the archivolt, and the architrave of the order, as when there is a key; or, at leaft, half that diftance: for when they are clofe to each other, their junction forms an acute and difagreeable angle.

The void or aperture of arches, fhould never be much more in height, nor much lefs, than double their width: the breadth of the pier fhould feldom exceed two thirds, nor be lefs than one third, of the width of the arch; according to the character of the compofition: and the angular piers, fhould be broader than the reft, by one half, one third, or one fourth. The archivolt and impoft muft be proportioned to the arch; due care being however taken, to keep them fubfervient to the cornice, the architrave, and other principal parts of the order. For this reafon the height of the impoft, fhould not be more than one feventh, nor need it ever be lefs than one ninth of the width of the aperture; and the archivolt muft not be more than one eighth, nor lefs than one tenth, thereof. The breadth of the confole or mafk, which ferves as a key to the arch, fhould at the bottom, be equal to that of the archivolt; and its fides muft be drawn from the center of the arch. The length thereof, ought not to be lefs than one and a half of its bottom breadth, nor more than double.

The thicknefs of the piers, depends on the width of the portico, and the weight which the arcade has to carry above; for they muft be ftrong enough to bear the burthen, and to refift the preffure of the portico's vault. But, with regard to the beauty of the building, it fhould not be lefs than one quarter of the width of the arch, nor more than one third. And when arches are clofed up, to receive doors, windows, or niches, the receffes fhould be deep enough, at leaft, to contain the moſt prominent parts of what is placed in them; otherwiſe the architecture will appear flat, and the cornices of the niches, or windows, projecting before the fronts of the arches, will become too principal and ſtriking in the compoſition; as may be ſeen in the ſecond order of the Farneſe at Rome.

THESE dimenſions are general: but for a more accurate detail, the annexed deſigns * may be conſulted, where the proper meaſures of every part are expreſſed in figures.

VIGNOLA, in all his orders, excepting the Corinthian, makes the height of the arch double its width. His piers when the columns have no pedeſtals, are always three modules, and four modules when they have pedeſtals; his impoſts are all of them one module in height, and the archivolts are either one module, or half a module, as they belong to arches with, or without pedeſtals.

PALLADIO has given deſigns only of arches with pedeſtals. Their height is from one and two thirds, to two and a half of their width; and his piers are all of them, nearly three modules and three quarters; excepting in the Compoſite order, where they are four and four fifths.

SCAMOZZI'S Tuſcan arch is, in height, ſomewhat leſs than double its width; which height he increaſes gradually, till, in the Corinthian arch with pedeſtals, it is nearly twice and one half the width. His piers diminiſh in proportion to the increaſe of delicacy in the orders: his Tuſcan pier in arches without pedeſtals, being four modules and a half; and his Corinthian only three modules and three quarters. In arches with pedeſtals, his Tuſcan pier is four modules and two thirds; and his Corinthian only four modules. His impoſts and archivolts are likewiſe varied; and their proportions are relative to the width of the arches and the height of the piers: ſo that they are conſiderably larger in arches with pedeſtals, than in thoſe without.

VIGNOLA'S arches, being all of the ſame proportion, do not characterize the difference of the orders. His piers, in arches without pedeſtals, are too narrow; and his archivolts too ſlight. In his Doric arch without pedeſtals, the diſtance between the arch and architrave of the order is too conſiderable; as it is indeed, in ſeveral others of his arches; and, in his Doric with pedeſtals, the piers are much too broad. Palladio makes too great a difference between the height of his arches. His Tuſcan and Doric are too low; his Corinthian and Compoſite much too high. His piers bear a greater proportion to the void of the arch, in the delicate orders, than in the maſſive. His archivolts are ſlender, his impoſts clumſy, and ill profiled. The apertures of Scamozzi's arches, are well proportioned; except in the Corinthian order; where they are, like Palladio's, of an exceſſive height. His piers bear a proper relation to the arches; as do likewiſe his impoſts and archivolts, excepting in the arches with pedeſtals; where they are much too predominant, in regard to the other parts of his compoſition: and the members of which they conſiſt, are larger than thoſe of the cornice of the order: a fault, which Palladio has likewiſe been guilty of, to a very great exceſs.

* See Plate of Arches.

AT

Tuscan

Doric

Ionic

Corinthian

T. Gandon delin.

F. Patton sculp.

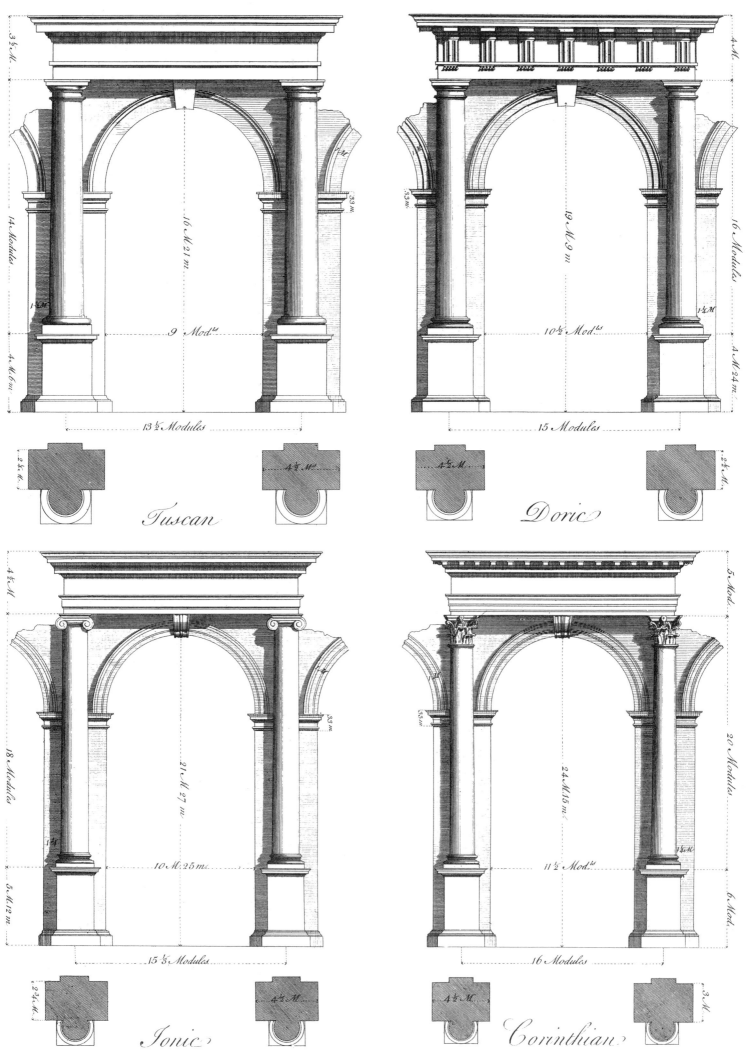

Tuscan

Doric

Ionic

Corinthian

T. Gandon delin.

F. Patton sculp.

AT firft fight, it appears extremely reafonable, to augment the fize of the impofts and archivolts of arches, in proportion to the increafe of the aperture; and in cafes where no order is employed, it ought always to be done: but when the arches are, not only adorned with impofts and archivolts, but are likewife furrounded with pedeftals, columns, and entablatures; it muft be very improper, to change confiderably, the proportions of any one of thefe parts; while all the reft remain unaltered; fince the confequence muft be a confiderable difparity between them: fo much the more ftriking, as they are near each other, and of fimilar natures; both circumftances tending to facilitate a comparifon: while, a trifling difproportion between the aperture of the arch, and its impoft, or archivolt, will feldom be perceived; and never can be very difpleafing to the eye.

IN the annexed * plates are given defigns of arches in all the orders, wherein it has been attempted to avoid the faults, with which the abovementioned mafters are charged. In the arches without pedeftals, their height is made equal to the length of the column; which height, is, in the Tufcan and Doric orders, fomething lefs than double the width of the arch, and in the Corinthian or Compofite, fomething more than double. And in arches with pedeftals, nearly the fame proportion between the height and the width of the aperture is obferved.

THE difference of width in the arches, (fuppofing the orders to be all of the fame height,) not being confiderable, I have conftantly obferved the fame dimenfions; as well in the piers, as in the impofts and archivolts; which is done to avoid a troublefome and needlefs detail; the characters of the different orders being fufficiently preferved without it. For though the Corinthian pier, contains in width the fame number of modules as the Tufcan; yet, as thefe modules diminifh, in proportion to the increafe of delicacy in the orders, the real fize of the one, is to that of the other, only as feven to ten.

IN the Doric order, the diftribution of the frize, makes it difficult to proportion the apertures of the arches well; either with, or without pedeftals: for the intervals of three or four triglyphs are too narrow, and thofe of four and five are rather too wide. Palladio, to conquer that difficulty, has at the Carita in Venice, omitted the ufual ornaments of the frize; and introduced, inftead of them, an imitation of thofe on the frize of the Sybil's Temple at Trivoli: having at the fame time made the diftance between the axis of the columns only eleven modules and a half, inftead of twelve and a half; which was the regular meafure. Le Clerc, in his defigns of the Doric order, has diminifhed the breadth of the metopes and triglyphs; and Scamozzi, has made his Doric columns feventeen modules high, inftead of fixteen, their ufual dimenfion, and raifed them on plinths; which laft expedient, Sangallo has likewife made ufe of, in the lower order of the Farnefe at Rome.

IN imitation of Sangallo, I have, in the Doric arch without pedeftals, raifed the columns on plinths; but avoided augmenting their height, as I did not incline

* See Plates of Arches without and with Pedeftals.

to change the eftablifhed proportions of the order, where there appeared fo little occafion for it. However, if the lownefs of the arch fhould be objected to, it may eafily be remedied, either by increafing the height of the column, as Palladio has done in his arch with pedeftals, or by diminifhing the breadth of the metopes and triglyphs, according to Le Clerc's method, or by employing both thefe artifices together: which laft, fhould be preferred; as it renders the change in the proportions of each particular part, lefs confiderable.

The fame expedients may be ufed in changing the meafures of the Doric arch with pedeftals, if they fhould not pleafe; obferving always, to divide the alteration proportionably, between the pedeftal, the column, and the frize of the order: by which means the height of the aperture may be brought to double its width, without apparent detriment to any other part: for many things, which in the ftrictnefs of theory appear licentious, are in reality of little or no confequence in the execution; becaufe they are not eafily perceptible.

The proportions of the Tufcan arch may likewife be changed, if required, and the height of the aperture be made nearer to double its width; which, as there are neither modillions nor dentils in the cornice, may be done without changing the proportion of any part of the order.

Should the breadths, which I have given to the piers of all the abovementioned arches, though they feem to me well proportioned, be thought too confiderable; they may be diminifhed, and, in arches without pedeftals, be reduced to three modules and three quarters, like thofe of Palladio; obferving in fuch cafe, to reduce the archivolts to twenty-fix minutes, inftead of the thirty, which they have in the annexed defigns. The piers of arches with pedeftals may likewife be leffened, and, inftead of four modules and a half, be only four in breadth; which may be done without changing the dimenfions of the archivolts: nor need, in either of the cafes, the impofts of any of the arches be altered.

When columns are engaged in the piers, their projection depends on that of the impoft, of which the moft prominent part, fhould be in a line with the axis of the column; at leaft in the Tufcan and Doric orders: but in the Ionic, Compofite, and Corinthian, it may project fomewhat beyond the axis, as in the Redentore at Venice, one of Palladio's beft works: becaufe, when the columns in thefe orders, are difengaged much above the half of their diameter, it occafions very difagreeable mutilations in the capitals; as may be obferved in the porch of St. George's, Bloomfbury, and at the Banquetting-Houfe, Whitehall.

In proportion to the increafe of delicacy in the orders, I have increafed the thicknefs of the piers; in each, a quarter of a module. Scamozzi's rule is quite oppofite to this: for he diminifhes his piers in thicknefs as well as in breadth, in the delicate orders; by which practice the real folidity of the ftructure is much affected: more particularly, as the columns, which may be confidered as parts of the piers, or as their abutments, are much weaker, in the Compofite and Corinthian, than they are in the Tufcan or Doric orders: whereas, according to the method here obferved, the folidity of all the piers, is nearly the fame; a circumftance, of far more confequence, than any trifling difproportion between the
thicknefs

thickneſs of the pier, and the diameter of the column; which can ſeldom be diſcovered, and never without a nicer inſpection than can take place, in obſerving the general effect of any compoſition.

WITH regard to the interior decoration of arcades, the portico may either have a flat ceiling, or be arched in various manners. When the ceiling is flat, there may be on the backs of the piers pilaſters; of the ſame kind and dimenſions, with the columns on their fronts; facing which pilaſters, there muſt be others like them, on the back wall of the portico. Their projection, as well as that of thoſe againſt the back of the piers, may be from one ſixth to one quarter of their diameter. Theſe pilaſters, may ſupport a continued entablature; or one interrupted, and running acroſs the portico over every two pilaſters, in order to form coffers. Or the architrave and frize only may be continued, while the cornice alone, is carried acroſs the portico, over the pilaſters as before; and ſerves to form compartments in the ceiling: as is done in the veſtibule of the Maſſimi Palace at Rome, and in the great ſtable of the King's Mews, near Charing Croſs.

WHERE the portico is arched, either with a ſemi-circular, or elliptical vault, the backs of the piers, and the inner wall of the portico may be decorated with pilaſters, as is above deſcribed, ſupporting a regular continued entablature; from a little above which, the arch ſhould take its ſpring, that no part of it may be hid by the projection of the cornice. The vault may be enriched with compartments of various regular figures, ſuch as hexagons, octagons, ſquares, and the like, of which and their decorations, ſeveral examples are given among the deſigns for ceilings. But when the vault is groined, or compoſed of flats, circular or domical coves, ſuſtained on pendentives, the pilaſters may be as broad as are the columns in front of the piers; but they muſt riſe no higher than the top of the impoſt, the mouldings of which, muſt finiſh and ſerve them inſtead of a capital: from whence the groins and pendentives are to ſpring, as alſo the bands, or *arcs doubleaux* which divide the vault.

IN the third plate of arches are ſix different deſigns of arcades, all of them compoſed by celebrated maſters, and perfect in their kind. Fig. 1, though leſs ſo than the reſt, is notwithſtanding the invention of Serlio; who recommends that manner of arching, in caſes, where columns are already provided, (as it frequently happens in places abounding with antiquities,) of which the length is not ſufficient for the intended purpoſe. And he obſerves, that, where theſe arches are uſed, it will be neceſſary to ſecure them with ſtrong abutments at each end. The great aperture of this kind of arch, may be from four and a half, to five diameters of the column in width, and in height, double that dimenſion; the width of the ſmall aperture muſt never exceed two thirds of that of the large one, and its height is determined by the height of the columns. To me, it ſeems, that this ſort of diſpoſition might be conſiderably improved, by adding an architrave cornice, or an entablature to the column, by omitting the ruſticks, and by ſurrounding the arches with archivolts.

FIG. 2, is of Vignola's invention, and executed by him in the Cortile of the caſtle at Caprarola. The arches are, in height, ſomewhat more than twice their width; the diſtance from the arch to the top of the cornice, is equal to one

U u third

third of the height of the arch; the breadth of the pier, is equal to the width of the arch; and the aperture of the window, occupies nearly one third of that breadth. Fig. 3, is an invention of Bramante, and executed in the Garden of the Belvidere at Rome. The height of the arch, is a trifle more than twice its width; the breadth of the pier, is equal to the width of the arch; and being divided into twelve parts, two of them are given to the parts of the pier fupporting the archivolts, four to the two columns, two to the intervals between the nich and the columns, and four to the nich. The height of the pedeftal is half the diameter of the arch; the columns are ten diameters in height; and the height of the entablature, is one quarter of the height of the columns: the impoft and archivolt are, each of them, equal to half a diameter of the column. Fig. 4, is very common in the works of Palladio, and has been often imitated by Inigo Jones. The height of the arch may be about twice its width, and the breadth of the pier fhould never be lefs than one, nor more than two thirds, of the width of the arch. Fig. 5, is a defign of Vignola, executed at Monte Dragone, a feat of the Princes Borghefi, near Frefcati. The height of the arch is fomething more than twice its width; and the breadth of the pier, including the columns that fupport the arch, is a trifle lefs than the width of the arch itfelf. Fig. 6, is an invention of Palladio, and executed by him in the Bafilica at Vicenza. The moft beautiful proportion for compofitions of this kind is, that the aperture of the arch be in height twice its width; that the breadth of the pier do not exceed that of the arch, nor be much lefs; that the fmall order be in height two thirds of the large columns; which height, being divided into nine parts, eight of them muft be for the height of the column, and the ninth, for the height of the archi-trave cornice; two fifths of which, fhould be for the architrave, and three for the cornice. The breadth of the archivolt, fhould be equal to the fuperior diameter of the fmall columns, and the key-ftone at its bottom, muft never exceed the fame breadth.

Of ORDERS above ORDERS.

WHEN two, or more orders are employed, and placed upon each other in a building; the laws of folidity require, that the ftrongeft fhould be placed lowermoft: wherefore the Tufcan is to fupport the Doric, the Doric the Ionic, the Ionic the Compofite or Corinthian, and the Compofite the Corinthian only.

THIS rule, however, has not always been ftrictly adhered to: moft authors place the Compofite above the Corinthian; and we find it fo difpofed in many modern buildings. There are likewife examples, where the fame order is repeated; as at the theatre of Statilius Taurus, and the Colifeum: and there are others, where an intermediate order is omitted, and the Ionic placed on the Tufcan, or the Corinthian on the Doric. But none of thefe practices are regular. The firft of them, is an evident trefpafs againft the rules of folidity, and fhould never be imitated; the fecond occafions a tirefome uniformity; and the laft cannot be effected without feveral difagreeable irregularities. For if the diameter of the fuperior order,

be

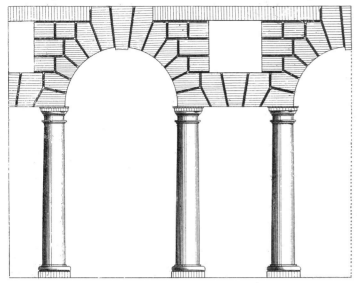

Fig. 1.

Fig. 2.

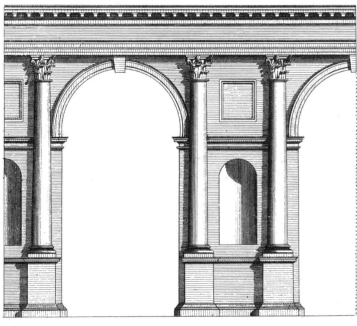

Fig. 3.

Fig. 4.

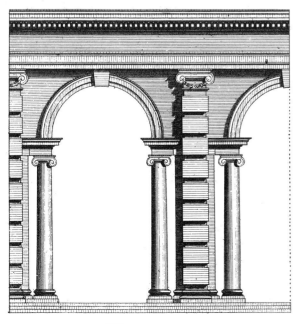

Fig. 5.

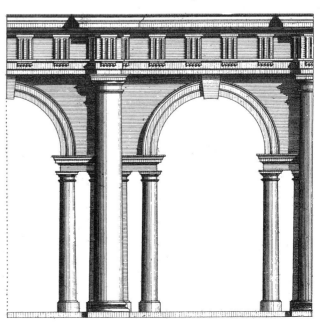

Fig. 6.

J. Gandon Delin.

S. Patton Sculp.

Columns upon Columns

Tuscan & Doric

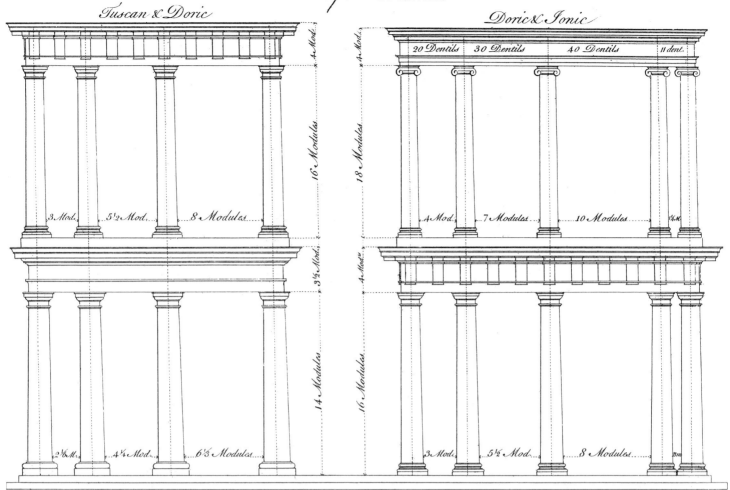

Doric & Ionic

Ionic and Composite, or Corinthian

Fig 1. Fig 2.

Composite and Corinthian

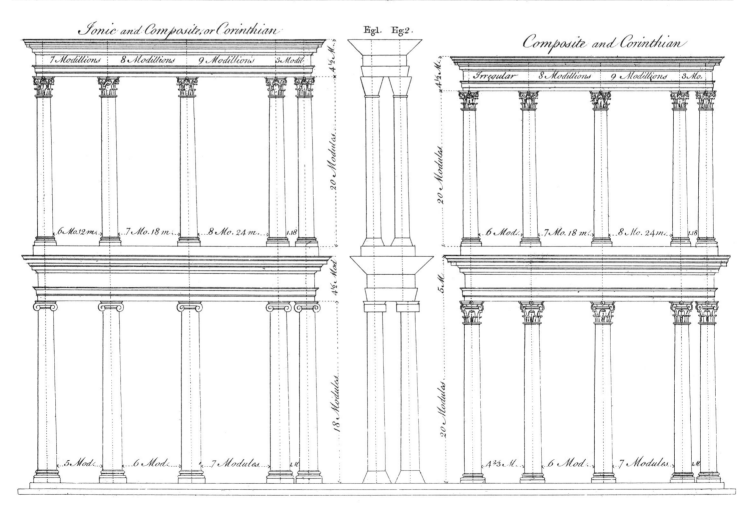

J. Gandon Delin.:   F. Patton Sculp

be in the fame proportion to that of the inferior, as if the fucceffion were regular; the upper order will be higher than the lower one; and if the diameter be leffened, in order to diminifh the height, the column will be too flender; the intercolumniation, which at beft, becomes too wide, will be ftill more enlarged; and the piers, if there be arches, will be confiderably too broad. Befides all which, the characters of the different orders will be much too oppofite, to be employed in the fame afpect, without being connected by fome preparatory decoration.

IN placing columns above each other, it is always to be obferved, that the axis of all the columns muft correfpond, and be in the fame perpendicular line, at leaft in front; in flank, they may or may not be fo, as fhall be moft convenient; though it is certainly more regular, as well as more folid, to place them on a perpendicular line in flank likewife. At the theatre of Marcellus, the axis of the Ionic column, is almoft a foot within that of the Doric one below it; which, as the columns are engaged, and the wall of the fecond ftory is confiderably retracted, could not well be avoided: and in cafes of a fimilar nature, where the folidity of the ftructure is not affected by it, the fame method may be taken; obferving, however, never to make the retraction greater, than it is at the theatre of Marcellus; where the front of the plinth, in the fecond order, is in a line with the top of the fhaft in the firft.

BUT wherever columns are detached, it will always be beft to place them exactly over each other, that fo the axis of all may form one continued perpendicular line: for then the ftructure will be folid, which it cannot be, when the fuperior column is placed confiderably within the inferior one; as a great part of it can then have no other fupport, than the entablature of the order below it. It is indeed true, that by fo doing, the bafes of the upper order will have a falfe bearing in front, as well as on the fides; but there being no poffibility of removing this inconveniency on the fides, it would be a matter of no confequence to remove it in front, where it is fcarcely perceptible.

VITRUVIUS, in the firft chapter of his fifth book, fays, that the columns in a fecond ftory fhould be lefs than thofe in a firft by one quarter; for the inferior parts being moft loaded, ought to be ftrongeft: and in the feventh chapter of the fame book, he repeats the fame precept; adding, that, if a third order, fhould be placed upon a fecond, its columns ought likewife to be lefs by one quarter than thofe of the fecond order. So that, according to this rule, the height of the column in the third order, would only be nine fixteenths of that in the firft: and, if the columns were placed on pedeftals; which, according to him, muft be lefs by one half in a fuperior, than in an inferior order; the height of the pedeftal and column, in the fecond order; would be to their height in the firft, as eleven to fixteen; and the height of the pedeftal and column, in the third order, would be to their height in the firft, nearly as fifteen to thirty-two: that is, lefs by more than one half. And further, if three orders of detached columns thus proportioned, were placed one above the other, as, for inftance, the Doric, Ionic, and Corinthian; and the lower intercolumniations were euftyle, or of two diameters and one third; the fecond intercolumniations would be aræoftyle, or of four diameters; and the third would be nearly of fix diameters and a half: a width of intercolumniation extremely unpleafing to the eye, at any rate unfolid, and, according to Vitruvius's own

X x

doctrine,

doctrine, not practicable but where the architraves are made of timber. And if, in like manner, three orders of engaged columns were placed above each other, either alone, or on pedeftals; and the lower intercolumniation, was of a proper width to admit a well proportioned nich, window, door or arch, it would be exceedingly difficult to decorate the fecond intercolumniation, and abfolutely impof-fible to decorate the third; which though confiderably wider than the firft, would be no more than about half as high.

I SHALL not trouble the reader with the various opinions and practices of the modern architects, with regard to the proportion of orders placed above each other: the curious may confult Blondel's cours d'architecture, where the greateft part of them are enumerated, and their merits nicely weighed; the whole difcuffion being fpun out, to the extent of feventy well filled folio pages. It will be fufficient to obferve, that Scamozzi's rule is univerfally efteemed the beft; being fimple, natural, and attended with fewer inconveniences than any other. It is built upon a paffage in the fifth book of Vitruvius, and imports, that the lower diameter of the fuperior column, fhould conftantly be equal to the upper diameter, of the inferior one; as if all the columns were formed of one long tapering tree, cut into feveral pieces.

ACCORDING to this rule, the Doric column will be to the Tufcan, as thirteen and one third to fourteen; the Ionic to the Doric, as fifteen to fixteen; the Compo-fite or Corinthian to the Ionic, as fixteen and two thirds to eighteen; and the Corinthian to the Compofite, as fixteen and two thirds to twenty.

IN this progreffion it appears, that when the Compofite and Corinthian are employed together, the relations between them are more diftant, than between any of the other orders. But this may be remedied by leffening the diminution of the inferior column, making its upper diameter fix fevenths, or feven eights of the lower one, inftead of five fixths: though, to fay the truth, the very beft expedient will be, never to ufe thefe two orders in the fame afpect; for they are fo much alike, that it differs little from a repetition of the fame object.

IT may probably be objected, that the inferior orders, according to the above-mentioned proportions, will not be fufficiently predominant. But if both the orders are continued throughout the front, this is of no confequence; there are many examples, where the difference between them is not greater, which yet fucceed perfectly well, and are generally efteemed. And if, the fuperior order only fubfifts in the middle, or at the ends, as is often the cafe; then the parts of the inferior order, over which no fuperior is placed, are generally finifhed with a baluftrade, levelling with the cills of the windows in the fecond order; which unites with, and is fufficient, to give a proper degree of predominance, to the lower part of the compofition.

IN England there are few examples of more than two ftories of columns in the fame afpect: and though in Italy, and other parts of Europe we frequently meet with three, and fometimes more; yet it is a practice by no means to be recom-mended, or imitated: for there is no poffibility of avoiding many ftriking inconfiftences; or of preferving the character of each order, in the intercolumnial decorations.

decorations. Palladio has attempted it at the Carita in Venice; Sangallo in the Palazzo Farnefe at Rome; Ammannato in the Cortile of the Pitti at Florence: but all unfuccefsfully. It is even difficult to arrange two orders with any tolerable degree of regularity, for the reafons already offered in the beginning of this chapter; which will remain in force, even when Scamozzi's rule is obferved, though the relations between the heights of the different orders, are then lefs diftant, than by any other method.

In the firft plate of orders above each other, I have given defigns of double colonades in all the orders; which are fo difpofed that the modillions, mutules, triglyphs, and other ornaments of the entablature, fall regularly over the axis of the columns, except in the Compofite and Corinthian combination; where, in the euftyle interval, the modillions of the fecond cornice do not exactly anfwer. But the diftance of the object from the fpectator's eye, makes this irregularity lefs important; more efpecially as a modillion will fall exactly over the axis of every third column. Neverthelefs, if a fcrupulous accuracy fhould be required, the entablature may be augmented, and made full five modules high; by which means, the diftribution will be perfectly regular.

Among the intercolumniations exhibited in the abovementioned plate, there are fome in the fecond orders extremely wide; fuch as the Ionic interval, over the Doric aræoftyle; the Compofite and Corinthian intervals, over the Ionic and Compofite aræoftyles; which having a weak, meagre appearance, and not being fufficiently folid, excepting in fmall buildings, are feldom to be fuffered, and fhould feldom be introduced. The moft eligible are, the euftyle and diaftyle for the firft order; which produce nearly the diaftyle and the aræoftyle in the fecond.

Many architects, among which number are Palladio and Scamozzi, place the fecond order of columns on a pedeftal. In compofitions confifting of two ftories of arcades, this cannot be avoided; but in colonades it may, and ought: for the addition of the pedeftal, renders the upper ordonnance too predominant; and the projection of the pedeftal's bafe, is both difagreeable to the eye, and much too heavy a load on the inferior entablature. Palladio, in the Barbarino Palace at Vicenza, has placed the columns of the fecond ftory on a plinth only; and this difpofition is beft: the height of the plinth being regulated by the point of view, and made fufficient to expofe to fight, the whole bafe of the column. In this cafe, the baluftrade muft be without either pedeftals or half balufters to fupport its extremities; becaufe thefe would contract, and alter the form of the column; its rail, or cap, muft be fixed to the fhafts of the columns, and its bafe made to level with their bafes; the upper torus and fillet of the columns being continued in the interval, and ferving as mouldings to the bafe of the baluftrade. The rail and balufters muft not be clumfy: wherefore it is beft to ufe double-bellied balufters; as Palladio has done in moft of his buildings, and to give to the rail, very little projection; that fo, it may not advance too far upon the furface of the column, and feem to cut into it. In large buildings, the center of the balufter may be in a line with the axis of the column: but in fmall ones, it muft be within it, for the reafon juft mentioned.

Y y

The

THE height of the baluſtrade is regulated, in a great meaſure, by its uſe; and cannot well be lower than three feet; nor ſhould it be higher than three and a half, or four feet. Neverthelefs, it muſt neceſſarily bear ſome proportion to the reſt of the architecture, and have nearly the ſame relation to the lower order, or whatever it immediately ſtands upon, as when a baluſtrade is placed thereon, chiefly for ornament. Wherefore, if the parts are large, the height of the baluſtrade muſt be augmented; and if they are ſmall, it muſt be diminiſhed, as is done in the Caſino at Wilton, where it is only two feet four inches high, which was the largeſt dimenſion that could be given to it, in ſo ſmall a building. But that it might, notwithſtanding its lowneſs, anſwer the intended purpoſe, the pavement of the portico is ſix inches lower than the baſes of the columns, and on a level with the bottom of the plat-band that finiſhes the baſement.

THE beſt, and indeed the only good diſpoſition, for two ſtories of arcades, is to raiſe the inferior order on a plinth, and the ſuperior one on a pedeſtal; as Sangallo has done at the Palazzo Farneſe: making both the ordonnances of an equal height, as Palladio has done at the Baſilica of Vicenza. In the ſecond plate of orders above each other, there are deſigns of arches upon arches for each order, which are perfectly regular, and well proportioned.

SCAMOZZI, in the thirteenth chapter of his ſixth book, ſays, that the arches in the ſecond ſtory ſhould not only be lower, but alſo narrower, than thoſe in the firſt; ſupporting his doctrine by ſeveral ſpecious arguments, and by the practice, as he ſays, of the ancient architects, in various buildings mentioned by him. In moſt of theſe however, the ſuperior arches are ſo far from being narrower, that they are either equal to, or wider than the inferior ones. In fact, his doctrine in this particular is very erroneous, entirely contrary to reaſon, and productive of ſeveral bad conſequences: for if, the upper arches be narrower than the lower ones, the piers muſt of courſe be broader; which is oppoſite to all rules of ſolidity whatever, and exceedingly ugly to the ſight. The extraordinary breadth of the pier on each ſide of the columns, in the ſuperior order, is likewiſe a great deformity: even when the arches are of equal widths, it is much too conſiderable. Palladio has, at the Carita in Venice, and at the Thieni Palace in Vicenza, made his upper arches wider than the lower ones; and I have not heſitated to follow his example: as by that means the weight of the ſolid in the ſuperior order is ſomewhat diminiſhed, the fronts of the upper piers bear a good proportion to their reſpective columns, and likewiſe to the reſt of the compoſition.

IN a ſecond ſtory of arcades, there is no avoiding pedeſtals. Palladio has indeed omitted them at the Carita: but his arches there, are very ill proportioned. The extraordinary bulk and projection of theſe pedeſtals are, as before obſerved, a conſiderable defect: to remedy which, in ſome meaſure, they have been frequently employed without baſes; as in the theatre of Marcellus, on the outſide of the Palazzo Thieni, and that of the Chiericato in Vicenza. This, however, helps the matter but little; and it will be beſt to make them always with baſes, of a moderate projection; obſerving at the ſame time, to reduce the projection of the baſes of the columns to ten minutes only, that the die may be no larger than is

abſolutely

Arches upon Arches

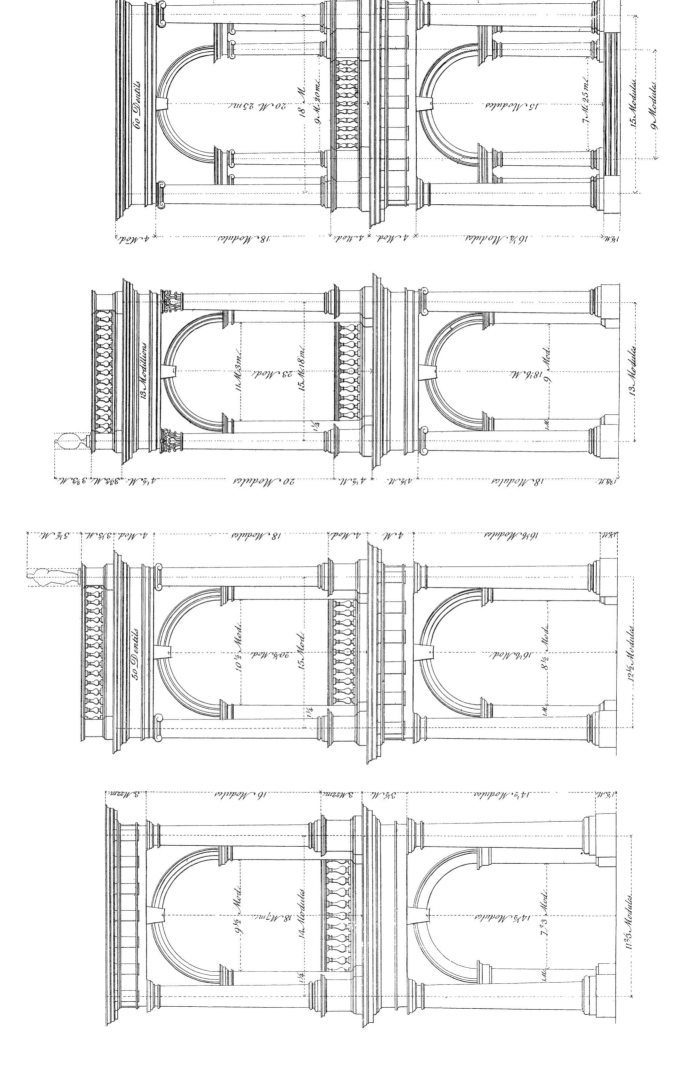

abfolutely neceffary, and in this cafe particular care muft be taken, not to break the entablature over each column of the inferior order; becaufe the falfe bearing of the pedeftal, in the fecond order, will by fo doing be rendered far more ftriking, and in reality more defective; having then no other fupport, than the projecting mouldings of the inferior cornice. There is no occafion to raife the pedeftals of the fecond order on a plinth: for, as they come very forward on the cornice of the firft order, and as the point of view muft neceffarily be diftant, a very fmall part only, of their bafes, will be hid from the eye.

THE baluftrade muft level with the pedeftals fupporting the columns; its rail or cornice, and bafe, muft be of equal dimenfions, and of the fame profiles, with theirs. It fhould be contained in the arch, and fet as far back as poffible; that the form of the arch may appear diftinct, and uninterrupted from top to bottom: for which reafon likewife, the cornice of the pedeftals muft not return, nor profile round the piers, which are to be continued in ftraight perpendicular lines, from the impofts to the bafes of the pedeftals. The back of the rail may either be made plain, or be funk into a pannel, in form of an open furbafe, for fo it will be moft convenient to lean upon, and it fhould be in a line with, or fomewhat receffed within the backs of the piers. The back part of the bafe of the baluftrade, may be adorned with the fame mouldings as the bafes of the piers; provided they have not much projection; but if that fhould be confiderable, it will be beft to ufe only a plinth, crowned with the two upper mouldings, that fo the approach may remain more free.

IN the Doric arch above the Tufcan, I have reduced the entablature to three modules, twenty-two minutes; which was neceffary, in order to have the arch well proportioned: and as its bearing is very confiderable, this licence feems the more excufable. The parts of the entablature have the fame proportion to each other as ufual; the only difference being, that, inftead of determining their meafures by the module of the column, they muft be determined by another module, made equal to one quarter of the height of the entablature. The pedeftals and the baluftrade are in this, as in the other arches, equal to the height of the entablature; which was done to preferve the fame general rule throughout: but as the entablature here bears a fomewhat larger proportion to the column than in the other orders, the height of the baluftrade is perhaps a trifle too confiderable, and may therefore, if required, be reduced to two ninths of the column, as in the Ionic order; and what is thus deducted from the height of the entablature, may be added to the height of the column, which by that means will acquire a more elegant proportion.

I HAVE reduced the Ionic, Compofite and Corinthian entablatures, in the fecond orders, to two ninths of the height of their refpective columns; and having allowed to each dentil with its interval, a breadth of nine minutes of the regular module of the column, the dentils and modillions anfwer exactly to almoft all the intercolumniations. In the defign of arches fupported by columns, the fmall order in the fecond ftory is a trifle lower than ufual; which cannot be avoided: for, if it be made two thirds of the large column, there will not be room above it for the circular part of the arch with its archivolt.

Of

Of BASEMENTS *and* ATTICS.

INSTEAD of employing feveral orders one above the other in a compofition, the ground floor, is fometimes made in the form of a continued bafe; called a Bafement: on which the order that decorates the principal ftory, is placed. The proportion of thefe bafements is not fixed, it depends on various circumftances, but chiefly on the nature of the apartments compofing the ground floor.

IN Italy, where their fummer habitations are very frequently on that floor, the bafements are fometimes very high. At the palace of the Porti in Vicenza, the height is equal to that of the order placed thereupon; and at the Thieni, in the fame city, its height exceeds two thirds of that of the order, although it be almoft of a fufficient elevation, to contain two ftories: but at the Villa Capra, and at the Loco Arfieri, both near Vicenza, the bafement is only half the height of the order; becaufe in both thefe, the ground floor confifts of nothing but offices.

IT will be fuperfluous to cite more examples of the diverfity of proportions, obferved by architects in this part of a building; as the four abovementioned, all of them eftimable works of the great Palladio, will fufficiently authorife any variations that it may be neceffary to make. It will not, however, on any occafion be advifable to make the bafement higher than the order it is to fupport: for the order being the richeft object of the compofition, and indicating the principal part in the fabrick, ought to be predominant. Befides, when the grand apartment is raifed too high, as is the cafe at Cazerta, where the afcent exceeds a hundred fteps; it lofes much of its importance, by the approach to it being rendered tediou, tirefome, and difficult. Neither fhould a bafement be lower than half the height of the order, if it is to contain apartments, and confequently have windows and entrances into it: for whenever that is the cafe, the rooms will be low, the windows and doors very ill formed, or not proportionate to the reft of the compofition, as is obfervable at Holkham: but if the only ufe of the bafement be to raife the ground floor, it need not exceed three, four, or at the moft five or fix feet in height; and be in the form of a continued pedeftal.

THE ufual manner of decorating bafements is, with ruftics of different kinds. The beft, in buildings where neatnefs and finifhing is aimed at, are fuch as have a fmooth furface. Their height, including the joint, fhould never be lefs than one module of the order placed upon the bafement, nor much more: and their figure may be from a triple fquare to a fefquialtera. The joints between them may either be fquare or chamfered: the fquare ones fhould not be wider than one eighth of the height of the ruftic, nor narrower than one tenth; and their depth muft be fomewhat lefs, or at moft equal to their width. Of thofe that have chamfered joints, the chamfer muft form a rectangle, and the width of the whole joint may be from one fourth to near one third of the height of the flat furface of the ruftic. In France we frequently fee only the horizontal joints of ruftics marked; the vertical ones being entirely omitted: and in Sir John Vanbrugh's works, the like is alfo

very

very common: but it has in general, a bad effect, and ftrikes as if the building were compofed of boards, rather than of ftone. Palladio's method feems far preferable, who, in imitation of the ancients, always marked both the vertical and horizontal joints; and whenever the former of thefe are regularly and artfully difpofed, the ruftic work has a very beautiful appearance. I have in the courfe of the work given various defigns of ruftic bafements*, diftributed in different manners, all which are collected from buildings of note.

THE bafement, when high, is fometimes finifhed with a cornice, as in the fecond figure of the third plate of arches, and as in the Strand front of Somerfet-Place: but the ufual method is only to crown it with a plat-band, as in the fourth figure of the fame plate; and as in the river front and fquare of the fame building: the height of which fhould not exceed the height of a ruftic with its joint, nor ever be lower than a ruftic exclufive of the joint. The zocholo or plinth at the foot of the bafement, muft at leaft be of the fame height with the plat-band, in general it fhould be fomewhat higher; and whenever there are arches in the bafement, the plat-band which fupplies the place of the impoft, muft be of the fame height as one of the rufticks, exclufive of its joint; and where a cornice is introduced to finifh the bafement, a regular moulded bafe to the fame muft alfo be introduced. To the height of the cornice may be given one feventeenth or eighteenth part of the whole bafement, and to that of the bafe about twice as much, divided into fix parts; of which the lower five fixths fhould form the plinth, and the upper fixth part, be compofed of mouldings.

IT is fometimes ufual, inftead of a fecond order to crown the firft with an attick; as Palladio has done at the Porti and Valmarino Palaces, in Vicenza, and Inigo Jones at Greenwich-Hofpital. Thefe atticks fhould never exceed, in height, one third of the height of the order on which they are placed; nor ever be lefs than one quarter. Their figure is that of a pedeftal. The bafe, dye, and cornice, of which they are compofed, may bear the fame proportions to each other as thofe of pedeftals do; and the bafe and cornice may be compofed of the fame mouldings, as thofe of pedeftals are. Sometimes thefe atticks are continued throughout, without any breaks; at other times parts project, and form pilafters over each column or pilafter of the order. The breadth of thefe pilafters is feldom made narrower than the upper diameter of the column or pilafter under them, nor ever broader. Their projection may be equal to one quarter of their breadth, or fomewhat lefs; and their fronts are fometimes adorned with pannels funk in and furrounded with mould-ings, as they were on the front of Powis-Houfe; but this, on moft occafions, as it looks too like joiners work; fhould be avoided as well as the capitals with which they are often adorned, particularly in France: becaufe they then approach too near the figure of regular pilafters of the orders, and being much broader than thefe, in proportion to their height; always carry with them the idea of a ftunted, clumfy, ill-proportioned compofition.

---

* See Plate 3 of Windows, and Plate 3 of Arches.

Of PEDESTALS.

APEDIMENT confifts of a horizontal cornice, fupporting a triangular or curvilineal fpace; either plain or adorned, called the Tympanum or Tympan; which is covered, either with two portions of ftraight, inclined cornice; or with one curvilineal cornice, following the direction of its upper outline. At each end of thefe cornices and on their fummit, are placed little plinths or pedeftals, called Acroterions or Acroters, ferving to fupport the ftatues, vafes, or other ornaments, which are ufed to enrich, and to terminate the pediment gracefully.

PEDIMENTS owe their origin, moft probably, to the inclined roofs of the primitive huts. Among the Romans they were ufed only as coverings to their facred buildings; till Cæfar, obtained leave to cover his houfe with a pointed roof, after the manner of temples. In the remains of antiquity we meet with two kinds of them; viz. triangular and circular. The former of thefe are promifcuoufly applied to cover fmall or large bodies: but the latter, being of a heavier figure, are never employed but as coverings to doors, niches, windows, or gates; where the fmallnefs of their dimenfions, compenfates for the clumfinefs of their form.

As a pediment reprefents the roof, it fhould never be employed but to terminate and finifh the whole compofition. Yet, in the churches of Rome and of Paris, we frequently fee one ufed to finifh the firft order of a porch; another to finifh the fecond order; and fometimes even 'a third or fourth above thefe: but this, however, is a practice which fhould not be imitated. Licinius, the mathematician, anciently reprehended Apaturius, the painter, merely for reprefenting an abfurdity of this kind in a picture: for who, faid he, ever faw houfes and columns built upon the roofs and upon the tylings of other houfes? Befides the inclined top of a pediment is, in appearance at leaft, a very unftable bafe for a range of columns or other heavy bodies.

NOR is it more reafonable to place two or three pediments one within another; as on one of the pavilions in the court of the Old Louvre at Paris, at St. Mary's in Campitelli, and at the church of the Great Jefu at Rome: fince the fame building can certainly want but one roof, to cover it.

ON circular bodies, pediments fhould never be applied, as at the church of St. Thomas in the Louvre at Paris; that kind of roof, being of a very improper conftruction for covering circles; and far from pleafing to the eye; as, in fuch cafes, they appear in almoft every view, contorted and irregular.

SOME writers there are, who object to pediments in interior decorations; becaufe, fay they, where the whole is covered and enclofed, there can be no occafion for coverings to fhelter each particular part. In this, however, they feem to carry their reafoning rather too far; a ftep farther would lead them into the fame

road

road with Father Laugier; who, having fagacioufly found out, that the firft buildings confifted of nothing but four trunks of trees, and a covering; confiders almoft
every part of a building, excepting the column, the entablature, and the pediment,
as licentious or faulty; and in confequence thereof, very cavalierly banifhes at once
all pedeftals, pilafters, niches, arcades, atticks, domes, &c. &c. It is only by
fpecial favour, that he condefcends to tolerate doors, or windows, or even walls.

THERE are many favourers of this writer's fyftem, who, like him, concentrate
all perfection in propriety. It were indeed to be wifhed that fome invariable
ftandard could be difcovered, whereby to decide the merit of every production of
the arts: but, certainly, Father Laugier has not hit the mark. Beauty and fitnefs,
are qualities that have very little connection with each other: in architecture they
are fometimes incompatible; as may eafily be demonftrated from fome of the Father's
own fingular compofitions; with a defcription of which, he has enriched his book.
And there are many things in that art, which though beautiful in the higheft
degree, yet carry with them in their application, an evident abfurdity: one
inftance whereof is the Corinthian capital; a form compofed of a flight bafket
furrounded with leaves and flowers. Can any thing be more unfit to fupport a
heavy load of entablature, and fuch other weights as are ufually placed upon it?
yet this has been approved and admired fome thoufand years, and will probably ftill
continue to be approved and admired, for ages to come.

LET it not be imagined, however, that it is by any means intended, entirely
to lay afide a regard to propriety; on all occafions it muft be kept in view: in
things defigned for ufe, it is the primary confideration; and fhould on no account
whatever be trefpaffed upon: but in objects merely ornamental, which are calculated
to captivate the fenfes, rather than to fatisfy the underftanding, it feems unreafon-
able to facrifice other qualities more efficacious, to fitnefs alone.

THE rigid ancient artifts, introduced but few pediments into their buildings;
ufually contenting themfelves with a fingle one, to diftinguifh and adorn the center
or principal part of the ftructure: but in the more licentious times of antiquity,
as well as in modern practice, and particularly amongft the Italians, fuch has been
the rage after pediments, that their buildings frequently confift of almoft nothing
elfe. At Rome the fronts of moft of their churches are covered with them; as are
likewife many of their palaces and private houfes, where they are feen of all fizes
and figures. For, befides the triangular and round, they have fome compofed of
both thefe forms; fome of an undulated figure; fome femi-hexagonal; fome with
the inclined cornice and tympan open in the middle, to receive a vafe, a buft, a
nich with a ftatue, or a tablet for an infcription; and others where the aperture
is left void, and the two ends of the inclined cornice are finifhed with a couple of
volutes, or fleurons. There is likewife a fort of pediment compofed of two half
pediments, which are not joined together to form a whole one, but reverfed; the
fummits being turned outwards. Of this kind there is one under the porticos of
the Gallery of Florence, with a buft wedged in between the two fections. England
is far from being free of thefe extravagances; the buildings of London exhibit
many examples of each kind, which not to offend, I fhall forbear to point out.

THE

THE beam, being a neceffary part in the conftruction of a roof, it is an impropriety to intermit or retrench, the horizontal entablature of a pediment, by which it is reprefented; either to make room for a nich, as at St. John's, Weftminfter; or for an arch, as in the cathedral church of St. Paul's; or for a window, as is cuftomary in moft of the new buildings in this city, where a femi-circular window is generally introduced, between the inclined cornice of the pediment and the aperture of the door, in order to gain light for the hall or paffage: and this licence is fo much the more reprehenfible, as it is extremely ugly; the two parts of the inclined cornice thus difunited, as it were untied, and unfupported, always ftriking the fpectator, with the idea of a couple of leavers, applied to overturn the columns on each fide. The making feveral breaks in the horizontal entablature, or cornice, of a pediment, as at the King's Mews near Charing Crofs, and on the pediments in the flanks of St. Paul's, is an impropriety of a fimilar nature, and equally unpleafing to the eye.

VITRUVIUS obferves, that the Greeks never employed either modillions or dentils in the horizontal cornices of their pediments; both of them reprefenting parts in the conftruction of a roof, which cannot appear in that view. This their practice, is obfervable in the temple of Minerva at Athens, and in fome other building yet ftanding in Greece; there is an ancient Roman inftance of it, in the temple of Scifi, mentioned by Palladio; and a modern one in the front of the Fueillants, near the Thuilleries at Paris, built by one of the Manfards.

ALL this is no doubt extremely proper, but at the fame time, it is as furely extremely ugly. The difparity of figure and enrichment, between the horizontal and inclined cornices, are fuch defects, as cannot be compenfated by any degree of propriety whatever: and therefore, to me it appears beft, in imitation of the greateft Roman and modern architects, always to make the two cornices of the fame profile; thus committing a trifling impropriety, to avoid a very confiderable deformity.

IN regular architecture, no other form of pediments can be admitted befides the triangular and round. Both of them are beautiful: and when a confiderable number of pediments are introduced, as when a range of windows are adorned with them, thefe two figures may alternately be employed; as they are in the niches of the Pantheon at Rome, and in thofe of the temple of Diana at Nimes.

IT is to be obferved, that the two uppermoft mouldings of the cornice are always omitted in the horizontal one of a pediment; that part of the profile being directed upwards, to finifh the inclined cornices. This difference of direction, increafes the height of the cyma very confiderably, and makes it far too large for the other parts of the entablature: to obviate which, fome architects have made a break in the cyma and fillet, as reprefented in the fourth figure, plate of pediments: but this being productive of a confiderable deformity; it will always be better, whenever the whole object is covered with a pediment, to make the profile of the cyma lower than ufual; by which means it may, notwithftanding the increafe occafioned by the difference of its direction, be made of a fize fuitable to the reft

of

of the cornice. But if the inclined cornice of the pediment be, on each fide, joined to horizontal ones, as is the cafe when the middle pavilion or other projecting parts are flanked with buildings, the only good method of leffening the abovementioned deformity, is to give very little projection to the cyma; by which means the increafe in its height may be rendered very trifling.

THE modillions, mutules, dentils, and other ornaments of the inclined cornice, muft always anfwer perpendicularly over thofe of the horizontal cornice, and their fides be always perpendicular to the horizon.

THE ancients judicioufly avoided the introduction of different fized pediments, in the fame compofition. Among the chafte remains of antiquity, I do not recollect any example, even of two different fizes in the fame afpect. Neither do we find that they ever adorned their niches, doors, or windows with pediments, when the whole front or any confiderable part thereof, was covered with one; juftly judging that the immenfe difparity, between the principal pediment and thofe that fhould cover the parts, could not but produce a difagreeable oppofition, in the fame manner as a pigmy and a giant, expofed to view at the fame time; are both made ridiculous by a comparifon.

THESE cautious proceedings of the ancient artifts, are good leffons to the moderns; which they would do well to have in memory, in all forts of compofi- tions. For, wherever there is a confiderable difference of dimenfion, in objects of the fame figure, both will equally fuffer by it: the largeft will appear infupportably heavy; the fmalleft ridiculoufly trifling: and wherever the difference of dimenfion is inconfiderable, it will always ftrike the beholder as the effect of inaccuracy in the workmen, or of inattention in the contriver: as may be verified by infpection of the arches in the bafement ftory of the Horfe Guards towards St. James's Park.

THE proportion of pediments depends upon their fize: for the fame propor- tions will not fucceed in all cafes. When the bafe of the pediment is fhort, its height muft be increafed, and when long it muft be diminifhed. For, if a fmall pediment be made low, the inclined cornice, which is always of the fame height, whatever may be the dimenfion of the pediment, will leave little or no fpace for the tympan; confequently little or no plain repofe, between the horizontal and inclined cornices. And if a large pediment be made high, it will have too lofty a tympan, and the whole compofition will appear ftraggling, and too heavy for that which is to fupport it. The beft proportion for the height, is from one fifth to one quarter of the bafe, according to the extent of the pediment, and the character of the body it ferves to cover.

THE face of the tympan, is always placed on a line perpendicular with the face of the frize; and, when large, may be adorned with fculpture, reprefenting the arms or cypher of the owner; trophies of various kinds, fuited to the nature of the ftructure; or bas-reliefs, either reprefenting allegorical or hiftorical fubjects: but when fmall, it is much better left plain.

VITRUVIUS determines the height of the acroters, by the height of the tympan; and Scamozzi, by the projection of the cornice; giving to the dye as much height

C c c

as

as the cornice has projection. But neither of thefe methods are well founded; for, when the building is terminated by a baluftrade, the pedeftals of the baluftrade ferve for the fide acroters, and that at the fummit muft be fuited to them. But when there is no baluftrade, the acroters muft always be of a fufficient height, whatever that height may be; to expofe to view the whole ftatue, or vafe, or other ornaments placed upon them, from the proper point of fight for the building.

Of BALUSTRADES.

BALUSTRADES are fometimes of real ufe in building, and at other times they are merely ornamental. Such as are intended for ufe; as when they are employed on fteps or ftairs, before windows, or to enclofe terraffes, or other elevated places of refort; muft always be nearly of the fame height: never exceeding three feet and a half, nor ever being lefs than three. That fo a perfon of an ordinary fize may, with eafe, lean over them, without being in danger of falling. But thofe that are principally defigned for ornament, as when they finifh a building; or even for ufe and ornament, as when they enclofe the paffage over a large bridge; fhould be proportioned to the architecture they accompany: and their height ought never to exceed four fifths of the height of the entablature on which they are placed; nor fhould it ever be lefs than two thirds thereof, without counting the zocholo, or plinth: the height of which, muft be fufficient to leave the whole baluftrade expofed to view, from the point of fight for the building. Palladio has in fome of his works, made the height of the baluftrade equal to that of the whole entablature; and Inigo Jones has followed his example in many of his buildings; particularly at the Ban-quetting Houfe: where befides this extraordinary loftinefs, it is raifed on a very high plinth. I do not think, either of thefe great artifts, are to be imitated in this practice, as it renders the baluftrade much too predominant, and very prejudicial to the effect of other parts in the compofition; particularly of the entablature to which it is contiguous.

THERE are various figures of balufters; the moft regular of which are deli-neated in the annexed plate. The handfomeft are the three in the firft row: their profiles and dimenfions are all different. The fimpleft of them, may ferve to finifh a Tufcan order; and the others may be employed in the Doric, Ionic, Compofite, or Corinthian orders; according to their degrees of richnefs.

THE beft proportion for baluftrades of this kind, is to divide the whole given height into thirteen equal parts; and to make the height of the balufter eight of thofe parts, the height of the bafe three, and that of the cornice, or rail, two. Or, if it fhould be required to make the balufter lefs, the height may be divided into four-teen parts, giving eight of thefe to the balufter, four to the bafe, and two to the rail: one of the parts may be called a module, and, being divided into nine minutes, ferve to determine the dimenfions of the particular members; as in the annexed defigns.

THE

Pediments and Imposts.

Figures of Pediments to be avoided

Tuscan Impost

Regular Pediments

Tuscan Impost & Archivolt

Doric Impost &c.

Ionic Impost &c.

Corinthian or Composite

Doric Impost

Ionic Impost

Corinthian or Composite

Chambers   P. Mazell sculp.

Ballusters &c.

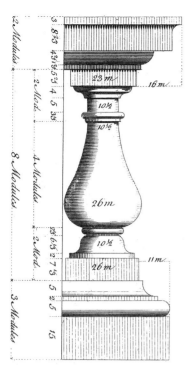
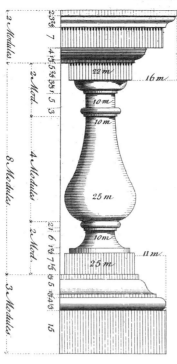

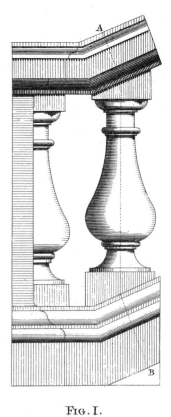

Tuscan Doric or Ionic Corinthian or Composite FIG. I.

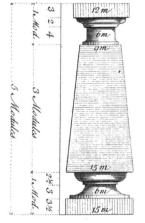
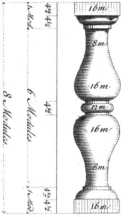
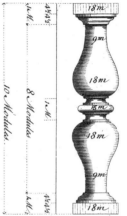
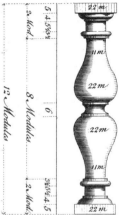

Tuscan Doric Ionic Corinthian

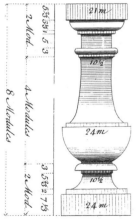
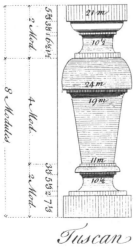
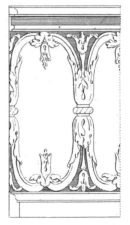

Tuscan Tuscan

W. Chambers.   J. Pass. Sculp.

THE other balusters exhibited in the same plate, are likewise perfect in their kinds, and collected from the works of Palladio, or other great masters. The double-bellied ones being the lightest, are therefore properest to accompany windows, or other compositions of which the parts are small, and the profiles delicate. The base and rail of these balusters may be of the same profile, as for the single-bellied ones; but they must not be quite so large. Two ninths of the baluster will be a proper height for the rail, and three for the base. The proportions of the balusters may easily be gathered from the designs, where they are marked in figures: the whole height of each being divided into such a number of parts, as is most convenient for the determination of the inferior divisions; one of these parts is the module: and is divided into nine minutes.

IN balustrades, the distance between two balusters should not exceed half the diameter of the baluster, measured in its thickest part; nor be less than one third of it. The pedestals that support the rail, should be at a reasonable distance from each other: for, if they be too frequent, the balustrade will have a heavy appearance; and if they be far asunder, it will be weak. The most eligible distance between them is, when room is left in each interval, for eight or nine whole balusters, besides the two half ones engaged in the flanks of the pedestals. But as the disposition of the pedestals depends on the situation of the piers, pilasters, or columns in the front; it being always deemed necessary to place a pedestal directly over the middle of each of these; it frequently happens, that the intervals are sufficient to contain sixteen or eighteen balusters. In this case, each range may be divided into two, or, which is better, three intervals; by placing a dye, or two dyes, in the range; each, flanked with two half balusters. The breadth of these dyes may be from two thirds to three quarters of the breadth of those of the principal pedestals. It will be best to continue the rail and base over and under them in a straight line, without breaks; for frequent breaks of any kind, tending to complicate without necessity, are defects; and most so, when of different dimensions; because they then complicate more, and serve to render the confusion greater.

THE breadth of the principal pedestals, when placed on columns, or pilasters, is regulated by them; the dye never being made broader than the top of the shaft, nor ever much narrower: and when there are neither columns, nor pilasters, in the composition, the dye should never be much broader than its height, and very seldom narrower: on the contrary, it is often judicious to flank the principal pedestals on each side with half dyes, particularly where the ranges are long, and divided in the manner abovementioned, as well to mark, and give consequence to these pedestals, as to support the ends of the rails; and give both apparent and real solidity. In such case, these principal pedestals must break forward more or less, as the nature of the design may require, and the base and rail must profile round them.

ON stairs, or other inclined planes, the same proportions are to be observed as on horizontal ones. It is indeed sometimes customary, to make the mouldings of the balusters follow the inclination of the plane: but this is difficult to execute, and when done, not very handsome; so that it will be better to keep them always horizontal, and shape the abacus and plinth in the form of wedges; as in figure A B, plate of balusters: making their height, at the axis of the baluster, the same

D d d   as as ufual. The diftance between two balufters on inclined planes, muft not be quite fo much as when they are in a horizontal fituation; becaufe the thickeft parts do not then come on the fame level. Le Clerc thinks it beft to finifh the inclined baluftrades of ftairs, or fteps, with horizontal pedeftals, placed on the floor, or pavement, to which they defcend. The method of joining the horizontal mouldings of thefe to the inclined ones of the rail and bafe of the baluftrade, is expreffed in figure A of the annexed plate.

As the intention of baluftrades is properly to enclofe terraffes, and other heights to which men refort, in order to prevent accidents; it is an impropriety, as D'Aviler obferves, to place them on the inclined cornices of pediments; as at Sta. Sufanna, and Sta. Maria de la Vittoria, near Dioclefian's baths at Rome; or in any other places, where it is not apparently, at leaft, practicable for men to walk.

WHEREVER baluftrades are ufed in interior decorations, as on ftairs, or to enclofe altars, thrones, tribunals, alcoves, buffets, or mufick galleries in publick affembly-rooms; or when, in gardens, they enclofe bafons of water, fountains, or any other decorations, the forms of the balufters may be varied; and enriched with ornaments properly adapted to the place they ferve to fecure and adorn.

WHEN ftatues are placed upon a baluftrade, their height fhould not exceed one quarter of the column and entablature, on which the baluftrade ftands. Their attitudes muft be upright; or, if anything, bending a little forwards, but never inclined to either fide. Their legs muft be clofe to each other; and the draperies clofe to their bodies: for whenever they ftand ftradling, with bodies tortured into a variety of bends, and draperies waving in the wind, as thofe placed on the colonades of St. Peter's, they have a moft difagreeable effect; efpecially at a diftance: from whence they appear like lumps of unformed materials, ready to drop upon the heads of paffengers. The three figures placed on the pediment of Lord Spencer's Houfe in the Green Park, which were executed by the late ingenious Mr. Spang, are well compofed for the purpofe. The height of vafes placed upon baluftrades, fhould not exceed two thirds of the height given to ftatues.

SOME there are, who think ftatues of the human figure, employed to decorate buildings, fhould never exceed the real human fize; alledging that they are the fcales by which we judge of grandeur, and that therefore any increafe of dimenfion in them, muft naturally leffen the grandeur of appearance, in the whole ftructure.

FOR my own part, I cannot be of their opinion; being perfuaded, that few, if any, judge by fuch far-fetched comparifons, and that no violent impreffions can be made upon the mind, by combinations which are too complicated to be inftantaneous: it is indeed true, that ftatues of an enormous fize, make the architecture which they accompany, appear trifling; but it is as true, that diminutive ones make it appear clumfy. Yet neither of thefe effects are owing to the forms, but entirely to the dimenfions of the objects; for it is very certain, that if inftead of ftatues, flower pots, bomb fhells, flaming altars, or any other things of a difproportionate fize were employed, they would produce the very fame effect, though they were ever fo unlike either the human figure, or any other animal being whatever. It will therefore be proper on all occafions, where ftatues are employed in decorations of

architecture,

architecture, to obferve the proportion above eftablifhed, which is built upon the practice of the greateft architects of preceding ages, whofe aim it conftantly was, to give to each object its due confequence in the compofition, without detriment to the reft; that fo all might equally contribute, to produce the general wifhed for effect.

OTHERS there are, who totally reject the practice of placing ftatues on the outfides of buildings, founding their doctrine, probably, upon a remark which I have fomewhere met with in a French author; importing, that neither men, nor even angels, or demi-gods, could ftand in all weathers, upon the tops of houfes and churches.

THE obfervation is wife, no doubt; yet, as a piece of marble or ftone is not likely to be miftaken for a live demi-god, and as ftatues, when properly introduced, are by far the moft graceful terminations of a compofition; one of the moft abundant fources of varied entertainment; and amongft the richeft, moft durable, and elegant ornaments of a ftructure; it may be hoped they will ftill continue to be tolerated.

IN interior decorations, it is fometimes cuftomary to employ inftead of baluf-ters, certain ornaments, called Frets, or *Guillochis*. I have in the plate of balufters, given fome defigns of fuch, for the ufe of thofe who incline to employ them, and many others may be found in le Pautres, and other ornamental publications. But it will be advifable to ufe them fparingly; for reprefenting leaves, ribbands, and flowers, they do not carry with them any idea of ftrength, and appear therefore nct calculated for a fence or anything to lean upon.

Of GATES, DOORS, *and* PIERS.

THERE are two kinds of entrances; doors, and gates. The former ferve only for the paffage of perfons on foot, but the latter are likewife contrived to admit horfemen and carriages. Doors are ufed as entrances to churches, and other public buildings, to common dwelling-houfes, and as communications between the different rooms of apartments. Gates ferve as inlets to cities, fortreffes, parks, gardens, palaces, and all places to which there is a frequent refort of carria-ges. The apertures of gates being always wide, they are generally made in the form of arches, that figure being the ftrongeft: but doors, which are ufually of fmaller dimenfions, are commonly of a parallelogram figure, and clofed horizontally. The ancients indeed, fometimes made their doors, and even their windows, narrower at the top than at the bottom: in the temple of Vefta at Tivoli, there are ex-amples of both; and Vitruvius, in the fixth chapter of his fourth book, lays down rules for the formation of Doric, Ionic, and Attic doors, by which the apertures of all, are made confiderably narrower at the top, than at the bottom. This oddity has been very little practiced by the modern artifts. Scamozzi difapproves of it; fo do feveral other writers: and it is a matter of furprife, that a perfon of fuch refined tafte, as the Earl of Burlington, fhould have introduced a couple of thefe ill-formed doors, in the *Cortile* of his houfe in Piccadilly.

IT muſt however be allowed that they, like ſome other uncouth things, have one valuable property; they ſhut themſelves: which in a country, where neither man nor woman takes thought, or trouble, about ſhutting doors after them, deſerves its praiſe; and was, perhaps, the original cauſe of their introduction among the ancients.

THE general proportion for the apertures, both of gates and doors, whether arched or quadrangular, is, that the height be about double their breadth, or a trifle more. Neceſſity probably, gave birth to this proportion, which habit confirmed and rendered abſolute. In the primitive huts, the entries were doubtleſs ſmall; perhaps, in imitation of thoſe to ſwallows neſts, no larger than was ſufficient for a man to creep through. For thoſe rude buildings being intended merely as retreats in the night, or in times of bad weather, it is natural to ſuppoſe they made the entrance to them as ſmall as poſſible, to exclude the air and rain. But when architecture improved, and methods were diſcovered of ſhutting the door occaſionally, they made it of ſuch a ſize as was neceſſary for giving admittance to a tall, bulky man; without ſtooping, or turning aſide: that is, they made it about three foot wide, and ſix foot high; or twice as high as broad; which proportion, being become habitual, was preferred to any other, and obſerved, even when the ſize of the entrance was conſiderably augmented, and other proportions would have been equally convenient.

WE may, I believe, look for the origin of many proportions in the ſame ſource; and of forms, in their aptitude to the purpoſes they ſerve: particularly with relation to ſuch objects as were, or are, of real uſe. And the pleaſure excited in us at their ſight, muſt, I am perſuaded, be aſcribed, rather to convenience, cuſtom, prejudice, or to the habit of connecting other ideas with theſe figures, than to any peculiar charm inherent in them, as ſome are diſpoſed to maintain.

THUS, when ſtruck with a fair female face, bright eyes, a florid complexion, good teeth, well turned limbs, a ſmooth unſpotted ſkin; it is not ſo much the form or colour, the elegant turn or ſmoothneſs of the frame, which affect us; as the inferences deduced from theſe appearances, of the general ſtate of mind; the bodily health and activity; the purity and fragrance; the ſenſibility and powers of communicating pleaſure, inherent in the beloved object: for if thoſe ſparkling eyes have borne falſe teſtimony; or thoſe limbs, which indicated agility and graceful motion, are found ſluggard, heavy, and aukward; if inſtead of purity and fragrance, their oppoſites offend the ſenſes; and inſtead of ſenſibility, dullneſs, or diſtaſte; our affection quickly abates, and the ſame object which commanded our love, ſoon excites no other emotion than that of indifference; perhaps of diſguſt; and even averſion.

AND thus with regard to ſtructures; whether conſidered in their general form, or ſeparately in their parts; whenever the maſſes and ſub-diviſions are few in number; firmly marked by quick and oppoſite tranſitions; the breadths and widths being predominant; we are impreſſed with ideas of grandeur, majeſty, manly ſtrength, and decorous gravity. And when the compoſition appears more detailed; the changes gradual and leſs contraſted; the heights predominant; we are impreſſed

with

with ideas of elegance, delicacy, lightnefs and gaiety. Exceffes in either of thefe cafes are equally dangerous, and productive of fenfations, though oppofite, yet equally difgufting: a ftep beyond the bounds of grandeur, finks into clumfinefs and ponderofity; a ftep beyond the limits of elegance, degenerates into weaknefs, triviality and affectation. Perfection confifts in mediums between extremes; and forcible effects are produced by verging towards them: all which, the rules of art tend to point out, and to explain.

OUR Saxon and Norman fore-fathers, ultimate corruptors of the almoft effaced Roman architecture; fufficiently prove, by the remains of their churches, monafteries, and caftles; to what extent barbarifm may carry deformity, gloom, unwieldy grandeur, and clumfy folidity. And their fucceffors of the thirteenth century, though following a manner infinitely more fcientifick and regular; often carried elegance, lightnefs, and exceffive decoration, far beyond their proper limits: till, in the fifteenth and fixteenth centuries, that manner had its laft polifh among us; was cleared of its redundancies; improved in its forms; fimplified and perfected in its decorations: in fhort, made what it is, in fome of the laft ftructures of that ftile; the admiration of all enlightened obfervers.

AMONGST the reftorers of the ancient Roman architecture, the ftile of Palladio is correct and elegant; his general difpofitions are often happy; his outlines diftinct and regular; his forms graceful: little appears that could with propriety be fpared, nothing feems wanting: and all his meafures accord fo well, that no part attracts the attention, in prejudice to any of the reft.

SCAMOZZI, in attempting to refine upon the ftile of Palladio, has over-detailed, and rendered his own rather trifling; fometimes confufed. Vignola's manner, though bolder, and more ftately than that of Palladio; is yet correct, and curbed within due limits; particularly in his orders: but in Michael Angelo's, we fee licence, majefty, grandeur, and fierce effect; extended to bounds, beyond which, it would be very dangerous to foar.

BUT whether there be any thing natural, pofitive, convincing and felf amiable, in the proportions of architecture; which, like notes and accord in mufick, feize upon the mind, and neceffarily excite the fame fenfations in all; or whether they were firft eftablifhed by confent of the ancient artifts, who imitated each other; and were firft admired, becaufe accompanied with other real, convincing beauties; fuch as richnefs of materials, brilliancy of colour, fine polifh, or excellence of workmanfhip; and were after, only preferred through prejudice or habit; are queftions which have much occupied the learned. Thofe who wifh to fee the arguments for, and againft, thefe refpective notions; are referred to Perrault, Blondel, and other writers upon the fubject. To the plurality of ftudents in the profeffion, it may be fufficient to obferve; without attempting to determine in favour of either fide; that both agree in their conclufion: the maintainers of harmonick proportions, proving their fyftem, by the meafures obferved in the moft efteemed buildings of antiquity; and the fupporters of the oppofite doctrine allowing, that as both artifts and criticks, form their ideas of perfection, upon thefe fame buildings of antiquity; there cannot be a more infallible way of pleafing, than by imitating that, which is fo univerfally approved.

IT

IT muſt however be obſerved, that ſounds operate very differently from viſible objects; the former of which affect all, and always in the ſame manner. The operation being merely mechanical, the ſame ſort of vibration, produces at all times the ſame effect; as equal ſtrokes upon a bell, produce the ſame ſounds. But viſible objects act differently. Their effect is not alone produced, by the image on the organ of ſight; but by a ſeries of reaſoning and aſſociation of ideas, impreſſed, and guiding the mind in its deciſion. Hence it is that the ſame object pleaſes one, and is diſliked by another; or delights to-day, is ſeen with indifference, or diſguſt, to-morrow. For if the object ſeen, had alone the power of affecting; as is the caſe with ſounds; it muſt affect all men alike, and at all times in the ſame manner, which by long and repeated experience, we know is not the caſe.

ONE certain ſource of general approbation, which admits of no diſpute, nor is ſubject to any exceptions, is, a ſtrict conformity of character, between the object and its application; between the whole, and the parts of which that whole is compoſed; the leaſt diſcord between theſe, immediately ſeizes upon the mind, and excites diſguſt, contempt, or ridicule; in proportion as the deviations appear greater or leſs; more unuſual, or more unnatural. And it is farther to be obſerved, that the ſame proportions, the ſame objects and combinations, which ſatisfy, even excite admiration in one caſe; or upon one occaſion; may excite diſlike in others, if erroneouſly applied; of which, there cannot be a ſtronger illuſtration than the human frame; male, and female; ſince almoſt every quality which conſtitutes perfection in one, becomes by being applied to the other, a ſtriking blemiſh; either of a diſguſting, or ridiculous nature.

THE uſual ornaments of gates; conſiſt of columns, pilaſters, entablatures, pediments, ruſticks of various ſorts, impoſts, archivolts, conſoles, maſks, &c. &c. and the common method of adorning doors; is, with an architrave ſurrounding the ſides and top of the aperture; on which are placed a regular frize and cornice. Sometimes too the cornice is ſupported by a couple of conſoles, placed one on each ſide of the door, and ſometimes, beſides an architrave, the aperture is adorned with columns, pilaſters, caryatides, or terms, ſupporting a regular entablature, with a pediment, or with ſome other termination either of architecture or ſculpture. In the two annexed plates are given various deſigns of gates and doors.

FIGURE 1, in the plate of doors, is a ruſtic door, compoſed by Vignola; in which the aperture occupies two thirds of the whole height, and one half of the whole breadth; the figure thereof being a double ſquare. The ruſtics may be either ſmooth or hatched, froſted or vermiculated, but their outline muſt be ſharp, and their joints muſt form a rectangle. Each joint may be in breadth, one third, or two ſevenths, of the vertical ſurface of a ruſtic. The joints of the *Claveaux* or archſtones, muſt be drawn towards the ſummit of an equilateral triangle, whoſe baſe is the top of the aperture. The architrave ſurrounding the aperture, may be compoſed either of a large oge and fillet, or of a plat-band, congé and fillet: its whole breadth muſt be one tenth of the breadth of the aperture, the remaining part of each pier being left for the ruſtics. The entablature is Tuſcan: the cornice thereof is to be one fifteenth of the whole height of the door; and what remains below it, being divided into twenty-one equal parts, the two uppermoſt of them will be for the frize

and

and architrave, and the remaining nineteen for the ruftics and plinth at the foot of the door. Fig. 2, is another very beautiful compofition of the fame great mafter, executed by him at the palace of Caprarola, in the Ecclefiaftical State; and copied by Inigo Jones in the hofpital at Greenwich: a circumftance which pleads ftrongly in its favour, though I cannot fay but our Englifh architect, has altered the proportions of the original, much for the worfe. The aperture is in the form of an arch, and occupies fomewhat more than two thirds of the whole height: it is adorned with two rufticated Doric pilafters, and a regular entablature. The height of the pilafters is fixteen modules; that of the entablature four. The width of the aperture is feven modules; its height fourteen: and the breadth of each pier is three modules. Fig. 3, is likewife a defign of Vignola's. It is of the Corinthian order, and executed in the *Cancellaria* at Rome. The height of the aperture is equal to double its width, and the whole ornament or entablature at the top, is equal to one third of the height of the aperture. The breadth of the architrave is one fifth of the width of the aperture; and the pilafters which fupport the confoles, are half as broad as the architrave. The whole is well imagined, but rather heavy; and it would fucceed better if the architrave were reduced to one fixth of the aperture, the whole entablature being proportionably diminifhed. The pilafters may remain of the breadth they now are, which is not too confiderable. Fig. 4, is a difpofition of Michael Angelo's. The windows of the Capitol are of this kind; and Sir Chriftopher Wren has executed doors of this fort, under the beautiful femi-circular porches in the flanks of St. Paul's Cathedral. The aperture of this defign may be a double fquare; the architrave one fixth of the width of the aperture, and the whole entablature one quarter of its height. The front of the pilafters or columns, on each fide, muft be on a line with the lower fafcia of the architrave; and their breadth muft be a femi-diameter. Fig. 5, is imitated from a defign of Philibert de l'Orme. It may ferve either for a gate or outward door: by obferving, in the former of thefe cafes, to raife the columns on plinths: and, in the latter, befides plinths, to place them on fteps, as all outfide doors ought to be; both becaufe the lower apartments fhould never be on a level with the ground, and becaufe this elevation will fhew the door, or indeed any other compofition, to more advantage. The aperture may be, in height, twice its width; the piers may be a little more than half that width, and the columne muft occupy half the breadth of the pier: their height may be eight diameters, or fomewhat more; the architrave and cornice muft bear the ufual proportion to the columns: the frize is omitted. The archivolt is in breadth, a femi-diameter of the column; and its whole curve being divided into thirteen equal parts, there will be room for feven *Claveaux*, and fix intervals. The fhafts of the column from the top of the impoft downwards, if divided into eight equal parts, will afford room for four intervals, and four ruftic cinctures; whereof that which levels with the impoft may be fquare, as in De l'Orme's defign; the reft of them being made either cylindrical or fquare, at pleafure. Fig. 6, is a door in the faloon of the Farnefe Palace at Rome, defigned by Vignola. The aperture forms a double fquare; and the entablature is equal to three elevenths of the aperture's height, the architrave being one of thefe elevenths; the whole ornament on the fides, confifting of the architrave and pilafters, is equal to two fevenths of the width of the aperture. The cornice is Compofite, enriched both with mutules and dentils; and the frize is in the form of a feftoon of laurel. Fig. 7, is copied from a door at Florence, faid to be a defign of Cigoli's. The height of the aperture is a trifle more than twice its width; it is arched. The impoft is equal to half a diameter; the columns

are

are Ionic, fomewhat above nine diameters high; and their fhafts are garnifhed, each with five ruftic cinctures. The entablature is lefs than one quarter of the column; and the length of the tablet, in which there is an infcription, is equal to the width of the aperture.

FIG. 8, is a compofition of Inigo Jones. The aperture may be a double fquare; the architrave may be from one fixth to one feventh of the width of the aperture, and the top of it muft level with the upper part of the aftragal of the columns. The columns are Corinthian, their height is ten diameters; and they muft be placed at a fufficient diftance from the architrave, to leave room for the projection of their bafes. The entablature may be two ninths, or one fifth, of the column, according to the character of the building in which the door is employed: and the height of the pediment may be one quarter of its bafe or fomewhat lefs.

FIG. 9, is a defign of Serlio's. The aperture may be either twice as high as broad, or a trifle lefs. The diameter of the columns may be equal to one quarter of the width of the aperture, and their height may be from eight diameters, to eight and a half. The entablature muft be fomewhat lefs than one quarter of the height of the columns; and the height of the pediment may be one quarter of its bafe, or a trifle lefs if required.

FROM thefe defigns and defcriptions, the manner of compofing doors may eafily be collected: and every man may invent a variety of other defigns, fuitable to the occafions on which they fhall be wanted. Yet fuch as are not endued with the talent of invention, will do well to copy thefe; which are all very excellent in their kind; and for more variety, they may recur to the defigns of windows contained in this work, which will, moft of them, anfwer equally well for doors.

IN the plate of gates and piers, fig. 1, is a pier, of which the diameter may be one quarter of its height, exclufive of the plinth and vafe placed upon it; the height of both which may be equal to one diameter of the pier. The ruftics may either be plain, chipped, frofted, or vermiculated; and the height of each courfe be one eleventh part of the height of the pier, counting to the top of the entablature; the entablature two elevenths; and the bafe of the pier one eleventh part: or if that fhould not be thought fufficient, one of the ruftick courfes may be left out, and the bafe be made two elevenths inftead of one. Fig. 2, is a gate, imitated from M. Angelo Buonaroti's defign for Cardinal Sermonetti. The height of the aperture is fomewhat more than twice its width; which width, occupies one third of the breadth of the whole compofition. The order is Compofite; and the height of the entablature is equal to one quarter of the height of the column. A break is made in it, over each column: but, unlefs the columns project confiderably, it will be as well to carry the entablature on in a ftraight line. The dimenfions of the particular parts may be meafured on the defign. Fig. 3, is a defign of piers executed at Goodwood, in Suffex. The diameter is one quarter of the height, exclufive of the finifhing, which is equal to one diameter; and the height of the pier, from the top of the entablature downwards, being divided into eleven parts and a half, one of them is given to the bafe, one to each courfe of ruftics, and one and a half to the aftragal, frize, and cornice. On many occafions however it may be proper to augment the height of the bafe, by omitting one of the ruftick courfes, and making it two parts inftead of

one.

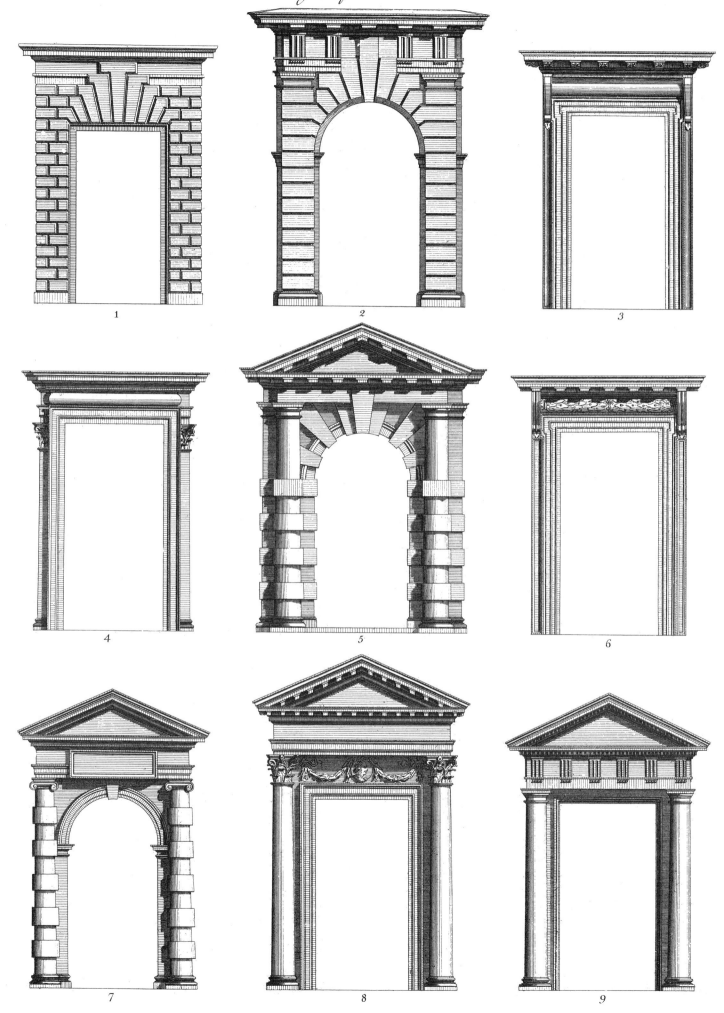

Designs for Doors.

1

2

3

4

5

6

7

8

9

W. Chambers delin.

F. Patton sculp.

1

2

3

4

5

6

W. Chambers.

T. Miller Sculp.

one. Fig. 4, is a compofition of the late Earl of Burlington's, which has been executed at his Lordfhip's Villa, near Chifwick, and likewife with fome little difference at Bedford Houfe, in Bloomfbury Square. Fig. 5, is an invention of mine, which has been feveral times executed; and fig. 6, is one of Inigo Jones's; which kind of pier he has executed at Aimfbury, in Wiltfhire, the feat of his Grace the Duke of Queenfbury.

AMONG the defigns at the end of this work, there are various other compofitions for gates; and any of the arches, either with, or without pedeftals, of which I have given defigns in treating of arcades, may likewife be employed as gates: obferving however, where the piers are weak, to fortify them; and make them at leaft equal to half the width of the aperture.

THE firft confideration, both in gates and doors, is the fize of the aperture; in fixing the dimenfions of which, regard muft be had to the bulk of the bodies that are to pafs through. For this reafon, infide doors, however fmall the building may be, in which they are ufed, fhould never be narrower than two foot nine inches; nor need they ever, in fmall private houfes, exceed three foot fix inches in width, which is more than fufficient to admit the bulkieft perfon, and enough for the paffage of two moderate ones. Their height fhould at the very leaft be fix foot nine inches, or feven foot; elfe a tall man with a hat, or a lady in feathers, cannot pafs without ftooping. In palaces, or great men's houfes, to which much company reforts, and all the doors of the ftate apartments are frequently thrown open, they are made much larger than above mentioned; often four, five, or fix foot wide, with folding doors, which fhut back in the thicknefs of the party wall, and leave a free paffage for the company from one room to another.

DOORS of entrance to private houfes, fhould not be lefs than three foot fix inches wide, nor more than fix foot; but to churches, palaces, and other publick ftructures, where there is a conftant ingrefs and egrefs of people, and frequently great crouds, the apertures muft be larger; and their width, cannot be lefs than fix feet, nor fhould it exceed ten or twelve.

THE fmalleft width that can be given to the aperture of a gate is nine foot; which is but juft fufficient for the free paffage of coaches: but if waggons and loaded carts are likewife to pafs, it muft not be narrower than ten or eleven foot. And gates of cities, or other entrances where carriages are liable to meet, fhould not be narrower than eighteen or twenty foot. The fame widths as are abovementioned, muft likewife be given to the intervals between piers, which equally ferve as entrances, and anfwer all the purpofes of gates.

In fettling the dimenfions of the apertures of doors, regard muft be had to the architecture, with which the door is furrounded. If it be placed in the intercolumniation of an order, the height of the aperture fhould never exceed three quarters of the fpace between the pavement and the architrave of the order; otherwife there cannot be room for the ornaments of the door. Nor fhould it ever be much lefs than two thirds of that fpace; for then there will be room fufficient, to introduce both an entablature and a pediment, without crouding: whereas if it be lefs, it will appear trifling, and the intercolumniation will not be fufficiently

H h h

filled.

filled. The apertures of doors, placed in arches, are regulated by the imposts; the top of the cornice being generally made to level with the top of the impost. And when doors are placed in the same line with windows, the top of the aperture should level with the tops of the apertures of the windows; or if that be not practicable, without making the door much larger than is necessary, the aperture may be lower than those of the windows, and the tops of all the cornices made on the same level.

WITH regard to the situation of the principal entrance, Palladio obferves that it should be so placed, as to admit of an eafy communication with every part of the building. Scamozzi compares it to the mouth of an animal; and, as nature, says he, has placed the one in the middle of the face, fo the architect ought to place the other in the middle of the front of the edifice; that being, the most noble situation; the most majestic, and convenient.

IN several of the palaces at Rome, as those of the Pamfilia in the Corfo, and of the Brachiano at Santi Apostoli, there are two principal entrances in the same aspect: but this, in general, ought to be avoided; as it leaves strangers in doubt where to seek for the state apartments, which should always be contiguous to the principal entrance. In interior difpositions, the doors of communication must be situated, as much as possible, in a line; the advantages of which are, that it contributes towards the regularity of the decoration, facilitates and shortens the passage through the apartments, and in summer, or on publick occasions, when the doors are set open, it produces a freer circulation of air; and likewise gives a much more splendid appearance to the apartments, by expofing to view at once, the whole series of rooms; which is more particularly striking, when the apartments are illuminated, as on occasion of balls, masquerades, routs, or other rejoicings. There should, if possible, be a window at each end of the building, directly facing the line of the doors of communication; that fo the view may be more extensive, and take in at once, not only all the rooms, but likewise parts of the gardens, or other prospects surrounding the building: and when ever this is not practicable, it will do well to place mirrours at each end of the apartment, or to counterfeit doors, and fill them with large plates of glafs, or with fashes and squares of looking glafs, (as is the custom in France;) which by reflection multiply the rooms, the doors, and other objects, making an apartment though limited, or fmall, appear very confiderable.

THE door of entrance from halls, vestibules, or antichambers, either to the principal apartment, or to any even of the inferior ones, should be in the middle of the room, if possible, and facing a window: those that lead to galleries, or any other long rooms, should be in the middle of one of the ends: and, in general, all entrances should be fo contrived, as to offer to view, at the first glance, the most magnificent, and extensive prospect of the place they open into. The doors of communication, from one room to another, of the fame apartment, must be at least two foot distant from the front walls; that the tables placed against the piers, between the windows, or other pieces of furniture put there, may not stand in the way of those who pafs. In bed rooms, care must be taken to make no doors on the sides of the bed; unlefs it be to communicate with a water closet, wardrobe, bath, or other conveniency of that kind; as well on account of the draught of

air,

air, as of the noife communicated through them, or attending their opening and fhutting: both which, are always troublefome, and on fome occafions dangerous. Neither ought doors to be placed near chimneys, for the fame reafons, and as the opening them, would difturb thofe who fit by the fire.

IN our northern climates, the fewer doors a room has, the more it will be comfortably habitable: for as we have much more cold than hot weather, it is very neceffary to make the rooms as clofe as poffible: otherwife they will not be fit to live in, the greateft part of the year. Wherefore it will be advifeable, never to make either more windows or doors, than are abfolutely neceffary: and the feigning doors, to correfpond with the real ones, may certainly be omitted on many, or on moft occafions. Here in England, the real and feigned doors of a room, with their ornaments, frequently cover fo great a part of the walls, that there is no place left, for either pictures or furniture: and one often fees, in houfes built forty or fifty years ago, particularly thofe defigned by Mr. Kent, or Lord Burlington; a hall, or a falon, large enough to receive a company of fixty or a hundred perfons; furnifhed with fix or eight chairs, and a couple of tables.

IN compofing doors, regard muft be had, both in their fize and their enrichments, to the place they lead to. Thofe that give entrance to palaces, churches, theatres, ftate apartments, or other places of confequence, muft be large, and profufely enriched; but fuch as open to humbler habitations, may be fmall and fparingly decorated: unlefs, the nature of the building fhould require otherwife. Where feveral doors are in the fame afpect, as on the infide of a hall, falon, or gallery, they fhould all be of the fame fize and figure; unlefs there be many, in which cafe the principal ones, provided they ftand in the middle of a fide, or in the middle of the ends of the room, may be larger; of a different form, and more abundantly adorned than the reft. But, whenever more than two forts are introduced in one room, it always tends to confufe the fpectator.

GATES in their compofition muft be characteriftick; exprefs the nature of the place they open to, and by their dimenfions, give fome idea of its extent and importance. Gates of cities, or of fortreffes, fhould have an appearance of ftrength and majefty; their parts fhould be large, few in number, and of a bold relief. The fame ought likewife to be obferved in the gates of parks, publick walks, or gardens; and thefe fucceed better when compofed of ruftick work, and of the maffive orders, than when they are enriched with nice ornaments, or delicate profiles. But triumphal arches, entrances to palaces, to magnificent villas, town, or country houfes; may with propriety, be compofed of the more delicate orders; and be adorned in the higheft degree.

THE gates of parks and gardens are commonly fhut with iron folding grates, either plain or adorned; thofe of palaces fhould likewife be fo, or elfe be left entirely open all day, as they are in Italy and in France: for the grandeur of the building, together with the domefticks, horfes, and carriages, with which the courts are frequently filled, give a magnificent idea of the proprietor, and ferve to enliven the fcenery.

IN

IN London, many of our Noblemen's palaces appear from the ftreet, like prifons, or gloomy convents ; nothing is feen but high black walls ; with one, two, or three ponderous caftle gates : in one of which there is a hole for the conveyance of thofe who afpire to get in, or wifh to creep out. If a coach arrives, the whole gate is indeed opened ; but this is a work of time, and hard labour : the more fo, as the porter exerts his ftrength to fhut it again immediately ; either in difcharge of his duty, or for fome other reafons. Few inhabitants of this city fufpect, and certainly fewer ftrangers ever knew ; that behind an old brick wall in Piccadilly, there is, (notwithftanding its faults,) one of the fineft pieces of architecture in Europe : and many very confiderable, fome even magnificent buildings, might be mentioned ; that were never feen by any, but the friends of the families they belong to, or by fuch, as are curious enough to peep into every out-of-the-way place, they happened to find in their way.

THE ancients frequently covered the clofures of their doors with plates, and baffo relievos of bronze. There are fome examples yet remaining of this practice, both at the Pantheon, and at St. John de Lateran ; the doors of which laft building formerly belonged to the temple of Saturn. The doors of St. Peter's of the Vatican are likewife covered with bronze ; and at Florence, thofe of the Baptiftery, fronting the cathedral, adorned with a great number of figures by Lorenzo Ghiberti, are much efteemed. Of thefe we have now in the collection of the Royal Academy, very perfect cafts. But the extraordinary expence, and great weight of fuch doors, have occafioned their being laid afide ; and wood alone is now ufed. The commoneft fort are made of deal, or wainfcot, painted in various manners ; and the better kind of them are of mahogany, or of different forts of rare wood inlaid.

WITH regard to their conftruction, Mr. Ware obferves that ftrength, beauty, and ftraitnefs are to be confidered ; all which purpofes are anfwered by compofing them of feveral pannels. The number of thefe muft depend on the fize of the door ; which fhould likewife regulate the thicknefs both of the pannels and the framing. If the doors be adorned with ornaments of fculpture, as is fometimes ufual in very rich buildings ; they muft either be funk in or kept very flat, upon the furface, both for the fake of lightnefs, and to prevent their being broken. The pannels may be either raifed or flat, and furrounded with one or two little plain or enriched mouldings, contained in the thicknefs of the framing ; not projecting beyond it, as is fometimes feen in old buildings.

DOORS that exceed three foot and a half in breadth, are generally compofed of two flaps ; by which means each part is lighter, when open doth not project fo far into the room, and when required, may be made to fold entirely into the thicknefs of the wall : as has been abovementioned. It is to be obferved that all doors fhould open inwards, otherwife in opening the door to give a perfon entrance, it muft open in his face ; and may chance to knock him down.

Of

Of WINDOWS.

THE firſt conſiderations with reſpect to windows, are, their number, and their ſize; which muſt be ſuch, as neither to admit more, nor leſs light than is requiſite.

IN the determination of this object, regard muſt be had to the climate, the aſpect, the extent and elevation of the place to be lit, to its deſtination, and, in a certain degree, to the thickneſs of the walls in which the windows are made; as on that circumſtance, in ſome meaſure depends, the greater or leſs quantity of light, admitted through the ſame ſpace. In hot countries, where the ſun is ſeldom clouded, and where its rays dart more intenſely upon the earth, the light is ſtronger than in thoſe which are temperate, or cold; therefore, a ſmaller quantity of it will ſuffice: and more than ſufficient ſhould not be admitted, as the conſequence is the admiſſion of heat likewiſe. The ſame is the caſe with a ſouthern aſpect, which receives more heat, and conſequently more light, than a northern, or even an eaſtern or weſtern one. A large lofty ſpace, requires a greater quantity of lighting than one circumſcribed in its dimenſions; and art demands, that the quantity introduced, ſhould be regulated ſo, as to excite gay, cheerful, ſolemn, or gloomy ſenſations in the mind of the ſpectator; according to the nature and purpoſes, for which the ſtructure is intended.

WHEREVER ſunſhine predominates, light muſt be admitted and diſtributed with caution; for when there is an exceſs, its conſtant attendant heat, becomes inſufferably incommodious, to the inhabitant. In Italy, and ſome other hot countries, although the windows be leſs in general than ours, their apartments cannot be made habitable, but by keeping the window ſhutters almoſt cloſed, while the ſun appears above the horizon. But in regions where gloom and clouds prevail eight months of the year, it will always be right to admit a ſufficiency of light for theſe melancholy ſeaſons; and have recourſe to blinds, or ſhutters, whenever the appearance of the ſun renders it too abundant.

Palladio, in the xxvth chapter of his firſt book obſerves, that no certain determinate rule can be eſtabliſhed concerning the height and width of the apertures of windows; but that to him it appeared proper, in conformity to the doctrine of Vitruvius, l. 4, c. vi, to divide the ſpace between the floor and ceiling, into three parts and a half, and give to the height of the window two of theſe parts, and to its width one of them, leſs one ſixth. In another part of the ſame chapter, he ſays, the windows ſhould not be wider than one quarter of the width of the room, nor narrower than one fifth; and that their height ſhould be double their width, more one ſixth; but as in every houſe, ſays he, there are large, middling, and ſmall rooms; " And it is yet neceſſary to keep all the windows on the ſame " levels of the ſame form, I prefer thoſe rooms for determining their meaſure, " of which the length is to the width, as five to three: thus, when the width of " the room is eighteen foot, and the length thirty; I divide the width into four

K k k   " parts

" parts and a half, giving one of these parts to the width of each window ; to its
" height two of them, more one sixth ; and make all the other windows on the
" same floor, of the same dimensions."

THIS last rule, which neither determines the number of windows, the height
of the room, nor the side on which the light is to be admitted; is surely too vague,
and subject to error: I have somewhere seen a better rule, but cannot remember
where. To the best of my recollection, it proportions the quantity of light to be
thrown in, to the number of square feet contained on the plan of the room ; by
which method, supposing due attention given to the height and depth of the room,
something more certain may be attained than by that of Palladio.

IN the course of my own practice I have generally added the depth and the
height of the rooms on the principal floor together, and taken one eighth part
thereof, for the width of the window; a rule, to which there are but few objections;
admitting somewhat more light than Palladio's, it is, I apprehend, fitter for our
climate than his rule would be.

HERE in England, our apartments are seldom made so lofty as in Italy, those
of our smaller dwelling houses often do not exceed ten foot, and are seldom higher
than twelve or fourteen. In such, the windows may be from three to four foot
wide, and in the rooms on the upper floor double, or somewhat more than double
of that in height: by which means, when the window cill is placed at a proper
distance from the floor, for a grown person to lean upon, the aperture will rise to
within eighteen inches, or two foot of the ceiling, and leave sufficient space above it,
for the cornice of the room, and the architrave or mouldings which surround the
window. But in more considerable houses, where the apartments are large, and
run from sixteen to twenty foot high; or sometimes more; the windows should
never be narrower than four foot; they often require to be made four and a half,
sometimes even five, or five and a half foot wide, and high in proportion. These
dimensions are sufficient for dwelling houses of any size in this country, when they
are larger, they admit too much of the cold air in winter, and are troublesome to
manage ; but churches, banquetting rooms, or other buildings of a publick nature;
may have much larger windows, and proportioned to the architecture, of which
such structures are composed, the parts whereof are generally large.

WITH regard to the beauty of exterior decorations, if an order comprehends
two stories, the apertures of the windows with which it is accompanied, should not
much exceed three modules in width, but when it contains only one story, their
width may be four and a half, or even five modules. Windows contained in
arches, may have from two fifths to three sevenths of the arch in width; and their
height must be such, that the last horizontal moulding of their cornice may answer
to the top of the impost of the arch: the whole pediment being contained in the
circular part. The pediment must be triangular; for curves above each other,
unless they be similar and parallel, do not succeed.

THE proportions of the apertures of windows, depend upon their situation:
their width in all the stories must be the same, but the different heights of the apartments, make it necessary to vary the heights of the windows likewise.

IN

In the principal floor, it may be from two and one eighth of the width, to two and one third, according as the rooms have more or lefs elevation; but in the ground floor, where the apartments are ufually fomewhat lower, the apertures of the windows fhould feldom exceed a double fquare; and when they are in a ruftick bafement, they are frequently made much lower. The windows of the fecond floor may be, in height, from one and a half of their width, to one and four fifths; and thofe of atticks or mezzanines, either a perfect fquare, or fome-what lower. The character of the order in which the windows are employed, and that of the profiles with which they are enriched, muft likewife in fome meafure be confulted, and the apertures be made more or lefs elevated, as the order of the whole decoration, or of the window itfelf, is more or lefs delicate.

The windows of the principal floor are generally moft enriched. The fimpleft method of adorning them is, with an architrave furrounding the aperture, covered with a frize and cornice fuited thereto : but, when the aperture is remarkably high with refpect to its width, it becomes neceffary to fpread the ornaments on the fides thereof, by flanking the architrave with columns, pilafters, or confoles, in order to give the whole compofition an agreeable proportion. The windows of the ground floor are fometimes left entirely plain, without any ornament whatever; at other times they are furrounded with an architrave, or with rufticks, or have a regular architrave, crowned with its frize and cornice. Thofe of the fecond floor have gene-rally an architrave, carried entirely round the aperture; and the fame is the method of adorning attick or mezzanin windows: but thefe two laft have feldom or ever either frize or cornice; whereas the fecond floor windows, whenever their aperture approaches a double fquare, are often adorned with both. As at the Banqueting-Houfe, and in many other buildings of note.

The cills of all the windows on the fame floor, fhould be on the fame level; and raifed above the floor, from two foot nine inches, to three foot, at the very moft. When the walls are thick, they fhould be reduced under the apertures of of the windows for the conveniency of looking out: and feats may be contrived to fit thefe receffes, as is the cuftom in many of our modern Englifh houfes. In France, and now too often here, the windows are carried quite down to the floor; which when the building is furrounded with gardens, or other beautiful profpects, renders the apartments exceedingly pleafant in fummer, but then they become exceedingly cold in winter. And the iron-work, which in France, and latterly very much here, is placed on the outfide; by way of fence againft accidents: ought never to have place, where regular architecture is intended: for all the gilding and flourifhing in the world, can never make it tolerably accordant with the reft of the compofition.

In regular built houfes, the cills of the windows on the ground floor, fhould be raifed fix foot above the pavement on the outfide of the building; to hinder paffengers from looking into the apartments. But when this cannot be done, without raifing the floor itfelf more than may be neceffary, the lower parts of the windows may be furnifhed with blinds. The tops of the apertures of windows, fhould never, within the apartments, be carried clofe up to the cornice of the room: a fufficient fpace ought always to be left for an architrave, or at leaft two or three

L l l

mouldings

mouldings to furround them, without crouding upon the cornice: between which and thefe architraves the laths whereon the curtains faften are generally placed.

The interval between the apertures of windows depends, in a great meafure, on their enrichments. The width of the aperture, is the fmalleft diftance that can be between them; and twice that width, fhould in dwelling houfes, be the largeft; otherwife the rooms will not be fufficiently lighted, and the building will have rather the appearance of a prifon, than of a ftructure calculated for the conveniences, and enjoyments of life. The purpofe for which the building is intended fhould, as has been before obferved, regulate the quantity of light to be introduced: and therefore in dwelling houfes, and all places where comfort and pleafure are the main purpofes, there cannot well be too much: but in facred ftructures, which fhould affect the mind with awe and with reverence, or in other great works, where grandeur of ftyle is aimed at, it fhould be cautioufly and rather fparingly diftributed.

The windows neareft to outward angles, muft be at leaft the width of their aperture diftant from the angle; and a larger fpace will be ftill more feemly, and render the building more folid. In all the ftories of the fame afpect, the windows muft be placed exactly one above the other; and thofe to the left fymmetrize, with thofe to the right, both in fize, fituation, number, and figure. The reafons for all thefe things are obvious enough, and therefore it is needlefs to mention them. The licentious practice of intermitting the architrave and frize of an order, in the intervals between the columns or pilafters, to make room for windows and their enrichments, which are carried clofe up to the cornice, can on no account whatever be fuffered in regular architecture; it being in the higheft degree abfurd to carry the windows above the ceiling; and great want of judgment in an architect, to inter-mix crouded together, fuch a number of rich complicated parts, as are thofe of the entablature of the order, and the entablatures of the windows. Befides the whole beauty of the order, when fo mutilated, is deftroyed; its proportions and figure being entirely changed. An interruption of the whole entablature, to make room for a window, and converting it into an impoft to the archivolt, as we fee done on the flanks of the Manfion Houfe, is a licenfe equally unpardonable. Sir Chriftopher Wren was extremely fond of thefe mutilations; and every lover of architecture, while he admires the exterior of St. Paul's, muft owe him fome grudge, for having fo unmercifully mangled many parts of the infide, of that fplendid ftructure.

The common fort of builders in this country, are extremely fond of variety in the ornaments of windows, and indeed in every other part of a building; imagining, probably, that it betrays a barrennefs of invention, to repeat the fame object fre-quently. There is a houfe near Berkley Square, with only eleven windows in the whole front, and yet they are of feven different forts. At Ironmonger's Hall in the City, the cafe is the fame; there being feven or eight forts of windows in the fame afpect: and the like is to be met with in many other buildings, both in town, and in the country.

These inventive gentlemen would do well to give their attention to fome pro-feffors of the mechanic arts, who, though exercifing their talents on meaner objects,

are

are neverthelefs worthy of their imitation. No taylor thinks of employing feven or eight kinds of buttons on the fame coat: a cutler will not make ten different forts of knives for the fame fet; and if a cabinet maker be trufted to furnifh a room, he feldom introduces more than one or two forts of chairs. Their practice is founded on experience; the general approbation of mankind is the ftandard they go by.

WE do not difcover, either in the works of antiquity, or thofe of the great modern architects, any traces of this childifh hankering after variety. The fame object is frequently by them, repeated a hundred times over; and this is one of the caufes of that amazing grandeur, that noble fimplicity, fo much to be admired in their productions.

THIS famenefs muft however have its limits: for when carried too far, the imagination of the beholder ftagnates, for want of occupation. In the moft admired works of architecture, we find the fame object, generally continued throughout the fame level: thus one order, and one fort of windows, or niches, generally reign throughout the ftory: but in the other ftories, where the eye, and the imagination, neceffarily affume a frefh courfe, the decoration is altered.

SCAMOZZI, and fome other eminent architects, both in their doctrine and practice, are fond of diftinguifhing the middle of every compofition, by an object different from the reft. Thus, in a range of windows, the middle one is generally either Venetian, or in the form of an arch; though all the reft are fquare. How this may affect others, I do not well know: but for my own part, I do not like the practice, excepting where it may be abfolutely neceffary. Every one from his own experience muft, I think, have felt a fudden uneafinefs arifing, on finding a ftyle, a ditch, or other impediment of that nature, in his way; and the mind is equally difturbed, when thus violently and unexpectedly interrupted, in contemplating the parts of a building.

SOMETIMES, however, it may be neceffary to increafe the fize, and vary the figures of the windows, either in the center break, or in fome other prominent part of a front; in order to light a falon, a gallery, or a hall, higher than the reft of the rooms. But then it will always be advifeable to repeat the fame form if fimple, as an arch; three, five, or more times, according to the extent of the plan, as has been done on the fouth front of Holkham: that fo, the mind may be in fome degree fatiated, before it is conducted to a new object.

VENETIAN windows, and Venetian doors too, are on fome occafions neceffary; particularly, in fmall buildings; to light a hall, a veftibule, or fuch other rooms, as cannot admit of two windows, and yet would not be fufficiently lit with one. But where they can be avoided, it is beft: for the columns which feparate the large interval, from thofe on the fides, form fuch flender partitions, that, at a diftance, they are fcarcely perceived; and the whole looks like a large irregular breach made in the wall.

AND however advifeable it may be to repeat the fame form, as has above been mentioned, the repetition of thefe Venetian windows, fhould always be avoided.

M m m   In

In the north front of Holkham, there are no lefs than feven of them, which added to the quantity of trifling breaks, and ups, and downs, in the elevation, keep the fpectator's eye in a perpetual dance to difcover the outlines: than which, nothing can be more unpleafing, or deftructive of effect. Indeed Mr. Kent, who was the defigner of this building, though we have it publifhed under another name; was very fond of puzzling his fpectators: witnefs the Horfe Guards, Holkham, the Treafury, and other of his works: which certainly would have added more to his fame, had they been lefs complicated and abundant in variety.

THE fafhes of windows are generally made of wainfcot, or mahogany, and fometimes of copper, or other metals: the London artificers excel in thefe works: they make them very neatly, and though in appearance flight, very ftrong. The fquares of glafs are proportioned to the fize of the windows; there being commonly three in the width, and four in the height, whatever be the dimenfions of the window: each fafh is compofed of two equal parts, placed one above the other, and either the lowermoft, or both of them, being hung on pullies, and counterpoifed with weights, are moved up or down with great eafe: both the cords and the weights being concealed. Thefe are much neater, and much more convenient, than the French ones; which are compofed of two vertical divifions, turn on hinges, and are fhut with an apparatus of ironwork always in the way, and weighing almoft a hundred weight. The fhutters are always within the apartments, wherever beauty is aimed at; thofe on the outfide deftroying the appearance of the front. They are divided into feveral vertical flips, folding behind each other, for the conveniency of ranging or boxing them when open, in the thicknefs of the wall. Each flip or fold is framed and compofed of feveral pannels, either raifed or flat, furrounded with fmall mouldings contained in the thicknefs of the framing: which, when the profiles in the room are enriched, fhould likewife be fo; at leaft on the fold that faces the aperture, when the fhutters are turned back; the front of which muft ftand flufh with the inner edge of the architrave furrounding the window, all the other folds being ranged behind it.

IN the three annexed plates of windows, I have given a great variety of defigns. Fig. 1, in the firft of thefe plates is imitated from the lower windows of St. Peter's, compofed by M. Angelo Buonaroti. The aperture is fomewhat lower than a double fquare in height: the architrave is one feventh of the width of the aperture, which is likewife the breadth of the pilafters: the confoles, both at bottom and top of the window, are, in length, one third of the width of the aperture; and the whole entablature is equal to one quarter the height thereof. Fig. 2, is a compofition of Bartolomeo Amanato, executed in the ground floor of the Mattei Palace at Rome. The whole defign, and particularly the lower part is well compofed: but rather approaching towards the heavy: the parts made fomewhat lefs would fucceed better, as would alfo a pediment inftead of the floped covering at top. Fig. 3 and 4, are both of them compofed by Bernardo Buontalenti, and executed in different places. The aperture of this fort of window may be a double fquare, or a trifle more; the architrave from one fixth to one feventh of the width of the aperture, and the pilafters either the fame; or lefs by one third, one quarter, or one fifth, according as the architrave is broader or narrower, there being very few cafes, in which both together, fhould exceed one third of the width of the aperture, at the moft. The height of the whole entablature, fhould not exceed one quarter of the height of
the

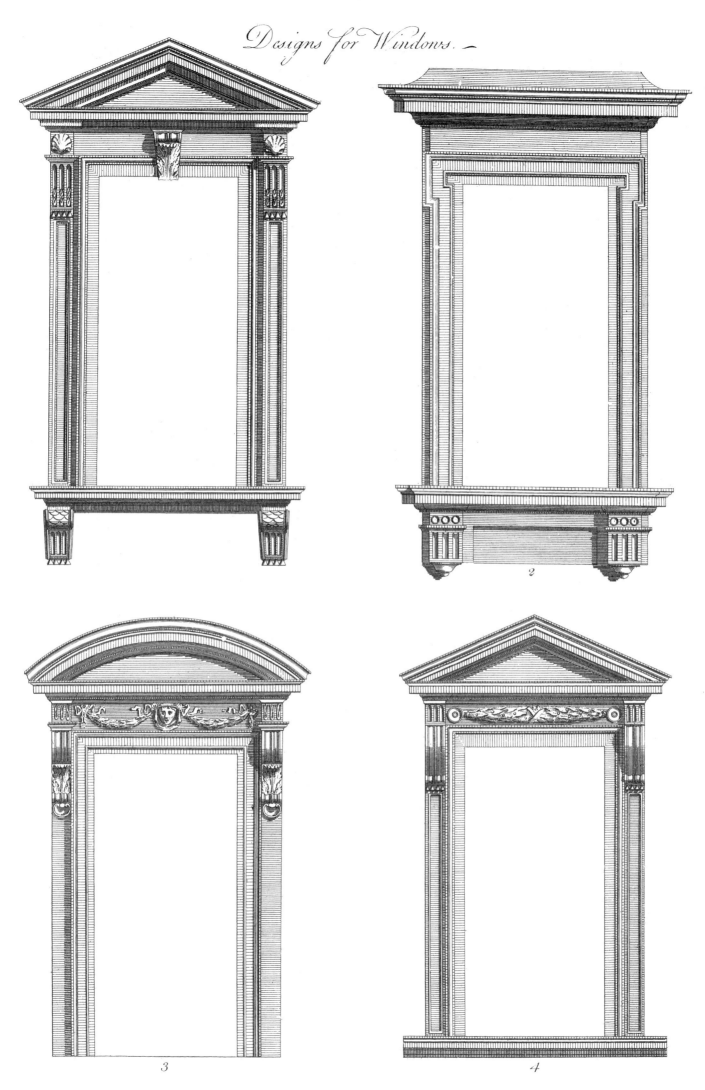

Designs for Windows.

Mr Chambers

F. Patton sculp.

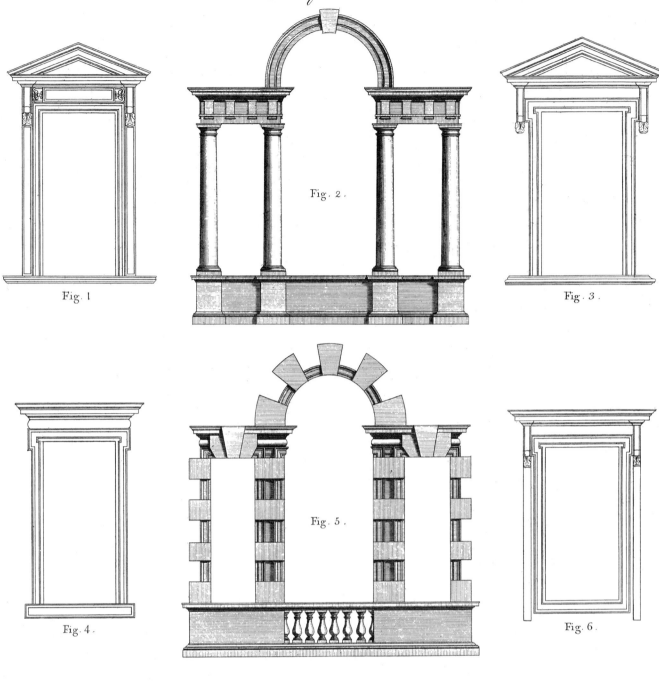

Fig. 1.

Fig. 2.

Fig. 3.

Fig. 4.

Fig. 5.

Fig. 6.

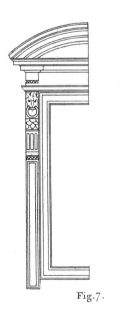

Fig. 7.

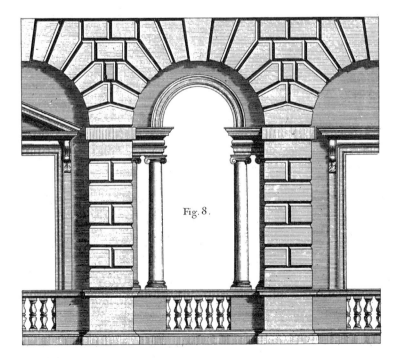

Fig. 8.

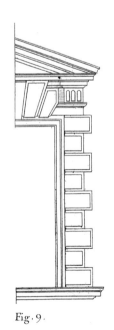

Fig. 9.

J. Miller Sculp.

the aperture, nor ever be much lower: the confoles may be equal in length to half the width of the aperture at moft, and to one third of it at the leaft.

In the fecond plate, fig. 1, is a defign of P. Lefcot, abbot of Clagny, executed in the Old Louvre at Paris. The proportions may be the fame, as in the two laft mentioned ones. Fig. 2, is what we commonly call, in England, a Venetian window. It is an invention of Scamozzi's. The height of the arched aperture, is twice, and one half its width: thofe on the fides, are half the width of that in the middle; and their height is regulated by the height of the columns. The breadth of the archivolt, is equal to the fuperior diameter of the columns. Fig. 3, is a defign of Palladio's, executed by him in many of his buildings. The aperture is a double fquare, the breadth of the architrave, is one fixth of the width of the aperture; the frize and cornice together, are double the height of the architrave; and the breadth of the confoles, is two thirds of the breadth of the architrave. This fort of window fucceeds much better without breaks in the architrave, which only ferve to render it top heavy; and the confoles when placed on pilafters feem more fupported, and ferve to give a better form to the whole, than when they are only ftuck on the wall: the breaks though frequently introduced by Inigo Jones, and other copyers or imitators of Palladio, are always unnatural; and can only be tolerated for the fake of variety, or with a view of fpreading a compofition in itfelf too lean elevated. Fig. 4, is likewife a defign of Palladio's, executed at the Chiericato in Vicenza. Its proportions differ very little from the former; the plat-band that fupports the window is equal to the breadth of the architrave. Fig. 5, is a Venetian window, invented, I believe, by Mr. Campbell. Fig. 6, is a defign of Inigo Jones's, executed at the Banqueting Houfe. I do not know exactly what proportions he has obferved, having never had an opportunity of meafuring the original: but the aperture may be a double fquare, the architrave one fixth of the aperture's width, and the whole entablature one quarter of its height; the breadth of the confoles may be two thirds of the breadth of the architrave. Fig. 7, is a defign of M. Angelo Buonaroti, executed at the Farnefe Palace in Rome. For the beautiful difpofition reprefented in fig. 8, we are indebted to the late Mr. Kent; and it is executed with fome little difference at the Horfe Guards, in St. James's Park. Its proportions may be collected from the defign. Fig. 9, is a defign of Ludovico da Cigoli, and executed in the ground floor of the Ranunchini Palace at Florence. In the third plate of windows, fig. 1, is imitated from a defign of Raphael Sanzio da Urbino, executed in the principal floor of the Pandolfini Palace at Florence. The height of the aperture, is a trifle more than twice its width; the architrave is equal to one feventh of the width of the aperture; the columns are Ionic, and will fucceed beft if entirely detached; yet that cannot well be, excepting on a ground floor: their height is nine diameters, their diftance from the architrave of the window is a quarter of a diameter, which is likewife the diftance of the entablature from the top of the fame architrave. The height of the whole entablature, is equal to two ninths of the column; and the height of the pediment is one quarter of its bafe, or a trifle lefs: the pedeftals and baluftrades are in height, one quarter of the column and entablature taken together. Fig. 2, is an invention of Andrea Palladio's, executed with fome little difference in the Porto Barbarino Palace at Vicenza. Inigo Jones has very judicioufly introduced the fame defign in the flanks of Greenwich Hofpital, and managed all the parts of it more gracefully than in the original. Fig. 3, is imitated from the windows in the principal floor of the Bracciano Palace at Rome, defigned

by

by Bernini. Fig. 4, is an invention of Palladio's, and the defign here given is very accurately meafured and copied from the Thieni Palace at Vicenza; in the principal floor of which it is executed. The height of the aperture is two and one tenth of its width, the columns are Ionic, one quarter engaged in the wall, and nine diameters high: the bottoms of the capitals are on a line with the top of the aperture, they have angular volutes, with an aftragal and fillet below the volute; the bafes are Tufcan: there are five ruftick dyes on the fhaft of each column, which are all of an equal breadth; the inner fides of them are on a line with the fides of the aperture; and their projection is equal to that of the plinth of the bafe, which is one fifth of a diameter of the column. The key-ftones are diftributed in the manner reprefented in the defign; they incline forwards towards the top, their furface is rough, and hatched irregularly with long chops, as are likewife the dyes on the columns, their angles alone being left fmooth and with a fharp outline; which roughnefs, makes an agreeable oppofition to the fmooth finifhing of the other parts. The entablature is Ionic, the architrave compofed of two fafcias only; the frize is fwelled, and the dentil-band is placed immediately on the frize, without any moulding to fupport it; a fingularity which Palladio has repeated in others of his defigns, though it has but an indifferent effect. The pedeftals and baluftrade, are a trifle higher than one third of the columns; the dyes and balufters, are placed immediately on the plat-band that finifhes the bafement: which is not fo well, as if there had been a bafe: but has been done, in order to diminifh the projection. This beautiful window, differs confiderably from the defign given of it in Palladio's book, and is undoubtedly fuperior to it. Fig. 5, is likewife a defign of Palladio's, copied from the Porti Palace at Vicenza; and fig. 6, is, I believe, an original invention of Inigo Jones's, which has been executed in many buildings in England.

I HAVE given in all, nineteen defigns for windows, and for greater variety, the figures 3, 4, 6, 7, 8, 9, in the plate of doors may be employed; they being equally proper either for windows or doors.

Of NICHES and STATUES.

ARCHITECTURE, as Daviler obferves, is indebted to fculpture for a great part of its magnificence; and, as the human body is juftly efteemed the moft perfect original, it has been cuftomary, in all times, to enrich different parts of buildings with reprefentations thereof. Thus the ancients adorned their temples, bafilicas, baths, theatres, and other publick ftructures, with ftatues of their deities, philofophers, heroes, orators, and legiflators; and the moderns ftill preferve the fame cuftom; placing in their churches, palaces, houfes, fquares, gardens, and publick walks, the bufts and ftatues of illuftrious perfonages, or bas-reliefs, and groupes, compofed of various figures, reprefenting memorable occurrences, collected from the hiftories, fables, or traditions of particular times.

SOMETIMES thefe ftatues or groupes, are detached; raifed on pedeftals, and placed contiguous to the walls of buildings; by the fide of flights of fteps or ftairs;

at the angles of terraces; in the middle of rooms, or of court, and publick fquares: but moft frequently they occupy cavities made in walls, which are called niches. Of thefe there are various forts: fome for the reception of ftatues or groups, being formed like arches in their elevation, and either femi-circular, femi-elliptical, or fquare in their plan: others, ufed for the fame purpofe; are of a parallelogram figure, both in the plan and elevation: And others, for the difpofal of bufts or vafes, are circular or oval, fquare or oblong in the elevation, and either funk fquarely or fpherically into the walls.

THE proportion of the former forts of thefe, depends on the characters of the ftatues, or on the general form of the groups placed in them: the loweft, are at leaft, a double fquare in height; and the higheft never exceed twice and one half of their width. With regard to thofe intended for bufts, they are always nearly proportioned alike; being made to fit the fhape of the things placed in them, either a trifle above a fquare in height, or circular, or oval, more or lefs elevated. The manner of decorating high niches, if alone in a compofition; as they are in the principal front of the Old Louvre at Paris: is generally, to enclofe them in a deco-ration or pannel, formed and proportioned like the aperture of a window; which is adorned in the fame manner, and bears the fame proportion to the architecture they accompany, as a regular window would. The nich contained in them, is more or lefs receffed, and is carried quite to the bottom: but on the fides, and at the top, there is a fmall fpace left between the nich and the architrave of the pannel. When niches are intermixed with windows, as they were in the front of Old Somerfet Houfe, towards the river; and as they are at St. Paul's; they may be adorned in the fame manner as the windows; provided the ornaments can be of the fame figure and dimenfions; but when the fpace between two windows is not fufficient to admit of this, it is much better to make the niches entirely plain, or furrounded only with rufticks, than to contract the aperture, and by that means make the decoration narrower than thofe of the windows, as Inigo Jones had done, at Old Somerfet Houfe; or than to adorn the niches in a different manner, as Sir Chriftopher Wren has at St. Paul's: for both thefe expedients are irregular, and occafion confufion. The tops and bottoms of thefe plain niches, muft level with the tops and bottoms of the apertures of the windows, and neither be raifed above or funk below them, as Daviler teaches: for on this, and on all other occafions of the like nature, a con-tinuity of ftraight horizontal lines muft conftantly be aimed at: it being certain, that whenever the eye of the fpectator is forced to dance up and down, and hunt, if I may be allowed fo to call it, for an outline; the operation is always painful: and the images raifed in the mind, are always confufed. To this, in a great meafure, may be attributed the general diflike to the Horfe Guards, in St. James's Park; which is a building of fo complicated a figure, both in plan and elevation, that it is im-poffible to form a diftinct idea of the whole at once.

THE fame kind of plain niches, may likewife be employed in narrower inter-columniations: but care muft withal be taken, not to fqueeze them in, between the columns or pilafters. And therefore, when the interval is not fufficient to afford room for a well proportioned nich, and a fpace on each fide between it and the columns, of at leaft two thirds of a module, it will be better to have no niches at all.

THE fize of the ftatue depends upon the dimenfions of the nich: it fhould neither be fo large as to feem rammed into it, as at Santa Maria Majore in Rome; nor fo fmall as to feem loft in it, as in the Pantheon; where the ftatues do not occupy above three quarters of theh eight of the nich, and only one half of its width. Palladio in arched niches, makes the chin of his ftatues on a level with the top of the impoft: fo that the whole head is in the coved part. In the nave of St. Peter's at Rome, the fame proportion has been obferved; and it has a very good effect. The diftance between the outline of the ftatue, and the fides of the nich, fhould never be lefs than one third of a head, nor more than one half; whether the nich be fquare or arched: and when it is fquare, the diftance from the top of the head to the foffit of the nich, fhould not exceed the diftance left on the fides. The ftatues are generally raifed on a plinth; the height of which, may be from one third to one half of a head: and fometimes, where the niches are very large in propor- tion to the architecture they accompany; as is the cafe when an order comprehends but one ftory; the ftatues may be raifed on fmall pedeftals; by which means they may be made lower than ufual, and yet fill the nich fufficiently; it being to be feared left ftatues of a proper fize to fill fuch large niches, fhould make the columns and entablatures appear trifling. The fame expedient muft alfo be made ufe of, whenever the ftatues in the niches, according to their common proportion, come confiderably larger than thofe placed at the top of the building: A trifling difparity, will not be eafily perceived, on account of the diftance between their refpective fituations; but if it be great, it muft have a very bad effect: and therefore this muft be well attended to, and remedied: either by the abovementioned method, or by entirely omitting ftatues at the top of the building; leaving the baluftrade either free, or placing thereon vafes, trophies, and other fimilar ornaments.

SOME writers there are, who give to thefe ornaments the preference at all times; alledging that it is abfurd to fuppofe horfes and men conftantly ftanding on the roofs, or ftuck up in the niches of a fecond or third ftory, in fituations fhocking and frightful to the imagination. De Cordemoy advifes by all means, to avoid placing ftatues too far from the ground; and Le Clerc is for having nothing but tutelar angels on the tops of houfes.

TO me, there appears fomething ridiculous in this affectation of propriety; and, I believe, it may in general be eftablifhed; that, whenever the image is fo different from the original it reprefents, as not to leave the leaft probability of its being ever miftaken for the real object; this ftrict adherence to propriety, is very fuperfluous.

THE character of the ftatue fhould always correfpond with the character of the architecture with which it is furrounded. Thus, if the order be Doric; Hercules, Jupiter, Pluto, Neptune, Mars, Efculapius, or any male figures, reprefenting beings of a robuft and grave nature, may be introduced: if Ionic; then Apollo, Bacchus, Ceres, Minerva, Mercury: and if Corinthian; Venus and the Graces, Flora, or others of a delicate kind and flender make, may properly have place.

NICHES being defigned as repofitories for ftatues, groups, vafes, or other works of fculpture, muft be contrived to fet off the things they are to contain, to
the

1

2

3

4

5

6

W. Chambers

J. Fougeron sculp.

Designs for Chimney Pieces.

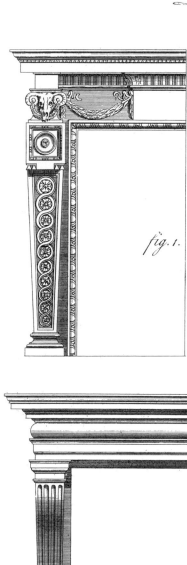

fig. 1.

fig. 2.

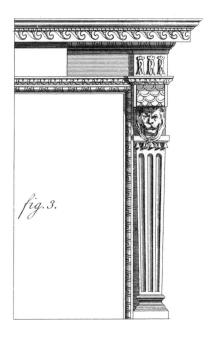

fig. 3.

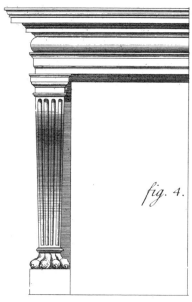

fig. 4.

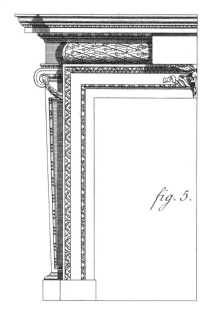

fig. 5.

fig. 6.

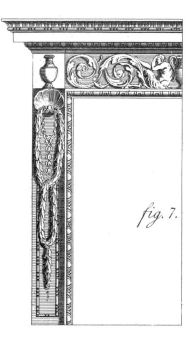

fig. 7.

fig. 8.

fig. 9.

Chambers

T. Miller Sculp.t

the beſt advantage; and therefore, no ornaments ſhould ever be introduced within them, as is ſometimes injudiciouſly practiſed: the cove of the nich being either filled with a large ſcallop ſhell; or the whole inſide, with various kinds of projecting ruſ-ticks; with moulded compartments either raiſed or ſunken; or compoſed of different coloured marbles: for all theſe ſerve to confuſe the outline of the ſtatue or group. It is even wrong to continue an impoſt within the nich; for even that, is of con-ſiderable diſadvantage to the figures; which never appear ſo perfect, as when backed and detached on a plain ſmooth ſurface. An exceſs of ornaments round the nich ſhould likewiſe be avoided; and particularly maſks, buſts, boys, or any repreſenta-tions of the human figure; all which ſerve to divide the attention, and to divert it from the principal object.

THE depth of the nich ſhould always be ſufficient to contain the whole ſtatue, or whatever elſe it is to contain; it being very diſagreeable to ſee ſtatues, or any other weighty objects, with falſe bearings; and ſupported on conſoles or other projections, as is ſometimes done: and in the caſe of niches, the ſide views become exceedingly uncouth; for in theſe, a leg, an arm, a head, in ſhort, thoſe parts alone which project beyond the nich, appear, and look like ſo many fragments, ſtuck irregularly in the wall.

Of CHIMNEY PIECES.

AS the Egyptians, the Greeks, and the Romans, to whom architecture is ſo much indebted in other reſpects, lived in warm climates; where fires in the apartments were ſeldom or never neceſſary; they have thrown but few lights on this branch of architecture. Amongſt the antiquities of Italy, I do not recollect any remains of chimney pieces. Palladio indeed mentions two; the one at Baia, and the other near Civita Vechia; which ſtood in the middle of the rooms, and conſiſted of columns ſupporting architraves, whereon were placed the pyramids or funnels, through which the ſmoak was conveyed: much after the manner of the fire place in the Rotunda of Ranelagh Gardens. Scamozzi takes notice of three ſorts of chimney pieces, uſed in Italy in his time. One of theſe he calls the Roman, the aperture of which is ſurrounded only with a clumſy architrave; another he calls the Venetian, which is likewiſe adorned with an architrave, upon which are placed a frize and cornice, and on the ſides thereof are pilaſters with conſoles. The third ſort he calls a *Padiglione.*

THIS laſt he particularly recommends, where the walls are thin; it being not hollowed into the wall, as both the other ſorts are; but compoſed of a projecting entablature, ſupported by conſoles, terms, or caryatides, on which the pyramid is placed. This ſort of chimney piece is ſtill very common in Italy, the Dutch are very fond of it, and we find it in many of our old Engliſh country houſes. The figures 4 and 9 in the annexed plate, are the lower parts of two of them, deſigned by Palladio, and executed, the one in the Caſa Treviſan, in the iſland of Murano; and the other in the Valmarani Palace at Vicenza.

NEITHER the Italians nor the French, nor indeed any of the continental nations, have ever excelled in compofitions of chimney pieces: I believe we may juftly confider Inigo Jones as the firft who arrived at any great degree of perfection, in this material branch of the art. Others of our Englifh architects, have fince his time, wrought upon his ideas; or furnifhed good inventions of their own: and England, being at prefent poffeffed of many ingenious and very able fculptors, of whom, one chief employment is to execute magnificent chimney pieces, now happily much in vogue; it may be faid, that in this particular we furpafs all other nations; not only in point of expence, but likewife in tafte of defign, and excellence of workmanfhip. Scamozzi mentions a chimney piece, in one of the public buildings at Venice, executed from his defign; as a moft uncommon piece of magnificence: having coft upwards of a thoufand crowns. In this country, a much larger expence is very frequent; and many private gentlemens houfes, in moft parts of England; are furnifhed with feveral chimney pieces, at leaft as valuable.

THE fize of the chimney muft depend upon the dimenfions of the room wherein it is placed. In the fmalleft apartments the width of the aperture is never made lefs than from three foot, to three foot fix inches: in rooms from twenty to twenty-four foot fquare, or of equal fuperficial dimenfions, it may be four foot wide; in thofe of twenty-five to thirty, from four to four and a half; and in fuch as exceed thefe dimenfions, the aperture may be extended to five, or five foot fix inches: but fhould the room be extremely large, (as is frequently the cafe of halls, galleries, and falons,) and one chimney of thefe laft dimenfions, neither afford fufficient heat to warm the room, nor fufficient fpace round it for the company; it will be much more convenient, and far handfomer; to have two chimney pieces of a moderate fize, than a fingle one exceedingly large; all the parts of which, would appear clumfy and difproportioned to the other decorations of the room.

THE chimney fhould always be fituated fo, as to be immediately feen by thofe who enter; that they may not have the perfons already in the room, who are gene-rally feated about the fire, to fearch for. The middle of the fide partition wall, is the propereft place in halls, falons, and other rooms of paffage; to which the principal entrances are, commonly, in the middle of the front, or of the back wall: but in drawing rooms, dreffing rooms, and the like, the middle of the back wall is the beft fituation; the chimney being then fartheft removed from the doors of com-munication. The cafe is the fame with refpect to galleries and libraries, whofe doors of entrance are generally either at one, or at both ends. In bed chambers the chimney is always placed in the middle of one of the fide partition walls; and in clofets, or other very fmall places, it is, to fave room, fometimes placed in one corner.

WHENEVER two chimnies are introduced in the fame room, they muft be regularly placed, either directly facing each other, if in different walls; or at equal diftances from the center of the wall, in which they both are placed. The Italians frequently put their chimnies in the front walls, between the windows; for the benefit of looking out while fitting by the fire: but this muft be avoided; for by fo doing that fide of the room becomes crouded with ornaments, and the other fides are left too bare; the front walls are much weakened by the funnels; and the

chimney

chimney fhafts at the top of the building, which muft neceffarily be carried higher than the ridges of the roofs, have from their great length, a very difagreeable effect: and are very liable to be blown down.

In large buildings, where the walls are of a confiderable thicknefs, the funnels are carried up in the thicknefs of the wall; but in fmall ones, this cannot be done: the flues and chimney pieces, muft neceffarily advance forward into the rooms; which, when the break is confiderable, has a very bad effect: and therefore, where room can be fpared, it will always be beft, either in fhow or ftate apartments; to make niches or arched receffes on each fide: and in lodging rooms; preffes or clofets, either covered with the paper, or finifhed in any manner fuited to the reft of the room. By thefe means, the cornice, or entablature of the room, may be carried round without breaks; the cieling be perfectly regular; and the chimney piece have no more apparent projection, than may be neceffary, to give to its ornaments their proper relief.

The proportion of the apertures of chimney pieces, of a moderate fize, is generally near a fquare: in fmall ones a trifle higher, and in large ones fomewhat lower. Their ornaments confift of architraves, frizes, cornices, columns, pilafters, terms, caryatides, confoles, and all kinds of ornaments of fculpture, reprefenting animal or vegetable productions of nature; likewife vafes, pateras, trophies of various kinds, and inftruments or fymbols of religion, arts, arms, letters and commerce. In defigning them, regard muft be had to the nature of the place where they are to be employed. Such as are intended for halls, guard rooms, falons, galleries, and other confiderable places; muft be compofed of large parts, few in number, of diftinct and fimple forms, and having a bold relief: but chimney pieces for drawing rooms, dreffing rooms, bed chambers, and fuch like; may be of a more delicate and complicated compofition. The workmanfhip of all chimney pieces muft be perfectly well finifhed, like all other objects liable to a clofe infpection: and the ornaments, figures, and profiles; both in form, proportions, and quantity, muft be fuited to the other parts of the room; and be allufive to the ufes for which it is intended. All nudities, and indecent reprefentations muft be avoided both in chimney pieces and in every other ornament of apartments, to which children, ladies, and other modeft grave perfons, have conftant recourfe: together with all reprefentations capable of exciting horror, grief, difguft, or any gloomy unpleafing fenfations.

Chimney pieces, are either made of ftone, of marble, or of a mixture of thefe; with wood, fcagliola, or-moulu, or fome other unfragile fubftances. Thofe of marble are moft coftly, but they are alfo moft elegant; and the only ones, ufed in high finifhed apartments: where they are feen either of white, or variegated marbles, fometimes inlaid and decorated, with the materials juft mentioned. All their ornaments, figures, or profiles, are to be made of the pure white fort, but their frizes, tablets, pannels, fhafts of columns, and other plain parts, may be of party-coloured marbles, fuch as the yellow of Sienna, the Brocatello of Spain, the Diafpers of Sicily, and many other modern as well as antique marbles, frequently to be had in England. Feftoons of flowers, trophies and foliages, frets and other fuch decorations, cut in white ftatuary marble and fixed on grounds of thefe, have a very

Q q q   good

good effect. But there should never be above two, or at the utmost three different forts of colours in the fame chimney piece; all brilliant, and harmonizing with each other.

IN the two annexed plates are eleven different designs for chimney pieces; some of them composed by Palladio and Inigo Jones, the rest by me. Their proportions may be gathered from the designs, which are executed with tolerable accuracy. Some other chimney pieces will be found among the designs at the end of the book.

THE shafts of the chimney funnels should be regularly disposed on the roofs of buildings, and all of them be made of the fame height, breadth, and figure. They are handsomest when made of stone, of a cubical figure, and finished with a light cornice, composed of few mouldings. Scamozzi recommends obelisks and vases; Serlio has given several designs for decorating the tops of funnels, which resemble towers; and Sir John Vanbrugh frequently converted his into castles: as may be seen at Blenheim, Castle Howard, and others of his numerous stately works.

NEITHER the Italians above cited, nor the Englishman, have been very successful in their designs; but upon the fame ideas, good ones might be composed; and made to terminate a structure with grace and propriety.

Of PROFILES for DOORS, WINDOWS, NICHES, CHIMNEY PIECES, &c.

WHEN any of the abovementioned objects are very large, the profiles of the orders are employed in their decoration: but when small, as is more frequently the cafe; other profiles, of a lefs complicated figure are ufed. Palladio has in his first book, given designs of several; three of which are exhibited in the annexed plate. Fig. 1, is the richest of the three, and very proper for windows, or doors, of the Corinthian order. The account given by that author of its proportions being very tedious and somewhat confused, is here omitted. But all the operations for proportioning the different members by equal parts, are expressed on the design.

FIG. 2, may be employed in an Ionic, or rich Doric order. Its architrave is to be divided into four parts; the frize to be made equal to three, the cornice to five of these parts. For the subdivisions fee the plate, or consult Palladio's book: his whole text upon so flight a subject, being too long to be inserted here.

FIG. 3, is proper in a Doric order. Its divisions are lefs complicated than the former two, and may easily be collected from the design.

IN the beginning of this work, I have pointed out the trouble and tediousness of determining proportions by equal parts; those who perufe the three paragraphs

in

W. Chambers Architectus

P. Fourdrinier Sculp.

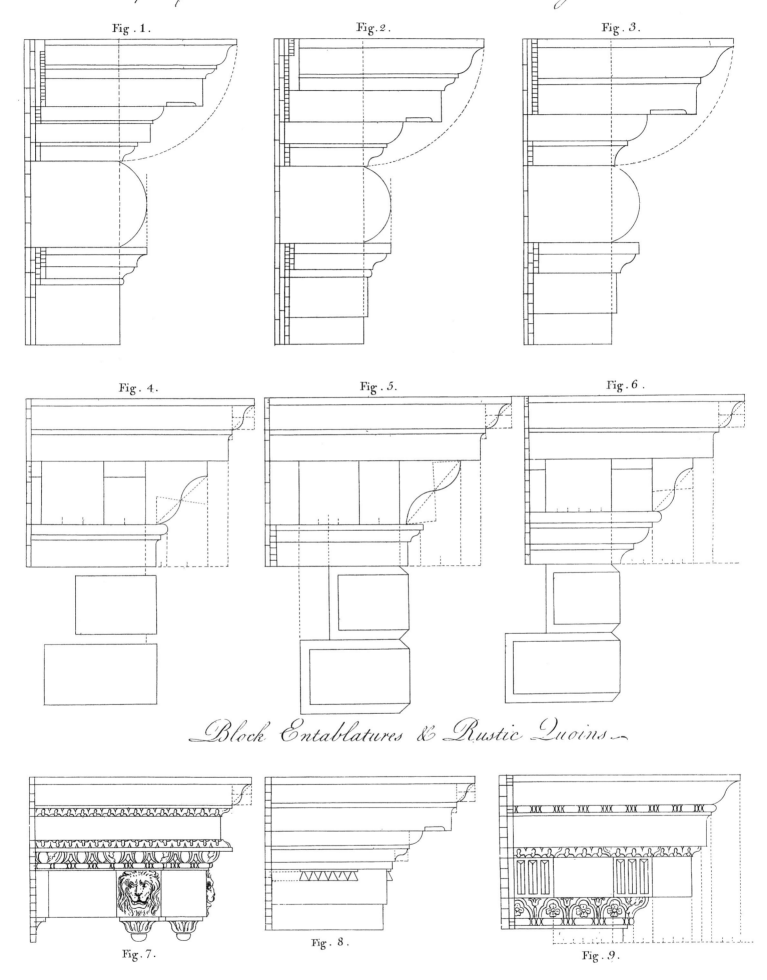

Profiles for Windows, Doors, Niches, or Chimney Pieces.

Fig. 1.   Fig. 2.   Fig. 3.

Fig. 4.   Fig. 5.   Fig. 6.

Block Entablatures & Rustic Quoins.

Fig. 7.   Fig. 8.   Fig. 9.

Block Cornice.   Architrave Cornice.   Block Cornice.

J. Jandon Delin.   J. Miller sculp.

in Palladio's work, employed in proportioning the three cornices juft mentioned, will, I think, have few doubts remaining upon that fubject. And for my own part, though I fee no objection to Palladio's great proportions, which are proper, in moft cafes, where fwelled frizes are ufed; and the architrave of the door, or window, is not lefs, nor much exceeds, one fixth of the width of the aperture; yet, for the parts, I venture to prefer employing the entablatures of the different orders of architecture, proportioned as they are; with the rejection of fuch mouldings or members as feem fuperfluous, and which, if introduced, would render the object confufed; and from the fmallnefs of its dimenfion, too diminutive to ftand a comparifon with other parts of the compofition.

THUS, for inftance, if the order in which the door, window, or nich is placed, be Compofite or Corinthian; the Compofite, or Corinthian entablature may be ufed for their dreffings, with the omiffion of either dentils or modillions. The Compofite architrave may be ufed as it is, but the Corinthian fhould be divefted of the lower fafcia, with the little aftragal by which it is feparated from the fafcia directly above it.

IN the Ionic order, the Ionic entablature may on fome occafions be ufed as it is, to drefs the doors and windows; provided the dentils be not cut: but in moft cafes, it will be propereft to leave out the dentil band, with the aftragal above it; and ftrengthen the fillet; which then, will make the feparation between the ovolo and the bottom moulding.

THE profiles of doors, of windows, of niches, and in fhort; the profiles of all fubfervient parts; muft not only be lefs in the whole, but likewife in each particular member, than thofe of the orders employed in the fame compofition: or than the cornice or entablature, which ferves as a finifhing to the whole defign: it being among the groffeft of errors, to make any ornaments belonging to the parts, more predominant than thofe which are particularly appropriated, to the embellifhment of the whole mafs, as Pietro da Cortona has done at St. Carlo in the Corfo at Rome, where the profiles of the great door, on the infide of the church, are confiderably larger than thofe of the order in which that door is contained.

THE ufual proportion given to architraves of outfide windows, niches, or doors, is from one feventh to one fifth of the width of the aperture. Where the architrave is fupported on each fide by pilafters, as is frequently the cafe; or where rufticks are applied, it may be a feventh, and fhould never exceed a fixth of the width of the aperture; but whenever it is unaccompanied, it ought never to be lefs than one fixth, nor fhould it ever exceed one fifth thereof. If the frizes be fwelled, their dimenfions, as well as thofe of the cornices, may be determined as Palladio directs; by dividing the breadth of the architrave into four parts, and giving three of thefe parts to the height of the frize, and five of them to that of the cornice: but if the frize be flat and upright, its height muft be equal to the breadth of the architrave.

THE pilafters which accompany the architrave, may be from one half to two thirds of its breadth. They commonly fupport confoles of various forms, equally broad with themfelves, and in length, generally from one half, to two thirds of the

R r r width

width of the aperture. Thefe fupport the corona of the cornice above, and reft below on mafks, fhells, leaves, bells, or drops.

IN interior decorations, where the eye is nearer the objects than in exterior; every thing fhould be more delicate, and calculated for clofer infpection; the door architraves there fhould never exceed a fixth of the aperture; and the frize and cornice may be proportioned to them, as is before directed.

IT is not ufual to employ either frize or cornice over infide windows, as they would ftand in the way of the curtains; and though the windows are in general made wider than the doors, their architraves are never made larger; on the contrary, they are often, for the advantage of having more room in the piers for large glaffes, reduced to three or four mouldings, furrounding the aperture, and forming boxes for the fhutters to fold into.

WITH refpect to chimney pieces, they are of fuch various compofitions; and fo great a latitude is allowed the compofer; that little can be determined concerning them. In general, their architraves fhould not be lefs than one fixth, nor exceed one fifth of the aperture's width; their frizes may be from two thirds to three fourths of the architrave, and their cornices fhould feldom or never be higher than the frize, but on moft occafions fomewhat lower; fince when they are large, and project much, they become inconvenient, and dangerous to the heads of the company.

Of BLOCK CORNICES and EXTRANEOUS ENTABLATURES.

BLOCK CORNICES and entablatures, are frequently ufed to finifh plain buildings, where none of the regular orders have been employed. Of this kind there is a very beautiful one compofed by Vignola, much ufed in Italy, and employed by Sir Chriftopher Wren to finifh the fecond order of St. Paul's. I have given a defign of it in the fecond plate of the Compofite order, with the meafures of all its parts, determined according to Vignola's method, by a module divided into eighteen minutes. When this entablature is ufed to finifh a plain building, the whole height is found by dividing the height of the whole front into eleven parts; one of which muft be given to the entablature, and the remaining ten to the reft of the front. And when it is employed to finifh an order; which however, may as well be let alone; it muft be fomewhat lefs in proportion to the columns, than a regular entablature would be: becaufe its parts are larger. The angles of the building, where this entablature is ufed, may be adorned with quoins; the fhort ones about a module long, and the long ones a module and a half; the height of each being to be, about three quarters of a module, including the joint.

AMONG the profiles for windows, &c. there are three other block entablatures, of a fimpler make; the fecond of which, Palladio has executed in a couple of houfes: the one at Vivaro, and the other at Monteccio, villages of the Vicentine. The other

two

two are not very different from that: the meafures of all of them, are taken from Mr. Gibbs's rules; and may eafily be collected from the defigns. Thefe entablatures need not exceed one thirteenth of the whole height of the front, nor fhould they ever be much lefs than one fifteenth. Fig. 7 and 9, in the fame plate, are two block cornices; the former of which is executed in a palace at Milan, and the other by Raphael, at a houfe in the Lungara at Rome: the height of thefe, need never exceed one fixteenth part of the whole front, nor fhould it be lefs than one eighteenth. Fig. 8, is an architrave cornice, which M. Angelo, Baldaffar Peruzzi, and Palladio, have employed in fome of their compofitions. This kind of profile is a proper finifhing for columns fupporting the archivolts of arches, as it approaches nearer the proportion of an impoft, than a regular entablature would: its height may be one eighth of the height of the column.

Of the PROPORTIONS of ROOMS.

THE proportions of rooms depend in a great meafure, on their ufe, and actual dimenfions: but with regard to beauty, all figures from a fquare to a fefquialteral, may be employed for the plan. Inigo Jones, and other great architects, have fometimes even exceeded this proportion, and extended the plan to a double fquare: but the great difparity between the width and length of this figure, renders it impoffible to fuit the height to both: the end views will appear too high, and the fide ones too low.

IT may perhaps to fome appear abfurd to make this objection; when galleries are frequently three, four, or five times as long as they are wide: but it muft be obferved, that, in this cafe, the extraordinary length renders it impoffible for the eye to take in the whole extent at once; and therefore the comparifon between the height and length, can never be made.

THE heights of rooms depend upon their figure: flat ceiled ones may be lower than thofe that are coved. If their plan be a fquare, their height fhould not exceed five fixths of the fide, nor be lefs than four fifths; and when it is an oblong, their height may be equal to their width. But coved rooms if fquare, muft be as high as broad, and when oblong, their height may be equal to their width; more one fifth, one quarter, or even one third, of the difference between the length and width: and galleries fhould, at the very leaft, be in height one and one third of their width, and at the moft, one and a half, or one and three fifths. Thefe proportions are all perfectly good, as they obviate any idea of confinement, and, at the fame time, render it practicable, for thofe who are in the room, to examine the figure and ornaments of the ceiling, without either pain or difficulty.

IT is not, however, always poffible to obferve exactly thefe proportions. In dwelling houfes, the height of all the rooms on the fame floor is generally the fame, though their extent be different; which renders it extremely difficult in large buildings, where there are a great number of different fized rooms, to proportion all

of

of them well. The ufual method, in buildings where beauty and magnificence are preferred to œconomy, is to raife the halls, falons, and galleries, higher than the other rooms, by making them occupy two ftories: to make the drawing rooms, or other largeft rooms, with flat cielings: to cove the middle fized ones a third, a quarter, or a fifth of their height, according as it is more or lefs exceffive: and in the fmalleft apartments, where even the higheft coves are not fufficient to render the proportion tolerable; it is ufual to contrive mezzanins above them: which afford fervants lodging rooms, baths, powdering rooms, wardrobes, and the like; fo much the more convenient, as they are near the ftate apartments, and of private accefs. The Earl of Leicefter's houfe at Holkham, is a mafter-piece in this refpect; as well as in many others: the diftribution of the plan, in particular, deferves much commendation; and does great credit to the memory of Mr. Kent: it being exceedingly well contrived, both for ftate and convenience. And, with regard to the whole interior decoration, it may certainly vie, in point either of magnificence, or tafte, with any thing now fubfiftent in England.

SINCE writing the above, thirty years have elapfed; and a very different ftile of decoration has been introduced: which, for richnefs and neatnefs of execution, far furpaffes any thing done at that time. The executive powers of our workmen are certainly much improved; yet, it is far from certain, that the tafte is better now, than it was then. That ftile, though fomewhat heavy, was great; calculated to ftrike at the inftant; and although the ornaments were neither fo varied, nor fo numerous as now; they had a more powerful effect: becaufe more boldly marked, lefs complicated in their forms, and lefs profufely applied. They were eafily perceptible without a microfcope, and could not be miftaken for filigrane toy work. Content with the ftores, which the refined ages of antiquity had left them, the architects of that day; ranfacked not the works of barbarous times; nor the port-folios of whimfical compofers; for boyifh conceits, and triflingly complicated ornaments.

THE coldnefs of our Englifh climate, and the frugality of thofe who build; are ftrong objections to high rooms: fo that we frequently fee the moft magnificent apartments, not above fifteen, fixteen, or at moft eighteen foot high; though the extent of the rooms would require a much more confiderable elevation. This practice is however not to be imitated, where beauty, or effect are aimed at. There are many good expedients for warming rooms, however fpacious or lofty; and to confider expence, in that particular alone, is an ill judged piece of parfimony; as it renders all other expence employed in the decoration of the room, ineffectual.

WHEN rooms are adorned with an entire order, the entablature fhould never exceed one fixth of the whole height, nor be much lefs than one feventh in flat ceiled rooms; and one fixth or feventh of the upright part in fuch as are coved. And, when there are neither columns nor pilafters in the decoration, but an entablature alone; its height fhould not be above one feventh or eighth of thefe heights. If rooms are finifhed with a fimple cornice, it ought never to exceed one fifteenth, nor ever be lefs than one twentieth part of the abovementioned heights: and when there is a frize added to the cornice, with an aftragal or other mouldings under it, as is fometimes cuftomary; the whole height of thefe, together with the cornice, fhould never exceed one eighth of the upright height of the room. In general, all
profiles

profiles within a building, muſt be more delicate than thoſe on the outſide: the architraves of the doors and windows ſhould never exceed one ſixth of the breadth of the aperture; on moſt occaſions, one ſeventh will be ſufficient; and all other parts muſt be diminiſhed proportionably.

Of   C I E L I N G S.

CIELINGS are either flat, or coved in different manners. The ſimpleſt of the flat kind are thoſe adorned with large compartments, either let into the cieling or being fluſh with its ſurface, and ſurrounded with one or ſeveral mouldings, as repreſented in the firſt, ſecond, and tenth, figures of the firſt plate of cielings: and when ſome of the mouldings which ſurround the compartments are enriched, and ſome of the compartments adorned with well executed foliages, or other ſtucco or painted ornaments, ſuch cielings have a very good effect; they are very proper for common dwelling houſes, and for all low apartments. Their ornaments and mouldings do not require a bold relief, but being near the eye, they muſt be finiſhed with taſte and neatneſs. For higher rooms, the kind of flat cielings repreſented in the third, fourth, ſeventh, and eighth figures, of the ſame plate; and in one of the figures of the ſecond plate, are more proper; as they have a much bolder relief. The uſe of theſe is frequent, both in Italy and England. They ſeem to be compoſed of various beams, framed into each other, and forming compartments of different geometrical figures. The deſigns which I have given, are all for ſquare cielings: but oblong, or thoſe of any other form, may be comparted in the ſame manner; the figures of the compartments being varied according to the fancy of the compoſer, and made either polygonal, circular, or ellyptical. The ſides of the beams forming theſe compartments, are generally adorned with mouldings; and repreſent, either a ſimple architrave, or an architrave cornice, according to the ſize of the compartments, and the height of the room. Sometimes the larger compartments are deeper than the ſmall ones, with which they are accompanied, and furrounded with a fuller profile: as in the flat cieling of the ſecond plate; which is a deſign of Baldaſſar Peruzzi, executed in the veſtibule of the Maſſimi Palace at Rome. The ſoffits of the beams are ſeldom left plain, but are adorned with *Guillochis* or frets of various kinds, of which I have given a good number of deſigns in the firſt and ſecond plates of cielings: and when the utmoſt degree of richneſs in the decoration is aimed at, the ground of the compartments is likewiſe adorned; either with paintings, or with baſſo relievos, repreſenting grotefque figures, foliages, feſtoons, tripods, vaſes, and the like; of which there are ſome deſigns in the firſt plate of cielings.

COVED CIELINGS are more expenſive than flat ones; but they are likewiſe more beautiful, ſufceptible of a greater variety of decorations, and in general, more ſplendid. They are promiſcuouſly employed in large or ſmall rooms, and occupy from one fifth to one third of the height of the room, according as that height is more or leſs conſiderable. If the room is low in proportion to its width, the cove muſt likewiſe be low; and when it is high, the cove muſt likewiſe be ſo: by which means the exceſs of height will be rendered leſs perceptible. But, where the

T t t   architect

architect is at liberty to proportion the height of the room to its fuperficial dimenfions, the moft eligible proportion for the cove, is one quarter of the whole height. In parallelogram figured rooms, the middle of the cieling is generally formed into a large flat pannel; as in the fifth and fixth figures of the firft plate of cielings; which is either left plain, or painted; adorned with coffers and rofes, or compartments, or with grotefque ornaments; according as the decoration is to be rich or fimple. This pannel, with the border that furrounds it, may occupy from one half to three fifths of the breadth of the room. The form of the cove is, generally, either a quadrant of a circle, or of an ellypfis, taking its rife a little above the cornice, and finifhing at the border furrounding the great center pannel; that fo the whole curve may be feen from the end of the room. This border is made to project fomewhat beyond the cove on the outfide, and on the fide towards the pannel, it is ufually made of a fufficient depth to admit the profile of an architrave, or of an architrave cornice.

THE coved part of the cieling, may either be left plain, as in one of the above-mentioned defigns; or adorned, as in the other; either, in the manner there reprefented, or in any other of the fame kind; or elfe with coffers of different polygonal figures, of which there is a great variety in the third plate of cielings; very proper, both for this purpofe, and likewife to adorn flat cielings.

IN England, circular rooms are not much in ufe: but they are neverthelefs very beautiful. Their height muft be the fame as that of fquare rooms: their cielings may be flat, but they are handfomer when coved, or of a concave form, whether of a femi-circular, or femi-ellyptical profile. In the fourth plate of cielings, I have given five different defigns for them, compofed by M. Angelo, Bartolomeo Amanato, Baldaffar Peruzzi, and Algardi: they are executed in the Capitol, the Mattei Palace, and the villa Pamphilia at Rome. Moft forts of compartments and coffers are likewife very proper for thefe circular coves; as well as for coves of octagonal, or other polygonal plans.

Arcs Doubleaux, or, as Mr. Gibbs calls them, foffits of arches, are frequently enriched. When narrow, their ornaments confift of *Guillochis* or frets: but when broad, they are adorned in a variety of different manners. I have given feveral defigns of them compofed by Raphael, Amanato, and M. Angelo, which are executed at St. Peter's, at the Pallazzo Mattei, and the villa Madama near Rome.

WHEN the profiles, or other parts of a room are gilt, the cieling muft likewife be fo; and that, full as profufely as the reft. The ufual method here, is to gild all the ornaments, and to leave the grounds white, pearl, ftraw colour, light blue, or of any other tint proper to fet off the gilding and ornaments to the beft advantage: but I have frequently feen that practice reverfed with more fuccefs, by gilding the grounds, and leaving the foliages white, party-coloured, or ftreaked with gold.

IT requires much judgment, to diftribute either gold or colours properly. Great care muft be taken not to leave fome places dull or bare, while others are fo much covered, that they appear like lumps of gold, or beds of gaudy flowers: in general, it is to be obferved, that wherever the gilding or colouring, tends in the leaft, to

confufe

Enrichments for Soffits of Arches, or Arcs Doubleaux.

Grignion Sculp.

Ornaments for Ceilings.

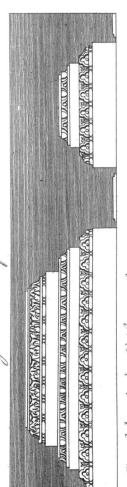

Enrichments for a Flat Ceiling.

Frets, or Guillochis of Various Sorts.

Chambers Delin.

Profile of the Ceiling above.

Ornaments for Ceilings.

Designs for flat Ceilings.

Designs for flat Ceilings.

Designs for Coved Ceilings.

Designs for flat Ceilings.

Soffits of Arches.

Design for a flat Ceiling.

Soffits of Arches.

Soffit of an Arch.

Various Ornaments for the Compartments of Ceilings.

W. Chambers delin.

C. Grignion sculp.

Ornaments for Circular Coved Ceilings &c.

Compartments for Coved Ceilings.

Octagons and Squares.

Hexagons and Lozenges.

Squares with Enriched Borders.

Squares, Octagons & Hexagons.

Octagons, Hexagons and Crosses.

Hexagons & Triangles.

Lozenges, with Enriched Borders.

Squares & Enwreathed Circles.

Squares & Stars, with Fleurons &c.

W. Chambers delin.

P. Mazel sculp.

confufe the defign, to give it a clumfy appearance, or to render the outline of any part indiſtinct; they are certainly ill employed.

PAINTED CIELINGS, which conſtitute one of the great embellifhments of Italian and French ſtructures, and in which, the greateſt maſters have difplayed their utmoſt abilities; are not in ufe among us. For one cannot fuffer to go by fo high a name, the trifling, gaudy, cielings now in fafhion: which, compofed as they are of little rounds, fquares, octagons, hexagons and ovals; excite no other idea, than that of a defert: upon the plates of which are difhed out, bad copies of indifferent antiques. They certainly have neither fancy, taſte, fplendour, execution, nor any other ſtriking quality to recommend them. But fhould the true ſtile of fuch compofitions ever come into fafhion, we might hope to fee hiſtory painting flourifh in England. Till then, it cannot reafonably be expected, while religion has banifhed pictures from churches, and the prejudices of connoiffeurs have excluded modern paintings from our houfes.

IT muſt however be allowed, that, fince the firſt publication of this book, the art of painting has taken a very different turn. At that time, little encouragement was afforded to any, but portrait painters; and to confefs the truth, very few, even of thefe, deferved much to be encouraged: but the inſtitution of a Royal Academy for the regular inſtruction of artiſts; the eſtablifhment of an exhibition under royal patronage, in which they are admitted to ſtand competitors for fame, with thofe moſt famed: the encouragement held forth to them by His Majeſty, the nobility, the gentry, and even by fome of their own profeffion: has roufed the genius, of our Englifh artiſts; ſtimulated their ambition; brightned up their profpects. Many of them now vie with the firſt of their cotemporaries in Italy, in France, or elfe-where: and fhould encouragement become yet more generally diffufed; it might reafonably be conjectured, from the rapid ſtrides already made towards perfection; that in the courfe of a few years, the Englifh fchool might afpire to ſtand unrivalled: or be at leaſt equal in fame, to any other of its time.

I HAVE now gone through the principal branches of the decorative part of architecture, which was all originally intended; my purpofe having then been to referve for a future occafion, whatever related to the convenience, ſtrength, or eco-nomical management of buildings. Ignorant how far I might be equal to the taſk undertaken, it feemed prefumptuous to come upon the publick with a bulky per-formance; poffibly of no merit: and it would have been imprudent to rifque my own fortune, in a bufinefs which might have been ruinous to me, without being profitable to others. What then was publifhed, I offered as a fpecimen of that which was farther intended, determined to be ruled by its reception, either to proceed or to defiſt.

THE concife manner in which it has been attempted to treat the fubject of the prefent publication, will, it is hoped, be fome inducement to perfons of diſtinction, to perufe the performance: and if the precepts are as clear and fatisfactory, as the author intended; the work may be of ufe, even to gentlemen; travellers in parti-cular; moſt of whom, from utter ignorance in architecture, as well as in other arts; have heretofore loſt half the fruits of their journies, returned unacquainted with the

U u u   moſt

moſt valued productions of the countries they had viſited; and perfectly diſſatisfied with expeditions, from which they had derived very little uſeful inſtruction, or real amuſement.

DESIGNS *for* CASINES, TEMPLES, GATES, DOORS, &c.

IN the firſt and ſecond plates, are the elevation and plans of a caſine erected at Marino, a villa belonging to the Earl of Charlemont, near Dublin.

THIS deſign was originally one of the end pavillions of a conſiderable compoſition, made ſoon after my return from Italy, for Edwyn Laſcells, Eſq; now Lord Harwood: which, among many others, his Lordſhip procured for Harwood Houſe. The ſame compoſition, with conſiderable variations, was afterwards wrought to the extent of a palace, for Her late Majeſty, the Dowager Queen of Sweden. The only part however, of either of the large deſigns which has been executed, is the preſent little publication, which was built by Mr. Verpyle with great neatneſs and taſte, after models made here and inſtructions ſent from hence.

IN the third plate are the plans and elevation of a caſine, built ſome years ago at Wilton, the ſeat of the Earl of Pembroke in Wiltſhire. It conſiſts of a ſmall ſalon and portico above, and of a little kitchen or ſervants waiting room below.

IN the fourth plate is the elevation of a hunting pavillion, deſigned many years ago for the Earl of Aileſbury: then Lord Bruce.

IN the fifth plate is a plan of the ſaid pavillion, and alſo of a kind of circular monopteros temple with two rooms adjoining to it, compoſed originally for Henry Willoughby, Eſq; now, Lord Middleton. The deſign was afterwards conſiderably augmented in its plan, and contrived for the reception of ſtatues and other valuable antiquities, belonging to the Earl of Charlemont's collection at Marino.

THE ſixth plate, exhibits an elevation of the ſaid circular monopteros compoſition.

IN the ſeventh plate are the elevation and plan of an octagon Doric temple, deſigned while at Florence, for the late Earl of Tylney: and propoſed to be executed in his Lordſhip's gardens at Wanſtead.

THE eighth plate exhibits the ſame diſpoſition, decorated in a different manner.

IN the ninth plate are deſigns of a Corinthian proſtyle temple, made for Her late Royal Highneſs the Princeſs Dowager of Wales, and propoſed to be erected in the gardens of Kew.

IN the tenth plate are the plan and elevation of a defign made for Sir Thomas Kennedy, late Earl of Caffils, with intention to be erected at his Lordfhip's feat in Scotland.

IN the eleventh plate are the plan and elevation of a maufoleum to the memory of Pope, Gay, and Swift; defigned for Kew Gardens.

IN the twelfth plate are two doors defigned by Andrea Palladio, and ferving as entrances to a garden near the Theatre at Vicenza.

IN the thirteenth plate is a Tufcan gate, imitated from one defigned by Palladio, which ferves as a back entrance to the Publick Garden at Vicenza. I have executed nearly the fame defign with additions at Blenheim: where it ferves as the principal entrance to the kitchen garden.

IN the fourteenth plate is the principal front and plan of a triumphal arch, compofed by me, and executed under my direction at Wilton.

IN the fifteenth plate are defigns of a ruftick Tufcan gate, imitated from Inigo Jones's York Stairs. An ancient infcription was by miftake put into the tablet, which could not be effaced without fpoiling the plate. I have fince executed nearly the fame defign in the embankment of Somerfet-Place, with the addition of lions over the columns of the order, medallions and vafes in the fide intercolumniations, and pedeftals under the columns: which, with the fteps down to the Thames, confiderably improve and augment the confequence of the compofition.

IN the fixteenth plate is a defign made by defire of his Grace the Duke of Richmond, for an entrance to Privy Garden, Whitehall.

IN the feventeenth plate is a tripod, defigned for his Grace the Duke of Marlborough, executed by Mr. Witton in Portland ftone, and erected in the gardens at Blenheim.

IN the eighteenth plate are various ornamental utenfils, defigned for the Earl of Charlemont, for Lord Melbourne, and for fome decorations in my own houfe.

IN the nineteenth plate are two defigns of chimney pieces, the one intended for Windfor Caftle, the other for Melbourne Houfe in Piccadilly.

A TWENTIETH plate was defigned, and partly engraved; it confifted of ornamental utenfils, invented for their Majefties, for his Grace the Duke of Marlborough, and for the Royal Academy. But the engraver Mr. Charles Grignion, finding it would have required more time to finifh in the manner he wifhed, than his other avocations would afford, declined to proceed: and the impoffibility of finding an equally able ornamental hand, to finifh what he had fo well begun, obliged me, though very reluctantly, to lay the publication afide.

F I N I S.

DIRECTIONS to the BINDER.

The PLATES reprefenting

PRIMITIVE BUILDINGS muft front page 1. Regular Mouldings, &c. p. 3. Orders of the Ancients, &c. p. 8. Tufcan Order, p. 15. Doric Order, p. 17. Doric Entablatures, p. 21. Ionic Order, p. 23. Goldman's Volutes, p. 24. Ionic Entablatures, p. 25. Compofite Order, p. 26. Compofite Entablatures, and Capitals, p. 28. Corinthian Order, p 29. Pilafter Capitals, p. 31. Perfians and Caryatides, p. 36. Intercolumniations, p. 42. Arches without Pedeftals, p. 46. Arches with Pedeftals, p. 48. Various Sorts of Arcades, p. 50. Columns upon Columns, p. 51. Arches upon Arches, p. 54. Pediments, &c. p. 58. Balufters, p. 61. Gates and Piers, p. 63. Doors, p. 65. Four Windows, p. 69. Nine Windows, p. 71. Six Windows, p. 72. Defigns for Chimney Pieces, p. 77. Lord Charlemont's Chimney Pieces, p. 79. Profiles for Doors, &c. p. 80. Ornaments for Flat Cielings, and for the Compartments of Cielings, p. 83. Enrichments for a Flat Cieling, and for Soffits of Arches, &c. p. 84. After which the Plate of Compartments, for Coved Cielings; and then that of Ornaments for Circular Coved Cielings.

Order of the DESIGNS at the End of the Book.

1ft. Elevation of Lord Charlemont's Cafine. 2d. Plans of the fame. 3d. Lord Pembroke's Cafine. 4th. Elevation of Lord Bruce's Cafine. 5th. Plan of the fame, and of Mr. Willoughby's Temple. 6th. Elevation of Mr. Willoughby's Temple. 7th. Lord Tilney's Temple. 8th. Defign infcribed to I. Hall Stevenfon, Efq; 9th. Defign infcribed to T. Worfley, Efq; 10th. Earl of Caffel's Defign. 11th. Defign infcribed to Sir Charles Hotham, Bart. 12th. Defign infcribed to Robert Wood, Efq; 13th. Defign infcribed to the Hon. Mr. Ward. 14th. Lord Pembroke's Triumphal Arch. 15th. Defign infcribed to Thomas Brand, Efq; 16th. Defign infcribed to his Grace the Duke of Richmond. 17th. Tripod. 18th. Ornamental Utenfils. 19th. Two Chimney Pieces for Windfor Caftle and Melbourne Houfe.

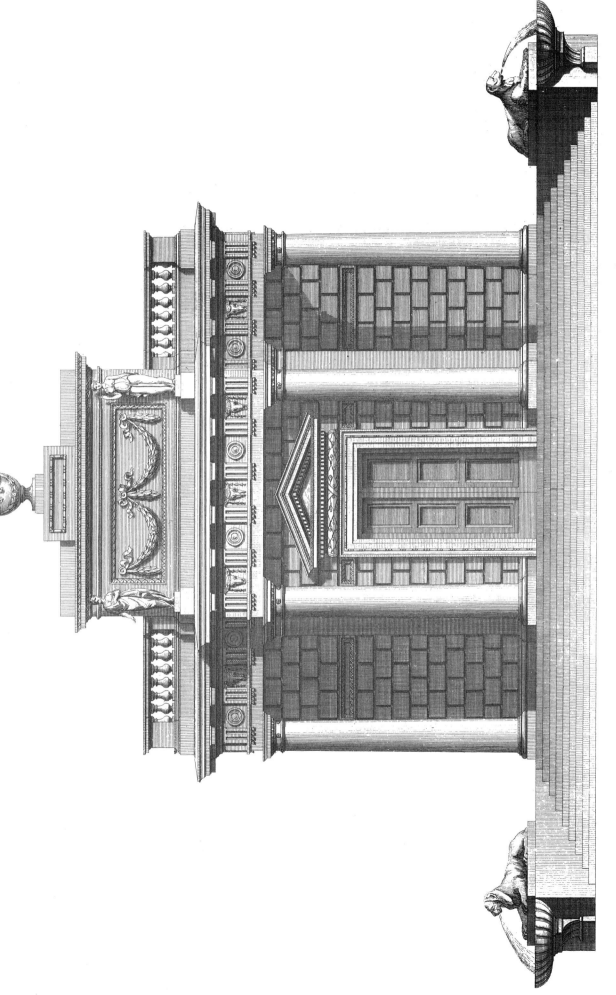

To the Lord Viscount Charlemont This Design of his Lordship's Casine at Marino.
is humbly Inscribed by his Lordships   most Obedient Servant, William Chambers.

W. Chambers Architect.

P. Fourdrinier Sculp.

5 10 15 20 25 30 Feet

Principal floor.

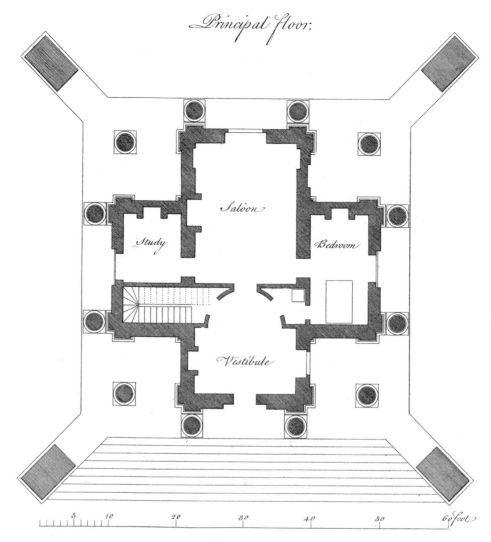

Saloon

Study

Bedroom

Vestibule

5 10 20 30 40 50 60 foot.

Cellar Story.

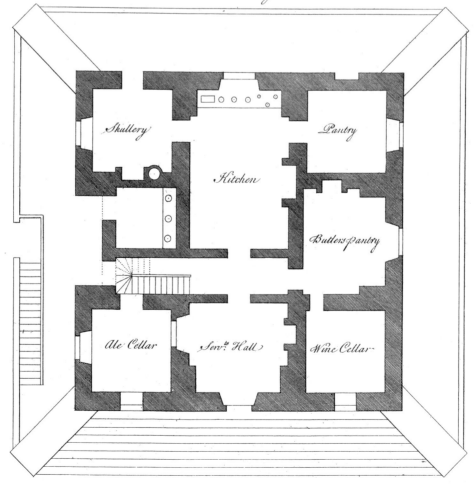

Skullery

Pantry

Kitchen

Butlers pantry

Ale Cellar

Servᵗ Hall

Wine Cellar

Plans of the Lord Viscount Charlemont's Casine at Marino.

Wᵐ Chambers Architectus

P. Fourdrinier Sculp.

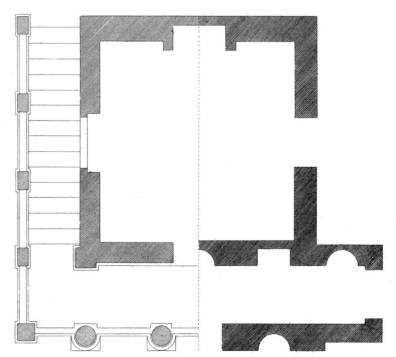

To the Countess of Pembroke, this Design of the Casine at Wilton, is humbly Inscribed, By her Ladyships most obedient Servant, William Chambers.

W. Chambers Architectus.   T. Patton Sculp.

To Lord Bruce, this Design for the Casine at Tanfield Hall in Yorkshire, is humbly Inscribed by his Lordships most Obedient Servant William Chambers.

W. Chambers.

F. Patton Sculp.

5   10   15   20   25   30   35   40 f.

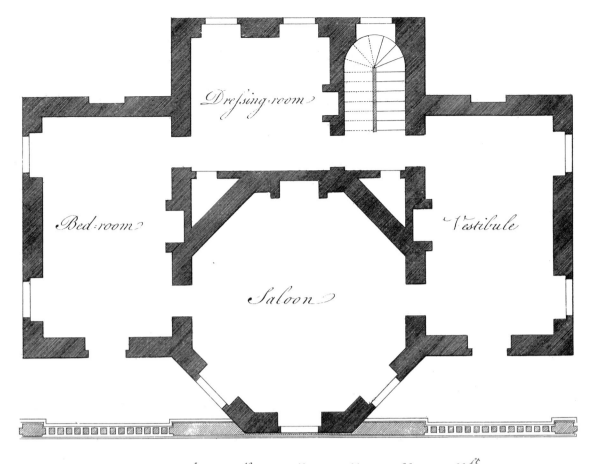

Dressing-room

Bed-room

Vestibule

Saloon

W. Chambers

J. Patton sculp.

The principal Floor of Lord Bruce's Casine.

Plan of M.ʳ Willoughby's Temple.

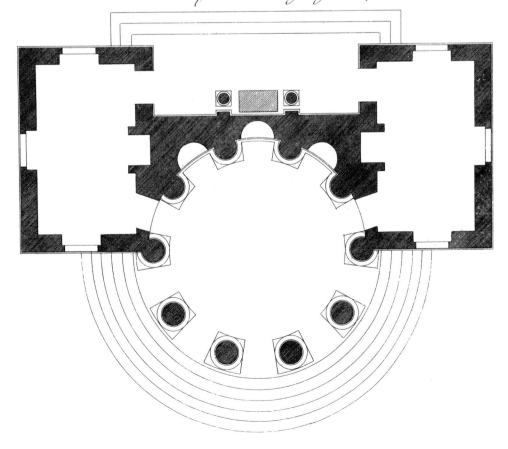

To Henry Willoughby Esqr: This Design is humbly Inscribed by his most Obedient Servant William Chambers.

To the Earl of Tilney, this Design is humbly Inscribed
by his Lordships most Obedient Servant, William Chambers.

W.ᵐ Chambers

P. Fourdrinier sculp.

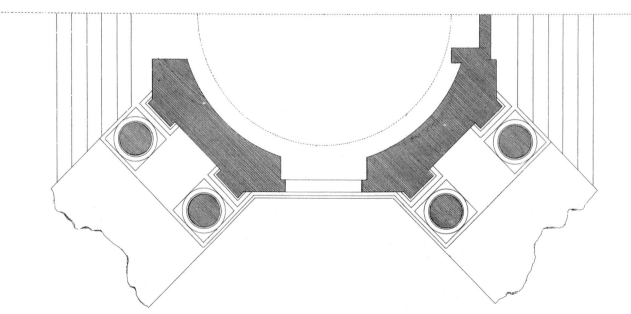

W.ᵐ Chambers   P. Fourdrinier sculp.

To Thomas Worsley of Hovingham Esqr. this Design is humbly Inscribed, by his most Obedient Servant, William Chambers.

P. Fourdrinier Sculp.

ALEXAN: POPE
POET: ANGELICÆ
SACRUM STO

T: SWIF
POE:

I: GAY
POE:

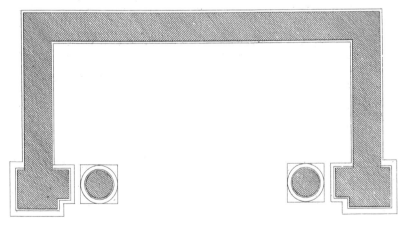

To Sʳ Charles Hotham Barᵗ this Design is humbly Inscribed

by his most Obedient Servant Willᵐ Chambers.

W. Chambers

P. Fourdrinier Sculp.

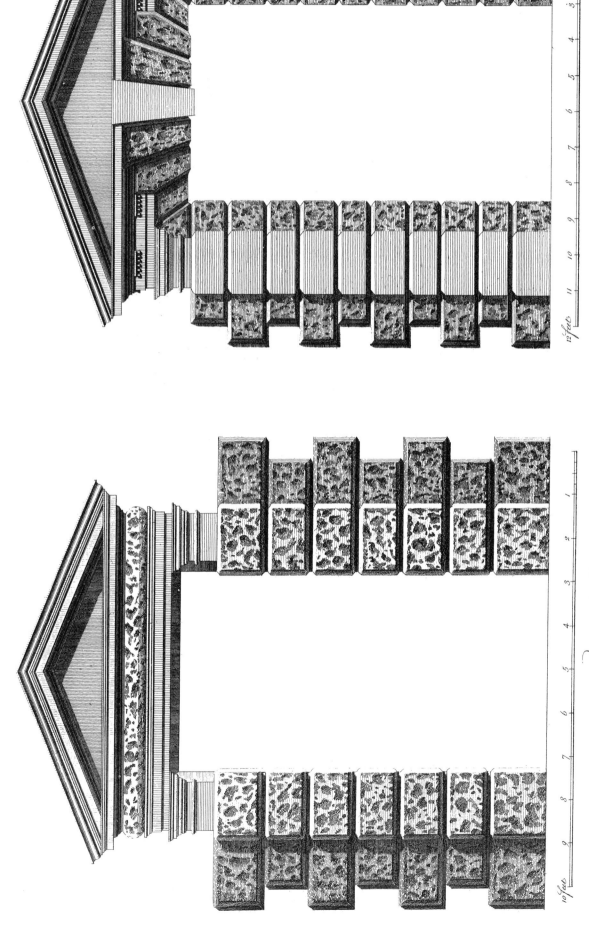

Rustick Doors to a Garden near the great Theatre at Vicenza.
By Andrea Palladio.

To Robert Wood Esq.r these Designs are humbly Inscribed by
his most Obedient Servant William Chambers.

W.m Chambers Delin.   P. Patton Sculp.

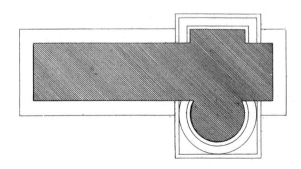

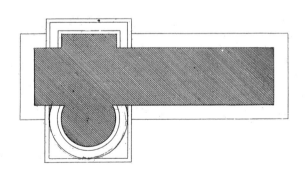

To the Honourable M.ʳ Ward, this Design
is humbly Inscribed by his most Obedient Servant, W.ᵐ Chambers.

M.ʳ Chambers   P. Fourdrinier Sculp.

IMPERATOR. MARCUS AURELIUS
PONT. OPT. MAXIM. TRI. POT
IV. C. IƆXXII

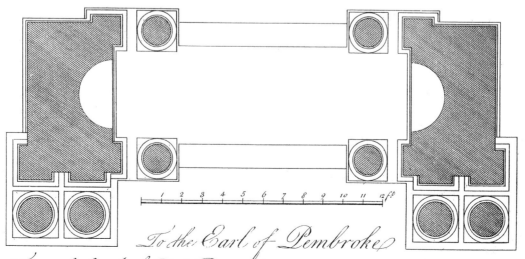

1 2 3 4 5 6 7 8 9 10 11 12ft

To the Earl of Pembroke,

this Design of the Triumphal Arch at Wilton, is humbly, Inscribed by his Lordships, most Obed.t Serv.t W.m Chamb.rs.

Wt. Chambers Architectus.   E. Rooker Sculp.

IMP. CAES. SEPTIMIUS. SEVER
PONT. MAX. TRIB. POT. X.

To Thomas Brand of the Hoo, in the County of Hertford Esq.ʳ
this Plate is humbly Inscribed by his most obedient Servant, W.ᵐ Chambers.

W. Chambers.

E. Rooker Sculp.

To His Grace the Duke of Richmond, Lenox, & Aubigny, this Design is humbly Inscribed by his Grace's most Obedient Servant, William Chambers.

M.ᵗ Chambers

E. Rooker Sculp.

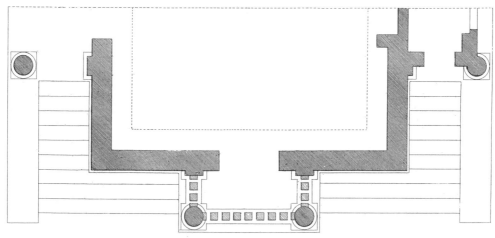

To S.ʳ Thomas Kennedy of Cullean Bar.ᵗ this Design is humbly Inscribed
by his most Obedient Servant, William Chambers.

W.ᵗ Chambers

P. Fourdrinier Sculp.

Pl.1.

Various Ornamental Utensils.

W. Chambers invt.

Bigby sculpt.

Pl. 2

Various Ornamental Utensils

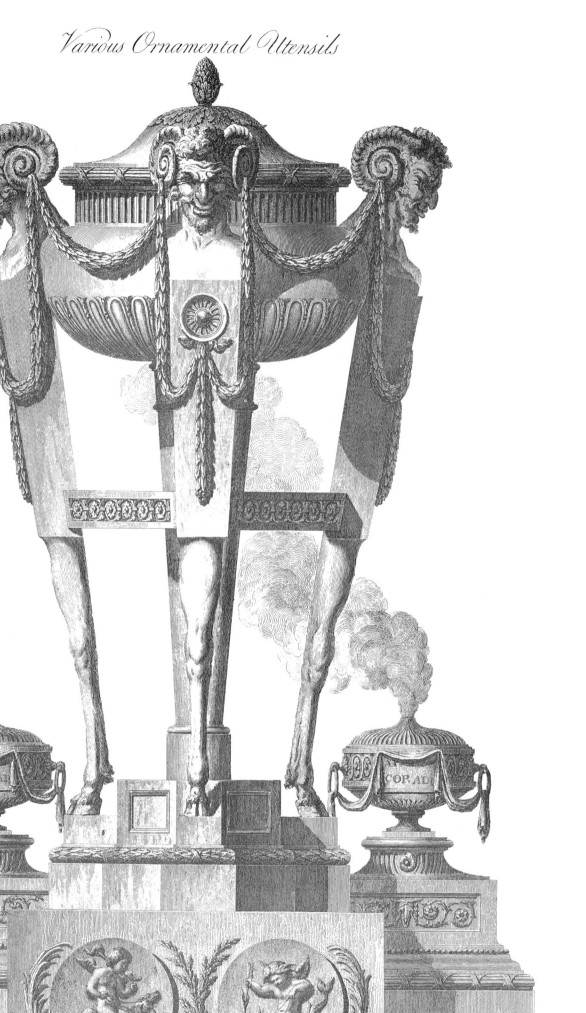

W. Chambers inv.

Bigby sculp.

Dover Books on Art and Art History

DE RE METALLICA, **Georgius Agricola.** One of the most important scientific classics of all time, this 1556 work on mining was the first based on field research and observation and the methods of modern science. 289 authentic Renaissance woodcuts. Translated by Herbert Hoover. Reprint of English (1912) edition. 672pp. 6¾ x 10¾. 60006-8

THE PIROTECHNIA, **Vannoccio Biringuccio.** History's first clear, comprehensive work on metallurgy, published in 1540, describing in detail the equipment and processes of 16th-century mining, smelting, and metalworking. 94 original woodcuts. Introduction. 507pp. 6⅛ x 9¼. 26134-4

THE ART OF BOTANICAL ILLUSTRATION: AN ILLUSTRATED HISTORY, **Wilfrid Blunt.** Surveys the evolution of botanical illustration from the crude scratchings of paleolithic man down to the highly scientific work of 20th-century illustrators. With 186 magnificent examples, more than 30 in full color. "A classic"—*The Sunday Times* (London). 372pp. 5⅜ x 8¼. 27265-6

IDOLS BEHIND ALTARS: MODERN MEXICAN ART AND ITS CULTURAL ROOTS, **Anita Brenner.** Critical study ranges from pre-Columbian times through the 20th century to explore Mexico's intrinsic association between art and religion; the role of iconography in Mexican art; and the return to native values. Unabridged reprint of the classic 1929 edition. 118 b/w illustrations. 432pp. 5⅜ x 8½. 42303-4

THE BOOK OF KELLS, **Blanche Cirker (ed.).** 32 full-color, full-page plates from the greatest illuminated manuscript of the Middle Ages; painstakingly reproduced from rare facsimile edition. Publisher's Note. Captions. 32pp. 9⅜ x 12¼. 24345-1

CHRISTIAN AND ORIENTAL PHILOSOPHY OF ART, **Ananda K. Coomaraswamy.** Nine essays by philosopher-art-historian on symbolism, traditional culture, folk art, ideal portraiture, etc. 146pp. 5⅜ x 8½. 20378-6

DALÍ ON MODERN ART, **Salvador Dalí.** Influential painter skewers modern art and its practitioners. Outrageous evaluations of Picasso, Cézanne, Turner, and more. 15 renderings of paintings discussed. 44 calligraphic decorations by Dalí. 96pp. 5⅜ x 8½. 29220-7

THE SECRET LIFE OF SALVADOR DALÍ, **Salvador Dalí.** One of the most readable autobiographies ever! Superbly illustrated with more than 80 photos of Dalí and his works, and scores of Dalí drawings and sketches. "It is impossible not to admire this painter as writer . . . (Dalí) communicates the snobbishness, self-adoration, comedy, seriousness, fanaticism, in short the concept of life and the total picture of himself he sets out to portray."—*Books.* 432pp. 6½ x 9¼. (Available in U.S. only) 27454-3

LEONARDO ON ART AND THE ARTIST, **Leonardo da Vinci (André Chastel, ed.).** Systematic grouping of passages of Leonardo's writings concerning painting, with focus on problems of interpretation. More than an anthology, it offers a reconstruction of the underlying meaning of Leonardo's words. Introduction, notes, and bibliographic and reference materials. More than 125 b/w illustrations. 288pp. 9¼ x 7⅜. 42166-X

LEONARDO ON THE HUMAN BODY, **Leonardo da Vinci.** More than 1,200 of Leonardo's anatomical drawings on 215 plates. Leonardo's text, which accompanies the drawings, has been translated into English. 506pp. 8⅜ x 11¼. 24483-0

THE BOOK BEFORE PRINTING: ANCIENT, MEDIEVAL AND ORIENTAL, **David Diringer.** Rich authoritative study of the book before Gutenberg. Nearly 200 photographic facsimiles of priceless documents. 604pp. 5⅜ x 8½. 24243-9

AMERICA'S OLD MASTERS: BENJAMIN WEST, JOHN SINGLETON COPLEY, CHARLES WILLSON PEALE AND GILBERT STUART, **James T. Flexner.** Concise biographies evaluate each painter, wellsprings of their art, interplay of native tradition and European influence, and more. 69 halftones. Bibliography. 448pp. 5⅜ x 8¼. 27957-X

GAUGUIN'S INTIMATE JOURNALS, **Paul Gauguin.** Revealing documents, reprinted from rare, limited edition, throw much light on the painter's inner life, his tumultuous relationship with van Gogh, evaluations of Degas, Monet, and other artists; hatred of hypocrisy and sham, life in the Marquesas Islands, and much more. 27 full-page illustrations by Gauguin. Preface by Emil Gauguin. 160pp. 6½ x 9¼. 29441-2

THE GEOMETRY OF ART AND LIFE, **Matila Ghyka.** Revealing discussion ranging from Plato to modern architecture. 80 plates and 64 figures, including paintings, flowers, shells, etc. 174pp. 5⅜ x 8½. 23542-4

THE LIFE OF WILLIAM BLAKE, **Alexander Gilchrist.** First full-length biography (1863) covers Blake's childhood, student years, trial for treason, his "madness," neglect by the public, declining health, and untimely death. Insightful commentary on the poet's works. 40 Blake illustrations. 640pp. 5⅜ x 8½. 40005-0

A MANUAL OF HISTORIC ORNAMENT, **Richard Glazier.** Hundreds of detailed illustrations depict painted pilasters from Pompeii, early Gothic stone carvings, a detail from a stained glass window in Canterbury Cathedral, and much more. Unabridged reprint of the 6th edition (1948) of *A Manual of Historic Ornament,* originally published in 1899 by B. T. Batsford, Ltd., London. Over 700 b/w illustrations. 16 plates of photographs. x+230pp. 6⅛ x 9¼. 42148-1

THE DISASTERS OF WAR, **Francisco Goya.** This powerful graphic indictment of war's horrors–inspired by the Peninsular War and the following famine–comprises 80 prints and includes veiled attacks on various people, the Church, and the State. Captions reprinted with English translations. 97pp. 9⅜ x 8¼. 21872-4

GREAT DRAWINGS OF NUDES, **Carol Belanger Grafton (ed.).** An impressive sampling of life drawings by 45 of the art world's greatest masters displays the styles of figure drawing across five centuries, from Dürer and Michelangelo to Modigliani and Derain. Featured artists include Raphael, Rubens, van Dyck, Hogarth, Constable, Ingres, Gauguin, Matisse, Rodin, and others. Captions. 48pp. 8¼ x 11. 42766-8

GREAT SELF-PORTRAITS, **Carol Belanger Grafton (ed.).** Unique volume of 45 splendid self-portraits encompasses pen, ink, and charcoal renderings as well as etchings and engravings. Subjects range from such 15th-century artists as da Vinci and Dürer to a host of 19th-century masters: Whistler, Rodin, van Gogh, Beardsley, and many more–Rembrandt, Rubens, Goya, Blake, Pissarro, and numerous others. 45 b/w illustrations. 48pp. 8¼ x 11. 42168-6

FORM, FUNCTION & DESIGN, **Paul Jacques Grillo.** One of finest modern analyses of design and its related variables–form, materials, climate, orientation, proportion, and composition. 422 illustrations. 238pp. 8¼ x 11. 20182-1

HAWTHORNE ON PAINTING, **Charles W. Hawthorne.** Collected from notes taken by students at famous Cape Cod School; hundreds of direct, personal aperçus, ideas, suggestions. 91pp. 5⅜ x 8½. 20653-X

MODERN MEXICAN PAINTERS, **MacKinley Helm.** Definitive introduction to art and artists of Mexico during great artistic movements of '20s and '30s. Discussion of Rivera, Orozco, Siqueiros, Galvan, Cantú, Meza, and many others. 95 illustrations. 228pp. 6½ x 9¼. 26028-3

MODERN ARTISTS ON ART, SECOND ENLARGED EDITION, **Robert L. Herbert (ed.).** Sixteen of the twentieth century's leading artistic innovators talk forcefully about their work–from Albert Gleizes and Jean Metzinger's 1912 presentation of Cubist theory to Henry Moore's comments, three decades later, on sculpture and primitive art. Four essays by Kurt Schwitters, Max Ernst, El Lissitzky, and Fernand Léger. 192pp. 5⅜ x 8½. 41191-5

A HISTORY OF ENGRAVING AND ETCHING, **Arthur M. Hind.** British Museum Keeper of Prints offers complete history, from 15th century to 1914: accomplishments, influences, and artistic merit. 111 illustrations. 505pp. 5⅜ x 8½. 20954-7

ART AND GEOMETRY, **William M. Ivins.** Stimulating, controversial study of interrelations of art and mathematics, Greek disservice and contribution. Renaissance perspective, Dürer and math, etc. 123pp. 5⅜ x 8½. 20941-5

CONCERNING THE SPIRITUAL IN ART, **Wassily Kandinsky.** Pioneering work by father of abstract art. Thoughts on color theory and nature of art. Analysis of earlier masters. 12 illustrations. 80pp. of text. 5⅜ x 8½. 23411-8

POINT AND LINE TO PLANE, **Wassily Kandinsky.** Seminal exposition of role of line, point, and other elements of non-objective painting. Essential to understanding 20th-century art. 127 illustrations. 192pp. 6½ x 9¼. 23808-3

Dover Books on Art and Art History

LANGUAGE OF VISION, Gyorgy Kepes. Noted painter, designer, and theoretician analyzes effect of visual language on human consciousness: perception of line and form, perspective, much more. Over 300 photos, drawings, and illustrations. 224pp. 8⅜ x 11¼. 28650-9

GOTHICK ARCHITECTURE: A REPRINT OF THE ORIGINAL 1742 TREATISE, Batty Langley and Thomas Langley. The architectural designs of Batty Langley greatly influenced England's Gothic Revival movement in the second half of the eighteenth century. This volume, which completely reproduces the author's most famous and influential work (beautifully engraved by his brother Thomas), displays columns, entablatures, windows, mantels, pavilions, and a host of other architectural features. This collection of permission-free illustrations will be welcomed by students and aficionados of eighteenth-century architecture, as well as designers and artists in search of period elegance. 80pp. 9 x 12. 42614-9

THE ART-MAKERS, Russell Lynes. Eakins, Hunt, French, Morse, Trumbull, and others, and their heroic struggle to make art respectable in 19th-century America. 211 illustrations. 526pp. 6⅛ x 9. 24239-0

THE LIFE OF WILLIAM MORRIS, J. W. Mackail. Classic biography of great Victorian poet, designer, and socialist. Childhood, education, embrace of socialism, Arts & Crafts movement, Kelmscott Press, much more. 22 illustrations. 800pp. 5⅜ x 8½. 28793-9

RELIGIOUS ART IN FRANCE OF THE THIRTEENTH CENTURY, Emile Mâle. Classic by noted art historian focuses on French cathedrals of the 13th century as apotheosis of medieval style. Iconography, bestiaries, illustrated calendars, gospels, secular history, and many other aspects. 190 b/w illustrations. 442pp. 5⅜ x 8½. 41061-7

VINCENT VAN GOGH: A BIOGRAPHY, Julius Meier-Graefe. Utterly engrossing account of legendary artist's entire life from birth to his suicide. Essential readings for anyone interested in van Gogh's life and art. 160pp. 5⅜ x 8½. 25253-1

THE GOLDEN AGE OF THE STEAM LOCOMOTIVE: WITH OVER 250 CLASSIC ILLUSTRATIONS, J. G. Pangborn. Long a collector's item, this book was originally conceived as a record of the Baltimore and Ohio Railroad's exhibit at the world's Columbian exposition of 1893 in Chicago. More than 250 illustrations showcase the locomotives and cars that existed from 1765 to 1893, among them, the *John Hancock, Londoner, Mud Digger, Old Ironsides, Robert Fulton, Tom Thumb,* and others. Unabridged reprint of the classic 1894 edition. 251 black-and-white illustrations. 176pp. 9⅜ x 12¼. 42824-9

PAINTERS OF THE ASHCAN SCHOOL, Bennard B. Perlman. Lively, beautifully illustrated study of 8 artists who brought a compelling new realism to American painting from 1870 to 1913. Henri, Glackens, Sloan, Luks, 4 more. 142 b/w illustrations. Bibliography. Introduction. 224pp. 9⅜ x 11¼. 25747-9

ROBERT HENRI: HIS LIFE AND ART, Bennard B. Perlman. A compelling new biography of the founder of the "Ashcan School," tracing Henri's life and art from his boyhood to his rise as an influential painter, teacher, and activist in the politics of art, and astutely appraising his pivotal role in American art. 79 illustrations, including 21 full-color and 9 black-and-white photos. Index. 208pp. 8⅜ x 11¼. 26722-9

COMPOSITION IN ART, Henry Rankin Poore. Learn principles of composition, classical and modern, through analysis of works from Middle Ages to present. 148 illustrations, 9 in color. 104pp. 8⅛ x 11. 23358-8

PERSPECTIVE IN ARCHITECTURE AND PAINTING: AN UNABRIDGED REPRINT OF THE ENGLISH-AND-LATIN EDITION OF THE 1693 "PERSPECTIVA PICTORUM ET ARCHITECTORUM," Andrea Pozzo. Influential classic spread Italian baroque style to northern Europe and Britain. Rare 1707 English edition. More than 300 decorative cuts and figures. 224pp. 9 x 12. 25855-6

PAINTERS ON PAINTING, Eric Protter. Fascinating insights as da Vinci, Michelangelo, Rubens, Rembrandt, Hogarth, Manet, Degas, Cézanne, van Gogh, Matisse, Pollock, Johns, and many other artists comment on their artistic techniques, objectives, other artists, and more. 68 illustrations. 312pp. 5⅜ x 8½. 29941-4

SHAKESPEARE'S A MIDSUMMER NIGHT'S DREAM, illustrated by Arthur Rackham. Shakespeare's romantic comedy takes on a new and vivid life with these brilliant images by of one of the twentieth century's leading illustrators. This faithful reprint offers a quality of printing and sharpness of reproduction that rivals the limited and first editions of 1908. Includes the complete text of the play, along with 40 full-color and numerous black-and-white illustrations. 176pp. 8⅜ x 11. 42833-8

THE ILLUSTRATOR AND THE BOOK IN ENGLAND FROM 1790 TO 1914, Gordon N. Ray. Combining essays, bibliographical descriptions, and 295 illustrations, this book by one of America's leading literary scholars and book antiquarians definitively chronicles a golden era in the art of the illustrated book. Artists range from Blake, Turner, Rowlandson, and Morris to Caldecott, Greenaway, Beardsley, and Rackham. 384pp. 8⅜ x 11¼. 26955-8

RODIN ON ART AND ARTISTS, Auguste Rodin. Wide-ranging comments on meaning of art; great artists; relation of sculpture to poetry, painting, music, philosophy of life, and more. 76 illustrations of Rodin's sculpture, drawings, and prints. 119pp. 8⅜ x 11¼. 24487-3

THE SEARCH FOR FORM IN ART AND ARCHITECTURE, Eliel Saarinen. Important philosophical volume by foremost architectural conceptualist emphasizes design on an organic level; interrelated study of all arts. 377pp. 5⅜ x 8½. 24907-7

THE SENSE OF BEAUTY, George Santayana. Masterfully written discussion of nature of beauty, form, and expression; art, literature, and social sciences all involved. 168pp. 5⅜ x 8½. 20238-0

PICASSO, Gertrude Stein. Intimate, revealing memoir of Picasso as founder of Cubism, intimate of Apollinaire, Braque, and others; creative spirit driven to convey reality of twentieth century. Highly readable. 61 black-and-white illustrations. 128pp. 5⅜ x 8½. 24715-5

ON DIVERS ARTS, Theophilus (translated by John G. Hawthorne and C. S. Smith). Earliest (12th century) treatise on arts written by practicing artist. Pigments, glass blowing, stained glass, gold and silver work, and more. Authoritative edition of a medieval classic. 34 illustrations. 216pp. 6½ x 9¼. 23784-2

VAN GOGH ON ART AND ARTISTS: LETTERS TO EMILE BERNARD, Vincent van Gogh. 23 missives—written during the years 1887 to 1889—radiate their author's impulsiveness, intensity, and mysticism. The letters are complemented by reproductions of van Gogh's major paintings. 32 full-page, b/w illustrations. xii+196pp. 8⅜ x 11. 42727-7

VASARI ON TECHNIQUE, Georgio Vasari. Sixteenth-century painter and historian on technical secrets of the day: gilding, stained glass, casting, painter's materials, etc. 29 illustrations. 328pp. 5⅜ x 8½. 20717-X

RECOLLECTIONS OF A PICTURE DEALER, Ambroise Vollard. Art merchant and bon vivant Ambroise Vollard (1867–1939) recounts captivating anecdotes from his professional and social life: selling the works of Cézanne; partying with Renoir, Forain, Degas, and Rodin; the studios and personalities of Manet, Matisse, Picasso, and Rousseau; and encounters with Gertrude Stein, Zola, and other noteworthies. 33 illustrations. 384pp. 5⅜ x 8½. 42852-4

ETCHINGS OF JAMES MCNEILL WHISTLER, James McNeill Whistler (selected and edited by Maria Naylor). The best of the artist's work in this genre: 149 outstanding etchings and drypoint, most in original size, all reproduced with exceptional quality. Popular individual prints include "Portrait of Whistler," "Old Battersea Bridge," "Nocturne," plus complete French set, Thames set, and two Venice sets. Introduction and an explanatory note for each print. 149 b/w illustrations. xviii+157pp. 9⅜ x 12¼. 42481-2

THE GENTLE ART OF MAKING ENEMIES, James McNeill Whistler. Great wit deflates Wilde, Ruskin, and Swinburne; belabors inane critics; also states Impressionist aesthetics. 334pp. 5⅜ x 7¼. 21875-9

PRINCIPLES OF ART HISTORY, Heinrich Wölfflin. Seminal modern study explains ideas beyond superficial changes. Analyzes more than 150 works by masters. 121 illustrations. 253pp. 6⅛ x 9¼. 20276-3

Medieval Art through Eighteenth-Century Art

Graphic Worlds of Peter Bruegel the Elder, Peter Bruegel. 63 engravings and a woodcut made from the drawings of the 16th-century Flemish master: landscapes, seascapes, stately ships, drolleries, whimsical allegories, scenes from the Gospels, and much more. Stimulating commentaries by H. Arthur Klein on individual prints, bits of biography on etcher or engraver, and comparisons with Bruegel's original designs. 176pp. 9⅜ x 12¼. 21132-0

Views of Venice by Canaletto, Antonio Canaletto (engraved by Antonio Visentini). Unparalleled visual statement from early 18th century includes 14 scenes down the Grand Canal away from and returning to the Rialto Bridge, 12 magnificent views of the inimitable *campi,* and more. Extraordinarily handsome, large-format edition. Text by J. Links. 50 illustrations. 90pp. 13¾ x 10. 22705-7

The Craftsman's Handbook, Cennino Cennini. This fifteenth-century handbook reveals secrets and techniques of the masters in drawing, oil painting, frescoes, panel painting, gilding, casting, and more. 142pp. 6⅛ x 9¼. 20054-X

The Book of Kells, Blanche Cirker (ed.). Thirty-two full-color, full-page plates from the greatest illuminated manuscript of the Middle Ages; painstakingly reproduced from rare facsimile edition. Publisher's Note. Captions. 32pp. 9⅜ x 12¼. 24345-1

The Complete Engravings, Etchings and Drypoints of Albrecht Dürer, Albrecht Dürer. This splendid collection reproduces all 105 of Dürer's works in these media, including such well-known masterpieces as *Knight, Death and Devil, Melencolia I,* and *Adam and Eve,* plus portraits of such contemporaries as Erasmus and Frederick the Wise; popular and religious works; peasant scenes, and the portentous works: *The Four Witches, Sol Justitiae,* and *The Monstrous Sow of Landser.* 120 plates. 235pp. 8⅜ x 11¼. 22851-7

The Human Figure, Albrecht Dürer. This incredible collection contains drawings in which Dürer experimented with many methods: the "anthropometric system," learned from Leonardo; the "exempeda" method, known to most as the man inscribed in a circle; the human figure in motion; and much more. Some of the life studies rank among the finest ever done. 170 plates. 355pp. 8⅜ x 11¼. 21042-1

Medieval Woodcut Illustrations, Carol Belanger Grafton (ed.). Selections from a 1493 history of the world features magnificent woodcuts of 91 locales, plus 143 illustrations of figures and decorative objects. Comparable to the Gutenberg Bible in terms of craftsmanship; designed by Pleydenwuff and Wolgemut. Permission-free. 194 b/w illustrations. 80pp. 8⅜ x 11. 40458-7

Engravings of Hogarth, William Hogarth. Collection of 101 robust engravings reveals the life of the drawing rooms, inns, and alleyways of 18th-century England through the eyes of a great satirist. Includes all the major series: *Rake's Progress, Harlot's Progress,* Illustrations for *Hudibras, Before and After, Beer Street,* and *Gin Lane,* plus 96 more with commentary by Sean Shesgreen. xxxiii+205pp. 11 x 13¾. 22479-1

The Dance of Death, Hans Holbein the Younger. Most celebrated of Holbein's works. Unabridged reprint of the original 1538 masterpiece and one of the great graphic works of the era. Forty-one striking woodcuts capture the motif *Memento mori*–"Remember, you will die." Includes translations of all quotes and verses. 146pp. 5⅜ x 8½. 22804-5

The Complete Woodcuts of Albrecht Dürer, Dr. W. Kurth (ed.). Superb collection of 346 extant woodcuts: the celebrated series on the *Life of Virgin, the Apocalypse of St. John, the Great Passion, St. Jerome in His Study, Samson Fighting the Lion, The Fall of Icarus, The Rhinoceros, the Triumphal Arch, Saints and Biblical Scenes,* and many others, including much little-known material. 285pp. 8½ x 12¼. 21097-9

Religious Art in France of the Thirteenth Century, Emile Mâle. This classic by a noted art historian focuses on French cathedrals of the 13th century as the apotheosis of the medieval style. Topics include iconography, bestiaries, illustrated calendars, the gospels, secular history, and many other aspects. 190 b/w illustrations. 442pp. 5⅜ x 8½. 41061-7

Great Scenes from the Bible: 230 Magnificent 17th Century Engravings, Matthaeus Merian (the Elder). Remarkably detailed illustrations depict Adam and Eve Driven Out of the Garden of Eden, The Flood, David Slaying Goliath, Christ in the Manger, The Raising of Lazarus, The Crucifixion, and many other scenes. A wonderful pictorial dimension to age-old stories. All plates from the classic 1625 edition. 128pp. 9 x 12. 42043-4

Medieval and Renaissance Treatises on the Arts of Painting: Original Texts with English Translations, Mary P. Merrifield. This rare 1849 work reprints treatises from the 12th–17th centuries (with the original-language version and its English translation on facing pages). Oil painting practices, methods of mixing pigments, and much more, with commentary on each treatise, plus excellent introduction discussing social history, artistic practices. 1,280pp. 5⅜ x 8½. 40440-4

Views of Rome Then and Now, Giovanni Battista Piranesi and Herschel Levit. Piranesi's masterful representations of architecture are reprinted in large format alongside corresponding recent photos. Monuments of ancient, early Christian, Renaissance, and Baroque Rome (Colosseum, Forum, fountains, etc.) with auxiliary notes on both the etchings and photos. 82 plates. 109pp. 11 x 14¾. 23339-1

The Notebooks of Leonardo Da Vinci, compiled and edited by Jean Paul Richter. These 1,566 extracts reveal the full range of Leonardo's versatile genius: his writings on painting, sculpture, architecture, anatomy, mining, inventions, and music. The first volume is devoted to various aspects of art: structure of the eye and vision, perspective, science of light and shade, color theory, and more. The second volume shows the wide range of Leonardo's secondary interests: geography, warfare, zoology, medicine, astronomy, and other topics. Dual Italian-English texts, with 186 plates and more than 500 additional drawings faithfully reproduced. Total of 913pp. 7⅞ x 10¾. Vol. I: 22572-0
Vol. II: 22573-9

On Divers Arts, Theophilus (translated by John G. Hawthorne and C. S. Smith). Twelfth-century treatise on arts written by a practicing artist. Pigments, glass blowing, stained glass, gold and silver work, and more. Authoritative edition of a medieval classic. 34 illustrations. 216pp. 6½ x 9¼. 23784-2

The Complete Etchings of Rembrandt: Reproduced in Original Size, Rembrandt van Rijn. One of the greatest figures in Western Art, Rembrandt van Rijn (1606–1669) brought etching to a state of unsurpassed perfection. This edition includes more than 300 works–portraits, landscapes, biblical scenes, allegorical and mythological pictures, and more–reproduced in full size directly from a rare collection of etchings famed for its pristine condition, rich contrasts, and brilliant printing. With detailed captions, chronology of Rembrandt's life and etchings, discussion of the technique of etching in this time, and a bibliography. 224pp. 9⅜ x 12¼. 28181-7

Drawings of Rembrandt, Seymour Slive (ed.) Updated Lippmann, Hofstede de Groot edition, with definitive scholarly apparatus. Many drawings are preliminary sketches for great paintings and sketchings. Others are self-portraits, beggars, children at play, biblical sketches, landscapes, nudes, Oriental figures, birds, domestic animals, episodes from mythology, classical studies, and more. Also, a selection of work by pupils and followers. Total of 630pp. 9⅜ x 12¼. Vol. I 21485-0
Vol. II 21486-9

The Materials and Techniques of Medieval Painting, Daniel V. Thompson. Sums up 20th-century knowledge: paints, binders, metals, and surface preparation. 239pp. 5⅜ x 8½. 20327-1

Drawings of Albrecht Dürer, Heinrich Wölfflin (ed.). 81 plates show development from youth to full style: *Dürer's Wife Agnes, Idealistic Male and Female Figures* (Adam and Eve), *The Lamentation,* and many others. The editor not only introduces the drawings with an erudite essay, but also supplies captions for each, telling about the circumstances of the work, its relation to other works, and significant features. 173pp. 8⅜ x 11. 22352 3

Write for ***free*** *Fine Art and Art Instruction Catalog to*
Dover Publications, Inc., Dept. ABI, 31 East 2nd Street, Mineola, NY 11501
Visit us online at ***www.doverpublications.com***

Nineteenth-Century Art

GREAT DRAWINGS AND ILLUSTRATIONS FROM PUNCH, 1841–1901, Stanley Appelbaum and Richard Kelly (eds.). Golden years of British illustration. 192 drawings by 25 artists: Phiz, Leech, Tenniel, du Maurier, Sambourne. 144pp. 9 x 12. 24110-6

BEST WORKS OF AUBREY BEARDSLEY, Aubrey Beardsley. Rich selection of 170 boldly executed black-and-white illustrations ranging from illustrations for Laclos' *Les Liaisons Dangereuses* and Balzac's *La Comédie Humaine* to magazine cover designs, book plates, title-page ornaments for books, silhouettes, and delightful mini-portraits of major composers. 160pp. 8⅛ x 11. 26273-1

THE RAPE OF THE LOCK, Aubrey Beardsley and Alexander Pope. Reproduction of "ideal" 1896 edition in which text, typography, and illustration complement each other. 10 great illustrations capture the mock-heroic, delicate fancy of Pope's poem. 47pp. 8⅛ x 11. 21963-1

SALOME, Aubrey Beardsley and Oscar Wilde. Lord Alfred Douglas' translation of Wilde's great play (originally written in French,) with all 20 well-known Beardsley illustrations including suppressed plates. Introduction by Robert Ross. xxii+69pp. 8⅛ x 11. 21830-9

DRAWINGS OF WILLIAM BLAKE, William Blake. Fine reproductions show the range of Blake's artistic genius: drawings for *The Book of Job, The Divine Comedy, Paradise Lost,* an edition of Shakespeare's plays, grotesques and visionary heads, mythological figures, and other drawings. Selection, introduction, and commentary by Sir Geoffrey Keynes. 178pp. 8⅛ x 11. 22303-5

SONGS OF INNOCENCE, William Blake. The first and most popular of Blake's famous "Illuminated Books" in a facsimile edition. 31 illustrations, text of each poem. 64pp. 5¼ x 7. 22764-2

A CÉZANNE SKETCHBOOK: FIGURES, PORTRAITS, LANDSCAPES AND STILL LIFES, Paul Cézanne. Experiments with tonal effects, light, mass, and other qualities in more than 100 drawings. A revealing view of developing master painter, precursor of cubism. 102 illustrations. 144pp. 8⅜ x 6⅜. 24790-2

GRAPHIC WORKS OF GEORGE CRUIKSHANK, George Cruikshank (Richard A. Vogler, ed.). 269 permission-free illustrations (8 in full color) reproduced directly from original etchings and woodcuts. Introduction, notes. 200pp. 9⅜ x 12¼. 23438-X

DAUMIER: 10 GREAT LITHOGRAPHS, Honoré Daumier. Works range from early and caustic anti-government drawings in 1831 to last works prior to retirement in 1872. Collection concentrates on liberated women, the French bourgeoisie, actors, musicians, soldiers, teachers, lawyers, married life, and myriad other creations by the "Michelangelo of the people." 158pp. 9⅜ x 12¼. 23512-2

DEGAS' DRAWINGS, H. G. E. Degas. Dancers, nudes, portraits, travel scenes, and other works in inimitable style, most not available anywhere else. 100 plates, 8 in color. 100pp. 9 x 12. 21233-5

THE DORÉ BIBLE ILLUSTRATIONS, Gustave Doré. 241 detailed plates from the Bible: the Creation scenes, Adam and Eve, horrifying visions of the Flood, the battle sequences with their monumental crowds, depictions of the life of Jesus, and visions of the new Jerusalem. Each plate is accompanied by the appropriate verses from the King James version. 241pp. 9 x 12. 23004-X

THE DORÉ GALLERY: HIS 120 GREATEST ILLUSTRATIONS, Gustave Doré (Carol Belanger Grafton, ed.). Comprising the finest plates from the great illustrator's work, this collection features outstanding engravings from such literary classics as Milton's *Paradise Lost, The Divine Comedy* by Dante, Coleridge's *The Rime of the Ancient Mariner, The Raven* by Poe, Sue's *The Wandering Jew,* and many others. Captions. 128pp. 9 x 12. 40160-X

DORÉ'S ILLUSTRATIONS OF THE CRUSADES, Gustave Doré. Magnificent compilation of all 100 original plates from Ichaud's classic *History of the Crusades.* Includes *The War Cry of the Crusaders, The Massacre of Antioch, The Road to Jerusalem, the Baptism of Infidels, the Battle of Lepanto,* and many more. Captions. 112pp. 9 x 12. 29597-4

DORÉ'S ILLUSTRATIONS FOR DON QUIXOTE, Gustave Doré. Here are 190 wood-engraved plates, 120 full-page: charging the windmill, traversing Spanish plains, valleys, and mountains; ghostly visions of dragons, knights, and flaming lake. Marvelous detail, minutiae, accurate costumes, architecture, enchantment, pathos, and humor. Captions. 160pp. 9 x 12. 24300-1

THE RIME OF THE ANCIENT MARINER, Gustave Doré and Samuel Taylor Coleridge. Doré's dramatic engravings for *The Rime of the Ancient Mariner* are considered by many to be his greatest work. The terrifying space of the open sea, the storms and whirlpools of an unknown ocean, the ice of the Antarctica, and more–all are rendered in a powerful manner. Full text. 38 plates. 77pp. 9¼ x 12. 22305-1

GAUGUIN'S INTIMATE JOURNALS, Paul Gauguin. Revealing documents, reprinted from rare, limited edition, throw much light on the painter's inner life, his tumultuous relationship with van Gogh, evaluations of Degas, Monet, and other artists; hatred of hypocrisy and sham, life in the Marquesas Islands, and much more. 27 full-page illustrations by Gauguin. Preface by Emil Gauguin. 160pp. 6½ x 9¼. 29441-2

NOA NOA: THE TAHITIAN JOURNAL, Paul Gauguin. Celebrated journal records the artist's thoughts and impressions during two years he spent in Tahiti. Compelling autobiographical fragment. 24 b/w illustrations. 96pp. 5⅜ x 8½. 24859-3

LOS CAPRICHOS, Francisco Goya. Considered Goya's most brilliant work, this collection combines corrosive satire and exquisite technique to depict 18th-century Spain as a nation of grotesque monsters sprung up in the absence of reason. Captions. 183pp. 6⅛ x 9¼. 22384-1

ORNAMENTATION AND ILLUSTRATIONS FROM THE KELMSCOTT CHAUCER, William Morris. Beautiful permission-free tailpieces, decorative letters, elaborate floral borders and frames, samples of body type, and all 98 delicate woodcut illustrations. xiv+112pp. 8½ x 12. 22970-X

WILLIAM MORRIS ON ART AND SOCIALISM, William Morris (Norman Kelvin, ed.). This outstanding collection of 11 lectures and an essay, delivered between 1881 and 1896, illustrates Morris' conviction that the primary human pleasure lies in making and using items of utility and beauty. Selections include: "Art: A Serious Thing," "Art Under Plutocracy," "Useful Work vs. Useless Toil," "The Dawn of a New Epoch," "Of the Origins of Ornamental Art," "The Society of the Future," and "The Present Outlook of Socialism." Introduction. Biographical Note. 208pp. 5⅜ x 8½. 40904-X

THE LIFE OF WILLIAM MORRIS, J.W. Mackail. Classic biography of great Victorian poet, designer, and socialist. Childhood, education, embrace of socialism, Arts & Crafts movement, Kelmscott Press, and much more. 22 illustrations. 800pp. 5⅜ x 8½. 28793-9

DEGAS, Julius Meier-Graefe. Famous art critic's lively, intimate, highly perceptive study of the artist's life and work. Many valuable insights and fascinating anecdotes. 40 finely reproduced black-and-white plates. 128pp. 5⅜ x 8½. 25702-9

GREAT BALLET PRINTS OF THE ROMANTIC ERA, Parmenia Migel. Sumptuous collection from 1830 to 1860. Taglioni, Elssler, Grisi, and other stars by such artists as Chalon, Grevedon, Deveria, etc. Introduction. 128pp. 9 x 12. 24050-9

GREAT LITHOGRAPHS BY TOULOUSE-LAUTREC: 89 PLATES, H. Toulouse-Lautrec. Exceptional sampling of some of finest lithographs ever. 89 plates, including 8 in full color. 88pp. 9⅜ x 12¼. 24359-1

CÉZANNE, Ambroise Vollard. French art dealer's intriguing memoirs of Cézanne–his life in Paris and Aix, friendship with Zola, passions, eccentricities. 20 paintings. 160pp. 5⅜ x 8½. 24729-5

DEGAS: AN INTIMATE PORTRAIT, Ambroise Vollard. Charming, anecdotal memoir by famous art dealer of one of the greatest 19th-century French painters. 14 illustrations. Introduction by Harold L. Van Doren. 96pp. 5⅜ x 8½. 25702-9

RENOIR: AN INTIMATE RECORD, Ambroise Vollard. Art dealer and publisher Vollard's splendid portrait of Renoir emerges in a long series of informal conversations with the Impressionist master that reveal intimate details of his life and career. 19 black-and-white illustrations of Renoir's paintings. 160pp. 5⅜ x 8½. 26488-2

THE LIFE AND WORKS OF AUGUSTUS SAINT GAUDENS, Burke Wilkinson. Critically acclaimed work, nominated for Pulitzer Prize in 1986, vividly evokes life and work of great American sculptor. 64 b/w photos. Notes. Index. 480pp. 6 x 9. (Not available in United Kingdom). 27149-8

VICTORIAN HOUSEWARE, HARDWARE AND KITCHENWARE: A PICTORIAL ARCHIVE WITH OVER 2000 ILLUSTRATIONS, **Ronald S. Barlow (ed.).** This fascinating archive, reprinted from rare woodcut engravings and selected from hard-to-find antique trade catalogs, offers a realistic view of the furnishings of a typical 19th-century home, including andirons, ash sifters, housemaids' buckets, buttonhole cutters, sausage stuffers, seed strippers, spittoons, and hundreds of other items. Captions include size, weight, and cost. 376pp. 9⅜ x 12¼. 41727-1

BEARDSLEY'S LE MORTE DARTHUR: SELECTED ILLUSTRATIONS, **Aubrey Beardsley.** His illustrations for the great Thomas Malory classic made Aubrey Beardsley famous virtually overnight–and fired the imaginations of generations of artists with what became known as the "Beardsley look." This volume contains a rich selection of those splendid drawings, including floral and foliated openings, fauns and satyrs, initials, ornaments, and much more. Characters from Arthurian legend are portrayed in splendid full-page illustrations, bordered with evocative and fecund sinuosities of plant and flower. Artists and designers will find here a source of superb designs, graphics, and motifs for permission-free use. 62 black-and-white illustrations. 48pp. 8¼ x 11. 41795-6

TREASURY OF BIBLE ILLUSTRATIONS: OLD AND NEW TESTAMENTS, **Julius Schnorr von Carolsfeld.** All the best-loved, most-quoted Bible stories, painstakingly reproduced from a rare volume of German engravings. 179 imaginative illustrations depict 105 episodes from Old Testament, 74 scenes from New Testament–each on a separate page, with chapter, verse, King James Text. Outstanding source of permission-free art; remarkably accessible treatment of the Scriptures. x+182pp. 8⅜ x 11¼. 40703-9

3200 OLD-TIME CUTS AND ORNAMENTS, **Blanche Cirker (ed.).** Permission-free pictures from 1909 French typography catalog: plants, animals, religious motifs, music, carriages, boats, sports, furniture, clothing; plus borders, banners, wreaths, and other ornaments. More than 3,200 b/w illustrations. 112pp. 9⅜ x 12¼. 41732-8

A DIDEROT PICTORIAL ENCYCLOPEDIA OF TRADES AND INDUSTRY, **Denis Diderot.** First paperbound edition of 485 remarkable plates from the great 18th-century reference work. Permission-free plates depict vast array of arts and trades before the Industrial Revolution. Two-volume set. Total of 936pp. 9 x 12.
> **Vol. I:** Agriculture and rural arts, fishing, art of war, metalworking, mining. Plates 1–208. 27428-4
> **Vol. II:** Glass, masonry, carpentry, textiles, printing, leather, gold and jewelry, fashion, miscellaneous trades. Plates 209–485. Indexes of persons, places, and subjects. 27429-2

BIRDS, FLOWERS AND BUTTERFLIES STAINED GLASS PATTERN BOOK, **Connie Clough Eaton.** 68 exquisite full-page patterns; lush baskets, vases, garden bouquets, birds, and more. Perfectly rendered for stained glass; suitable for many other arts and crafts projects. 12 color illustrations on covers. 64pp. 8¼ x 11. 40717-9

TURN-OF-THE-CENTURY TILE DESIGNS IN FULL COLOR, **L. François.** 250 designs brimming with Art Nouveau flavor: beautiful floral and foliate motifs on wall tiles for bathrooms, multicolored stenciled friezes, and more. 48pp. 9¼ x 12¼. 41525-2

CHILDREN: A PICTORIAL ARCHIVE OF PERMISSION-FREE ILLUSTRATIONS, **Carol Belanger Grafton (ed.).** More than 850 versatile illustrations from rare sources depict engaging moppets playing with toys, dolls, and pets; riding bicycles; playing tennis and baseball; reading, sleeping; engaged in activities with other children; and in many other settings and situations. Appealing vignettes of bygone times for artists, designers, and craftworkers. 96pp. 9 x 12. 41797-2

504 DECORATIVE VIGNETTES IN FULL COLOR, **Carol Belanger Grafton (ed.).** Permission-free Victorian images of animals (some dressed in quaint period costumes, others fancifully displaying brief messages), angels, fans, cooks, clowns, musicians, revelers, and many others. 40467-6

OLD-TIME CHRISTMAS VIGNETTES IN FULL COLOR, **Carol Belanger Grafton (ed.).** 363 permission-free illustrations from vintage publications include Father Christmas, evergreen garlands, heavenly creatures, a splendidly decorated old-fashioned Christmas tree, and Victorian youngsters playing with Christmas toys, holding bouquets of holly, and much more. 40255-X

OLD-TIME NAUTICAL AND SEASHORE VIGNETTES IN FULL COLOR, **Carol Belanger Grafton (ed.).** More than 300 exquisite illustrations of sailors, ships, rowboats, lighthouses, swimmers, fish, shells, and other nautical motifs in a great variety of sizes, shapes, and styles–lovingly culled from rare 19th- and early-20th-century chromolithographs. 41524-4

BIG BOOK OF ANIMAL ILLUSTRATIONS, **Maggie Kate (ed.).** 688 up-to-date, detailed line illustrations–all permission-free–of monkeys and apes, horses, snakes, reptiles and amphibians, insects, butterflies, dinosaurs, and more, in accurate, natural poses. Index. 128pp. 9 x 12. 40464-1

422 ART NOUVEAU DESIGNS AND MOTIFS IN FULL COLOR, **J. Klinger and H. Anker.** Striking reproductions from a rare French portfolio of plants, animals, birds, insects, florals, abstracts, women, landscapes, and other subjects. Permission-free borders, repeating patterns, mortised cuts, corners, frames, and other configurations–all depicted in the sensuous, curvilinear Art Nouveau style. 32pp. 9¼ x 12¼. 40705-5

ANIMAL STUDIES: 550 ILLUSTRATIONS OF MAMMALS, BIRDS, FISH AND INSECTS, **M. Méheut.** Painstakingly reproduced from a rare original edition, this lavish bestiary features a spectacular array of creatures from the animal kingdom–mammals, fish, birds, reptiles and amphibians, and insects. Permission-free illustrations for graphics projects; marvelous browsing for antiquarians, art enthusiasts, and animal lovers. Captions. 112pp. 9⅜ x 12¼. 40266-5

THE ART NOUVEAU STYLE BOOK OF ALPHONSE MUCHA, **Alphonse Mucha.** Fine permission-free reproductions of all plates in Mucha's innovative portfolio, including designs for jewelry, wallpaper, stained glass, furniture, and tableware, plus figure studies, plant and animal motifs, and more. 18 plates in full color, 54 in 2 or more colors. Only complete one-volume edition. 80pp. 9⅜ x 12¼. 24044-4

ELEGANT FLORAL DESIGNS FOR ARTISTS AND CRAFTSPEOPLE, **Marty Noble.** More than 150 exquisite designs depict borders of fanciful flowers; filigreed compositions of floral sprays, wreaths, and single blossoms; delicate butterflies with wings displaying a patchwork mosaic; nosegays wrapped in lacy horns; and much more. A graceful, permission-free garden of flowers for use by illustrators, commercial artists, designers, and craftworkers. 64pp. 8⅜ x 11. 42177-5

SNOWFLAKE DESIGNS, **Marty Noble and Eric Gottesman.** More than 120 intricate, permission-free images of snowflakes, based on actual photographs, are ideal for use in textile and wallpaper designs, needlework and craft projects, and other creative applications. iv+44pp. 8¼ x 11. 41526-0

ART NOUVEAU FIGURATIVE DESIGNS, **Ed Sibbett, Jr.** Art Nouveau goddesses, nymphs, florals from posters, decorations by Alphonse Mucha. 3 gorgeous designs. 48pp. 8¼ x 11. 23444-4

ANTIQUE FURNITURE AND DECORATIVE ACCESSORIES: A PICTORIAL ARCHIVE WITH 3,500 ILLUSTRATIONS, **Thomas Arthur Strange.** Cathedral stalls, altar pieces, sofas, commodes, writing tables, grillwork, organs, pulpits, and other decorative accessories produced by such noted craftsmen as Inigo Jones, Christopher Wren, Sheraton, Hepplewhite, and Chippendale. Descriptive text. 376pp. 8⅜ x 11¼. 41224-5

ART NOUVEAU FLORAL PATTERNS AND STENCIL DESIGNS IN FULL COLOR, **M. P. Verneuil.** Permission-free art from two rare turn-of-the-century portfolios *(Etude de la Plante* and *L'ornementation par le Pochoir)* includes 159 floral and foliate motifs by M. P. Verneuil, one of the Art Nouveau movement's finest artists. The collection includes 120 images of flowers–foxglove, hollyhocks, columbine, lilies, and others–and 39 stencil designs of blossoming trees, reeds, mushrooms, oak leaves, peacocks, and more. 80pp. 9¼ x 12¼. 40126-X